European Institute of Public Administration

Understanding State Aid Policy in the European Community

Perspectives on Rules and Practice

Edited by

Sanoussi Bilal and Phedon Nicolaides

KLUWER LAW INTERNATIONAL

THE HAGUE / LONDON / BOSTON

A C.I.P. Catalogue record for this book is available from the Library of Congress.

ISBN 90-411-1184-0

Published by Kluwer Law International,
P.O. Box 85889, 2508 CN The Hague, The Netherlands.

Sold and distributed in North, Central and South America
by Kluwer Law International,
675 Massachusetts Avenue, Cambridge, MA 02139, U.S.A.

In all other countries, sold and distributed
by Kluwer Law International, Distribution Centre,
P.O. Box 322, 3300 AH Dordrecht, The Netherlands.

Printed on acid-free paper

Printed in the Netherlands

To Vicky
and
Ans, Alexander and Ilse

TABLE OF CONTENTS

PART II: THE "GUIDELINE" MECHANISM: HORIZONTAL, SECTORAL AND REGIONAL GUIDELINES

PART III: FUTURE DEVELOPMENTS

ANNEXES   245

ACKNOWLEDGEMENTS

We wish to express our gratitude to the *Fundación Banco Bilbao Vizcaya* for its generous financial support. We are indebted to Roel Polmans for his extensive research assistance, to Jacqueline Walkden for her thorough editorial input and to Denise Grew for the preparation of the manuscript.

ACKNOWLEDGMENTS

LIST OF CONTRIBUTORS

Christian Ahlborn   Linklaters & Paines, London (UK)

Sanoussi Bilal   Senior Lecturer in Economics, European
                                   Institute of Public Administration,
                                   Maastricht (NL)

Guy Cox   Chef de Cabinet, Ministry of Employment and
                                   Labour, Belgium

Eduardo Fernández Ezkurdia   Consultant, Strategy and Finance Policy
                                   Advisers, Bilbao (E)

Alfons Guinier   Secretary General, European Community
                                   Shipowners' Associations – ECSA (B)

Carlos Lambarri   Member of the Board, General Director,
                                   Euskaltel; Former Deputy Minister of
                                   Finance, Basque Country (E)

Phedon Nicolaides   Professor of Economics and Head of Unit on
                                   EC Policies and the Internal Market, European
                                   Institute of Public Administration,
                                   Maastricht (NL)

Marco Nuñez Müller   Partner, Schön Nolte Finkelnburg & Clemm,
                                   Brussels (B)

Roel Polmans   Research Assistant, European Institute of
                                   Public Administration, Maastricht (NL)

Adinda Sinnaeve   Assistant Administrator, European
                                   Commission, Directorate General IV –
                                   Competition, Brussels (B)

Piet Jan Slot   Professor of Economic Law, University of
                            Leiden (NL)

Fiona G. Wishlade   Senior Research Fellow, European Policies
                            Research Centre, University of Strathclyde,
                            Glasgow (UK)

FOREWORD

The mission of the European Institute of Public Administration (EIPA) is to support the process of European integration by providing training, research and consultancy services to the administrations of the Member States and the Institutions of the European Union.

A prerequisite of the success of the integration process is a thorough assessment of the policies of the European Union and its Members. EIPA has often carried out such assessments and the present volume is one more example of our commitment to assist policy makers to evaluate and improve EU policies.

In the European Commission's Action Plan for the Internal Market, state aid was identified as one of the main policy areas where further effort was needed to remove vestigial barriers to trade and competition. Indeed, undistorted competition is one of the fundamental principles on which the Community is based. State aid policy will have to be streamlined otherwise current problems will only be exacerbated as the Union admits new Members. For this reason, in June 1998 we organised a Workshop in Maastricht where we invited academics, national policy makers, Community officials and practitioners to discuss the current Community policy on state aid and consider possible options for reform.

This volume contains the papers that were presented at the Workshop. Although the papers have been revised in the light of comments made at the Workshop, the editors have not sought to impose a single view. EIPA itself is prevented by its rules from having an institutional view of its own. That is why the various chapters put forth a range of perspectives on state aid policy.

The Workshop and the publication of this volume would not have been possible without the generous financial support of the Spanish *Fundación BBV*. We are grateful to *Fundación BBV* and to its President, Jose Angel Sanchez Asiain, and its Director, Maria Luisa Oyarzabal, for enabling us to carry out an important project with significant policy implications. We hope to continue our cooperation with *Fundación BBV* and to organise similar events in the future.

I would like also to thank the contributors to this volume, who, with their papers, have helped us to organise a successful Workshop. We intend to distribute this volume to Community and national policy makers who could not attend the Workshop so that they can also benefit from the views and analyses presented here.

Isabel Corte-Real
Director-General, EIPA

INTRODUCTION

INTRODUCTION

Sanoussi Bilal and Phedon Nicolaides

In a world shaped by the globalisation of economic activity and liberalisation and deregulation processes, most governments have declared their trust in and reliance on market forces, stricter control of public spending and ultimately the reduced direct involvement of the state in the economy. This process is particularly relevant in the European Union (EU) where the integration of the internal market is pursued by eliminating regulatory and technical barriers to the movement of goods, services, capital and people and to the freedom of establishment. The overall aim is to ensure the proper functioning of the market by adopting common rules and policies.

In this context, the continued intervention of the Member States of the EU in the market by granting state aid to support specific activities, sectors or regions is of particular interest. A question that naturally arises is why Member States still grant aid and whether it is compatible with the objective of integration which should result in a better allocation of resources.

In order to prevent "undue" distortions to trade and competition within the EU, the European Commission has the sole power to authorise national aid schemes. Hence, the European Community (EC) policy on state aid reflects this unique sharing of responsibility between the Member States, which design, finance and implement state aid schemes, and the Commission which has to approve them or not.

Indeed, most EC policies are implemented in conjunction with national policies. Only a few policies fall within the exclusive competence of the Community (e.g. common commercial policy, common agricultural policy, certain aspects of competition policy). In those areas where the Community has exclusive competence decisions are normally made by the Council on the basis of a qualified majority. Within the context of the Community decision-making procedures, the task of the Commission is to make proposals and

S. Bilal and P. Nicolaides (eds.), Understanding State Aid Policy in the European Community, 3–10.
© 1999 *Kluwer Law International. Printed in the Netherlands.*

implement, either by itself or through Member States, the decisions of the Council (and the European Parliament). In some cases, however, the Council has delegated the discretion to make decisions to the Commission (e.g. common agricultural policy).

In this respect, competition policy is rather unique because not only are certain aspects of it decided exclusively at the Community level, but also because in certain instances the decision-making responsibility rests solely with the Commission. The rules on state aid are a case in point. The Treaty confers on the Commission the right to vet state aid schemes and approve or prohibit them as appropriate.

In political terms, state aid rules place the Commission in a special position vis-à-vis the Member States. First, before they implement any measure that may contain an element of state aid they must notify it to the Commission and obtain its permission. In other areas where "secondary" legislation imposes similar reporting obligations on Member States (which are mostly limited in the internal market), they do not normally need to secure the prior approval of the Commission.

Second, when the Commission objects to national measures it normally issues "reasoned opinions" and ultimately it has to petition the Court to compel Member States to change the policies in question. This is not the case with state aid, where the Commission both investigates and decides either positively or negatively on state aid schemes. If Member States object to a decision of the Commission, it is they that have to resort to the Court to reverse it.

Third, in the area of state aid the Treaty allows the Commission to vet aid granted by any level of government within Member States (central, regional, local).

In economic terms, state aid rules are also significant because they apply to all sectors of the economy. Unlike other Treaty rules that apply to goods or services or particular sectors or industries, the rules on state aid cover all undertakings in all industries and all levels of government and their agencies. Perhaps more importantly, they cover any scheme that may contain any form of public assistance.[1]

Community policy on state aid has developed over a period of more than 30 years and there now exists a considerable body of law in the form of Commission decisions and Court rulings that has interpreted the general Treaty provisions in much detail. It would appear that the rules in this area should be, by now, very clear and well understood and that Community policy is mature with no need for further adjustments. Although EC policy is indeed well developed, it is still in a state of flux. More importantly and despite the Commission's numerous communications on the various aspects and forms of state aid, public understanding of the policy is still incomplete.

There are at least three reasons which have contributed to this state of affairs.

First, governments have been finding new and ingenious ways of assisting their industries. However, as the scope of the application of state aid rules expands, the measurement of aid becomes more problematic partly because quantifiable data are less readily available and partly because it is necessary to gauge the intentions of the aid-granting agencies and compare them to those of private investors in similar situations. As similar situations may not be easily identifiable, the criteria used to identify aid become more subjective.

Second, the Treaty allows certain exceptions to the general ban on state aid. Again a question arises as to how to reconcile such exceptions with, on the one hand, the need to maintain free competition and, on the other, the need to promote the development of economically backward areas of the Union. Since the regional development argument is used more frequently, even by the more prosperous Member States, one may conclude that more than 30 years of practice have not resolved all policy problems. This tension between free and fair competition is bound to become more pronounced as a result of monetary union and entry into the EU of new, poorer countries.

Third, the Commission has been operating, by necessity, in a "political/ legal vacuum" through the development of guidelines on the application of state aid rules without any prior, explicit mandate by the Council. There is now a need to streamline those guidelines and focus the activities of the Commission on the most serious cases of state aid. Commission resources will then be used more effectively. This streamlining would need explicit decisions by the Council and could involve greater delegation of responsibility to national authorities and courts.

Contents of the book

It follows that there is a need to promote better understanding of current state aid rules and procedures, to undertake critical analysis of the effectiveness of state aid rules and to stimulate discussion on the likely and/or necessary developments in the Community framework of controlling state aid.

To achieve those three objectives, the European Institute of Public Administration organised a European Workshop on "EC Policy on State Aid: Rules, Procedures, Results and Evolution", which took place in Maastricht on 25-26 June 1998. It brought together Community, national, regional and local officials, industry representatives, legal experts, consultants and academics to enable them to exchange views and debate the issues. Most of the papers in this book were presented during this workshop.

The main purpose of this book is to explain the principles and methods of EC state aid policy in a manner which is both accessible and useful to practitioners and policy makers. Moreover, it intends to analyse fundamental concepts and use case studies to illustrate them. It also identifies those aspects of EC policy which are under development and possibly subject to different interpretations.

In particular, the book examines both theory on the role and objective of public assistance and current practice controlling such assistance. It addresses the issue of state aid from an economic, legal and administrative perspective and offers detailed information on current practice through case studies. It also considers likely future developments in the Community framework of state aid control.

The book is organised into three parts. Part I consists of papers providing an overall description and assessment of the state aid rules and procedures. In Chapter 1, Adinda Sinnaeve, from Directorate-General IV on competition at the European Commission, introduces in a simple and systematic way the main objectives and procedures for the Commission's control of state aid under Art. 92-94 of the EC Treaty. She describes the role of state aid control and the approach adopted by the Commission to effect this. More importantly, she succeeds in presenting in a clear and concise way the intricate procedural framework derived from Art. 93.

In Chapter 2, Phedon Nicolaides and Sanoussi Bilal discuss the economic rationale for state aid in an attempt to assess whether state aid rules raise economic efficiency. After reviewing the various principles for granting state aid and briefly addressing the current practice in the European Union, they conclude that EC state aid rules tend to deviate from economic considerations. In particular, in evaluating aid cases, the Commission has a tendency to overlook the nature and the size (and sometimes even the presence) of market failure as a possible justification for state aid. Although aid schemes are often granted on the basis of broader objectives, the issue of proportionality between the means (i.e. the amount and modalities of state aid, as well as the distortion of competition that necessarily follows) and the objective pursued is not spelled out in the rules nor in practice. Finally, contrary to efficiency considerations, aid measures are often of a specific rather than a general nature, thereby introducing further distortive effects.

In Chapter 3, Sanoussi Bilal and Roel Polmans, working on data published by the Commission, attempt to evaluate the trends of state aid to industry in the Member States over the period from 1986 to 1996. They conclude that although declining, state aid remains a predominant feature of economic policy in most Member States of the EU, with global figures at the EU level masking significant differences overtime and between Member States in the trends and patterns of state aid. In particular, while there is a general tendency towards greater convergence in the degree of support to the manufacturing sector among Member States, country-specific characteristics continue to prevail in determining state aid policy, in spite the Commission's effort to control state aid.

In Chapter 4, Piet Jan Slot considers EC state aid procedures from a user's perspective. In view of the procedures and the case law, he discusses the rights of third parties, that is the possibilities for the intended beneficiaries of state aid and their competitors to express their views during the procedure and to defend their rights accordingly. In assessing the "user-friendliness" of these procedures, with reference to competition law, he concludes that although there is a rather well-developed system of legal protection of the procedural rights of third parties (mainly based on case law), there is a lack of transparency and openness in the procedures (exemplified by the absence of a right of access to the files) and the substantive soundness of the rules on state aid can also be questioned.

Part II consists of six papers presenting the implementation of state aid policy through the guideline mechanism. These papers consider the application of horizontal, sectoral and regional guidelines. Chapters 5 and 6 cover rules on the assessment of state aid with horizontal objectives, respectively research and development (R&D) aid and employment aid. In Chapter 5, Marco Núñez Müller analyses the recent practice of the Court and the Commission related to the Community framework for state aid for R&D. He reckons that the generally favourable attitude of the Commission towards R&D aid mainly stems from the importance given in the EC Treaty to the promotion and defence of R&D policy. Yet, state aid for R&D projects must comply with the relevant rules. In this respect, Núñez Müller argues that the R&D framework promotes clarity and legal certainty by setting the criteria adopted for aid evaluation, such as the aid intensity and the incentive effect. He also points out some of the weaknesses of this framework, such as the lack of proper operational distinction in the definition of various types of research (i.e. fundamental research, industrial research and pre-competitive development activity, on the one hand, and research by public non-profit-making entities and private entities, on the other hand).

In Chapter 6, Guy Cox, *Chef de Cabinet* of the Belgian Ministry of Employment and Labour, evaluates the guidelines on aid to employment. He proceeds by outlining the conditions under which horizontal subsidies for employment are allowed and deemed compatible with the common market and then by discussing the links between cost reduction and employment. He contends that to favour employment, governments have to adopt general and/or specific measures that reduce the cost of labour, in accordance with the guidelines set by the Commission. In his view, the difficulty for governments lies in the lack of transparency and simplicity of the rules, the vagueness of the distinction between general measures for labour cost reduction (allowed) and social measures (not allowed), and the harshness with which the

Commission implements these ill-defined rules. He therefore calls for new guidelines to restore clarity and confidence in the system.

The next two chapters illustrate cases of sectoral guidelines and rules on the assessment for the approval of aid to particular industries. In Chapter 7, Alfons Guinier, Secretary General of the European Community Shipowners' Associations (ECSA), presents the recent developments in the maritime policy of the EU through the changes in the guidelines for aid to shipping companies. After recalling the strategic importance of shipping activities for the EU and the difficulties faced by the maritime sector during the 1980s, he discusses the objectives and consequences of some of the major modifications introduced in the guidelines. He concludes that not only have the guidelines succeeded in providing sufficient scope for state intervention to prevent the decline of shipping activities in the EU, but they have also served as a clear incentive for Member States to take direct action to support the maritime transport sector. It remains to be seen, however, whether this state-aid-led recovery, long overdue according to Guinier, will lead to the EU shipping sector becoming more competitive internationally.

In Chapter 8, Piet Jan Slot analyses the application of state aid rules as a mechanism for supervising prices in the energy sector. To do so, he provides an extensive review of the main judgements of the European Court of Justice in this field. Piet Jan Slot concludes that the case law of the Court provides ample guidelines for the pricing of energy sources by government controlled public utilities, although no precise and definitive criteria can be laid down, the two main standards of references being the application of the market economy investor principle and the principle of non-discrimination. In his view, the main concern lies in the procedural level and the difficulty in practice of assessing *a priori* whether or not a commercial action in relation to energy prices amounts to state aid.

Finally, the last two chapters of this part address, from very different perspectives, the issue of regional aid guidelines. In Chapter 9, Carlos Lambarri (former Deputy Minister of Finance of the Basque Country) and Eduardo Fernández Ezkurdia discuss the tension in regional aid policy between efficiency considerations and distributive aspects, or how to achieve the goal of regional development without distorting competition. After briefly surveying the EC rules on regional aid, they introduce a broad notion of the competitiveness of a region which they use to identify the contradiction between the objective of regional development and the constraints imposed by the guidelines. They advocate more flexible and permissive rules on regional aid, extending the definition of aid to include tax measures, abolishing the limits on aid amounts, relaxing the control on proactive aid intended to attract investments and raising the level of aid concentration in order to favour the poorest regions.

In Chapter 10, Fiona Wishlade provides an extensive and systematic discussion of the guidelines on national regional aid, their impact on assisted area coverage in the EU, and the requirements they impose on area designation in terms of methodology, definition of territorial units and the statistical indicators adopted. Finally, she assesses, under the new Commission proposals, the so-called "coherence" of the national assisted areas with those aided under the Community Structural Funds (i.e. should the national assisted area maps coincide with the EC regional policy map?). Her main conclusions are: first, that regional policy is constrained in ways not warranted by competition concerns, as population coverage (the principal measure of regional discipline) is largely used in an arbitrary way; second, that the area designation methodology required appears to be contradictory to past practice and to the principle of subsidiarity; and finally, that the lack of coherence between national and Community assisted areas is not only due to arithmetical difficulties, but also results from a failure to adequately determine policy objectives and responsibilities at the national and Community levels.

Finally, the last part of the book contains two chapters on the future development of EC state aid policy. In Chapter 11 Adinda Sinnaeve presents the Commission's reform project on state aid procedures. With the objectives of increasing the efficiency of state aid control and improving transparency and legal certainty of state aid rules, the Commission decided to propose two major changes in the system, using Art. 94 as the legal basis (something that was never attempted before). First, it proposed introducing a block exemption covering certain categories of aid – the routine cases – a system of ex-post monitoring replacing the existing requirement of prior approval by the Commission (the so-called "Enabling Regulation"). The second proposal consists of a procedural regulation which brings the various procedural rules together in a coherent legal text. A version of "the proposal for a Council Regulation laying down detailed rules for the application of Art. 93 of the EC Treaty", as agreed upon by the Council on 16 November 1998 and submitted to the European Parliament for its opinion, can be found in a diagrammatic format as Appendix II. The reader should note that Appendix II is based on the draft that was approved by the Council in November 1998, which is still correct at the time of publication.

In Chapter 12, Christian Ahlborn offers a critical assessment of the reform project. He discusses some of the proposed changes introduced by the Commission and highlights some of the shortcomings of the reform. In particular, while praising the initial intention of the reform, he regrets the lack of political ambition to adopt major changes, the result of which being an incomplete codification of current practices, the neglect of some important issues (such as third party rights) and the inefficiency of some of the reforms.

The reforms proposed by the Commission certainly go in the right direction but they are unlikely to be the last policy change. The rules need to be tightened further. Their economic effects also need to be evaluated in a more detailed and systematic manner. It is to some extent surprising how large the legal literature is on state aid and how rare economic assessments of the impact of both state aid and the rules that purport to control aid are.

This book identifies the major weaknesses of the present system of state aid rules. We hope that by identifying those weaknesses we have also paved the way for proper economic analysis of the effects of forty years of state aid control in the European Community.

NOTE

1. Exceptions to this general principle are very few indeed and they cover only armaments production, certain aspects of public transport and certain forms of aid to providers of services of general economic interest.

PART I:

RULES AND PROCEDURES: DESCRIPTION AND ASSESSMENT

CHAPTER 1

STATE AID CONTROL: OBJECTIVES AND PROCEDURES

Adinda Sinnaeve *

1. Introduction

In recent years, the Commission's control of state aid under Arts. 92 – 94 EC Treaty has constantly been at the centre of attention, not only among competition lawyers but also among the public at large. The 40 years of EC competition policy show that this has not always been the case. For a long time, state aid control lived at the margin of competition policy. Even its status as part of competition policy was uncertain, the latter sometimes being considered as only dealing with Arts. 85 and 86. Moreover, while legislation in the anti-trust field was adopted very early,[1] its counterpart never benefited from the considerable momentum legislation can give to the development of a policy. Despite some unsuccessful attempts, Art. 94 remained a dead letter. This may indeed be surprising, as the logic of the Treaty is to ensure undistorted competition regardless of whether the distortion is caused by the behaviour of businesses or by the State. Both sections of the competition chapter of the Treaty should thus be equally important for competition policy. Nevertheless, it is only in the last two decades that state aid policy has gradually been able to establish its position as a fully-fledged, necessary pillar of competition policy. In the absence of formal legislation, this development is mainly built on soft law, for the material aspects of state aid control, and case law for the procedural part.

2. The role and purpose of state aid control

One of the basic reasons for having a system of state aid control is the risk of a subsidy race where Member States might outbid each other. This would not

S. Bilal and P. Nicolaides (eds.), Understanding State Aid Policy in the European Community, 13–27.

only be a waste of public money, but also in the long term would weaken the competitive position of European industry, as it would prevent the necessary restructuring and innovation needed to remain competitive. To ensure that Member States only grant aid in the interests of the Community as a whole, control by an independent authority acting on behalf of the Community is indispensable. Moreover, in the absence of state aid control, the gap between wealthier regions, which have more resources at their disposal, and others is likely to increase. State aid control is thus also a necessary instrument for a cohesion policy.

The importance of state aid control has been reinforced by several developments. First of all, the completion of the single market, culminating in the forthcoming economic and monetary union, makes the effective control of state aid more necessary than ever.[2] After the gradual abolition of other barriers, the granting of state aid is one of the few remaining tools for national governments to protect their national industry. Since state aid can be used to replace barriers to trade that have been dismantled in the single market integration process strict control is required. At the same time, the distortive effects of state aid are more visible and more directly felt by competitors in other Member States as markets become more integrated.

The introduction of the single currency will be a further step in the process of creating equal conditions for all players in the market. Where other factors determining the competitive position of enterprises are levelled out, the effects of state aid can be more distortive. Recent developments also seem to indicate that there is a realistic prospect of a limited alignment in fiscal areas. In particular, if the objective of a gradual abolition of schemes which are considered to constitute unfair tax competition – as confirmed by the Ecofin Council[3] – succeeds, another possible instrument of competition between Member States may disappear or lose most of its influence. Against this overall trend of creating a level European playing field for all enterprises, the potential effects of state aid are increasing accordingly. In addition, the budgetary constraints following from the convergence criteria may induce Member States to replace general measures and less harmful aid schemes by more distortive and hoc aid. Hence, the need for strict control is reinforced.

Finally, together with the completion of the single market, a process of liberalisation of certain hitherto protected sectors of industry has been taking place. Opening up new markets for competition inevitably enlarges the scope of state aid control. It has to be ensured that after liberalisation the previous restrictions on competition are not replaced by new distortions in the form of state aid.

In parallel to and in direct connection with these evolutions, Member States and industry are showing an increased awareness of the role of state aid policy. Competitors address themselves more easily towards the Commission with complaints about alleged illegal aid to other enterprises. They closely follow the Commission's policy and increasingly use their rights to challenge Commission decisions before the European Courts. This change in the general environment reflects the currently held expectations of the Commission as the independent arbiter in state aid control.

3. The Commission's approach in assessing state aid

Art. 92(1) of the EC Treaty provides that:

"save as otherwise provided in this Treaty, any aid granted by a Member State or through State resources in any form whatsoever which distorts or threatens to distort competition by favouring certain undertakings or the production of certain goods shall, in so far as it affects trade between Member States, be incompatible with the common market".

Unlike Art. 4(c) of the ECSC Treaty, this provision does not contain a direct prohibition against aid, but only a declaration of incompatibility with the common market. Although the Court of Justice has interpreted Art. 92(1) as an implied prohibition, it has always added that this prohibition is neither absolute nor unconditional.[4] The principle of incompatibility is tempered by automatic and discretionary exemptions set out in paragraphs (2) and (3) of Art. 92. The system of discretionary exemptions confers upon the Commission the power to evaluate whether aid is compatible or not with the common market, because it can be considered to fall under one of the following exemptions: (a) aid to promote the development of regions with an abnormally low living standard or serious underemployment; (b) aid to promote important projects of common European interest or to remedy a serious disturbance in the economy of a Member State; (c) aid to facilitate the development of certain economic activities or certain economic areas; and (d) aid to promote culture and heritage conservation.[5]

Although further analysis of the criteria used by the Commission to assess compatibility would go beyond the scope of this article, the basic principles and objectives of the Commission's policy should be recalled.

As the Court has constantly confirmed, the discretionary power the Commission has to apply Art. 92(3) is very wide. The exemptions are formulated in a general way and leave ample room for the Commission to take a range of social, economic and policy considerations into account. In exercising its discretion the Commission can thus develop a real policy based on Community objectives and an assessment of aid within the Community context. This policy will necessarily evolve in the same way as the common market, with which the aid should be compatible.

The principles, however, remain the same: the aid should contribute to the achievement of Community objectives in such a way that the distortion of competition is justifiable (the principle of compensatory justification).[6] By definition, all aid falling under Art. 92(1) distorts competition. The reason why it can, nevertheless, be approved lies in the fact that it promotes other objectives of the Community, such as regional development or employment, which outweigh the distortion.

In practice, the principle of compensatory justification is implemented via three criteria, which the aid should normally fulfil. First, the aid should serve a purpose that is recognised to be in the general interest of the Community. Second, it should be necessary to accomplish the relevant Community objective. If market forces alone are sufficient to attain the objective, no aid should be authorised. In cases, however, where market imperfections, such as externalities and misallocation of resources, prevent the social optimum from being achieved, corrections by state intervention may be needed. Finally, even if the necessity requirement is met, the intended result should be balanced against the distortion of competition it causes. Only if the aid is proportional to the objective and the benefits for the Community exceed those which would result from undistorted competition is authorisation justified.

The lack of compensatory justification explains why the Commission has always taken a very negative position on operating aid, i.e. aid which relieves an enterprise of the expenses it would itself normally have had to bear in its day-to-day management or its usual activities.[7] By its very nature such aid is not in the interests of the Community.

It is clear that these underlying principles of the Commission's policy need to be embodied in more operational criteria. The Commission has therefore translated the principles into concrete assessment criteria, which are laid down in guidelines, frameworks and communications. These quasi-legislative texts[8] define the conditions under which aid projects can be authorised for different types of horizontal, regional or sectoral aid. They aim at ensuring greater legal certainty for Member States and companies, predictability of decisions and equal treatment.

4. The Procedural Framework

4.1 THE PROCEDURE FOR NOTIFIED AID

4.1.1 Notification obligation and standstill clause. The cornerstones of the control system as foreseen by Art. 93 of the Treaty are the obligation to notify to the Commission about all plans to grant or alter aid, and the prohibition against putting them into effect before the Commission has authorised them.

As long as no block exemptions have been adopted,[9] these rules apply to all aid projects. The following two exceptions usually mentioned in this regard, are merely apparent exceptions:

– The *de minimis* rule states that no notification is needed for all aid not exceeding ECU 100,000 per enterprise over a period of three years.[10] This rule is based on the presumption that aid under this threshold does not affect intra-Community trade and/or does not distort or threaten to distort competition. As a consequence, Art. 92(1) can be said not to apply. Rather than being an exception to the notification obligation, the *de minimis* rule provides a clarification of the notion of aid within the meaning of Art. 92(1) and indirectly of the scope of Art. 93(3).

– Individual awards of aid on the basis of an approved aid scheme do not have to be notified. To examine all the individual applications of aid schemes would obviously be impossible for practical reasons. It would also be unnecessary because the notification of the scheme should already contain all the relevant criteria and conditions for the award of aid in particular cases. Therefore the mechanism of schemes is such that, in principle, with the approval of the scheme, the Commission implicitly approves its future applications.[11]

If the principle of the obligation to notify is clear, its scope is less so. In the absence of a definition of aid in the treaty, the notion has been developed on a case-by-case basis through Commission decisions and judgements of the Court. These have provided clarification on the characteristics of aid falling under Art. 92(1) (advantage, state resources, specificity, effect on intra-Community trade, risk of distortion),[12] for instance by introducing the private-investor criterion. However, there remain several grey areas.[13] The only way for a Member State to clear the doubts about whether a measure constitutes state aid in borderline cases, and thus to protect the interests of the beneficiaries, is notification. Legal certainty can only be provided by a Commission decision.

The standstill clause prohibits the Member State from putting the aid into effect until the Commission has authorised it. Putting aid into effect does not mean the actual granting of aid, but the prior action of instituting or implementing aid at the legislative level according to the constitutional rules in the Member State concerned. Aid is deemed to be put into effect as soon as the legislative machinery enabling it to be granted without further formality has been set up.[14] It follows that aid plans should either be notified at the drafting stage, or contain a special clause making their entry into force conditional upon the approval of the Commission.

4.1.2   Preliminary examination. The procedure to examine a notification is divided into two possible phases: a preliminary examination and a formal examination for cases which raise doubts as to their compatibility with the common market.

As early as the *Lorenz* case of 1973, the Court decided that the Commission should conclude its preliminary examination within a period of two months.[15] If no decision is taken within this time limit, the Member State may put the notified measure into effect, after giving prior notice to the Commission. The two-month rule has become established practice and should normally ensure a relatively fast and efficient procedure. However, a problem arises from the fact that this period can only start to run from the receipt of a *complete* notification, containing all the necessary information for the Commission to take a decision. If notifications are incomplete, the Commission will request additional information and, with the receipt of the Member State's reply, a new period of two months starts to run. Experience shows that, to some extent, delays on decisions can be attributed to the way notifications are prepared. The development of standard notification forms, such as already exist for certain types of aid, would seem to be useful in order to improve this situation.

The preliminary examination is closed either by a decision not to raise objections if the measure does not constitute state aid or is clearly compatible with the common market, or by a decision to open a formal investigation.

4.1.3   Formal investigation procedure. Where the Commission, after the preliminary examination of the notified measure, has doubts as to its compatibility with the common market, it is obliged to open a formal investigation, in accordance with Art. 93(2).[16] The decision to open proceedings is published in the Official Journal and the Member State concerned and interested parties are invited to submit their comments. This should allow the Commission to gather all the information it needs to assess the compatibility of the aid and have a complete picture of the case.[17] At the same time, interested parties are given the opportunity to make their views known and defend their interests. The notion of interested party is very wide in this context. According to the Court it is an indeterminate group of persons, including all persons, undertakings or associations whose interests might be affected by the grant of the aid, in particular competing undertakings and trade associations.[18] The Commission will normally examine all comments without submitting them to a strict admissibility test.

Unlike the preliminary examination, which is an internal Commission procedure, the formal procedure has a contradictory character in relation to the Member State concerned. The latter will receive all the comments from third parties and have the opportunity to reply. The Commission cannot base its decision on elements which the Member State has not been in a position to comment on.[19] The contradictory character of the procedure may also lead to negotiations between the Member State and the Commission, in particular, in cases where a conditional decision is envisaged or where a Member State prefers to modify its original aid project in order to get Commission approval.

As far as third parties are concerned, the procedure is not contradictory. They have a formal right to submit written comments, but are not informed about comments from other parties and are not involved in the further course of the procedure. This restrictive practice is often criticised: not only is the role of third parties already limited to cases where the Commission opens a procedure, but their means of action are also restricted during that procedure. If the role of third parties is to assist the Commission in its examination, one could indeed wonder why the Commission is hesitating to involve them more. Part of the explanation could be that comments from third parties have generally not been of great help in the Commission's assessment in state aid cases. Moreover, the practice shows that in nearly 50% of all cases, no comments from third parties apart from other Member States and beneficiaries are received. Aside from the general debate concerning the position of third parties in state aid procedures,[20] this low degree of participation among competitors and associations seems to make the claim for giving them more rights somewhat contradictory.

Four types of decisions can close the formal investigation procedure. The Commission can decide that the notified measure does not constitute state aid, it can take a positive decision, a conditional decision or a negative decision. Although it follows from Art. 92(1) that aid should in principle be prohibited, the number of negative decisions is very low.[21] This can be explained by the fact that the Commission's policy has become increasingly well known and hence Member States draw up projects which are in line with the criteria established in the guidelines and frameworks. It also happens that notifications are modified or withdrawn when it becomes clear that no approval is to be expected. Finally, the Commission may, instead of taking a negative decision, impose conditions designed to make the aid project compatible. The relatively small number of negative decisions does therefore not reflect the reality of strict control and the influence of the Commission's policy.

4.2 THE PROCEDURE FOR UNLAWFUL AID

4.2.1 The notion of unlawful aid. The notion of unlawful aid covers all aid which is put into effect in contravention of Art. 93(3). Although it is commonly referred to as unnotified aid, it also includes aid which is awarded after notification but before the Commission has reached a decision.

Figures show that a high proportion of the aid cases examined by the Commission are registered as involving unlawful aid.[22] Such cases may come to light following complaints, information in the press or any other source.

4.2.2 Differences from the procedure for notified aid. Where Member States have infringed Art. 93(3), the Commission is not bound by the time limit of two months for the preliminary examination. Otherwise, the procedure basically follows the same pattern as for notified aid, except for the following differences, which are a consequence of the illegality of such aid.

During the examination of the compatibility of the illegally granted aid, the Commission has the power to take interim decisions. It can order the Member State concerned to suspend the aid (*suspension injunction*) and to provide it with all the information necessary to examine the compatibility of the unlawful aid (*information injunction*).[23] If the Member State does not provide the necessary information, the Commission is entitled to take a decision on the basis of the information available.

Where aid has already been paid out, a suspension injunction is not a sufficient remedy against the infringement of the procedural rules, since it cannot be used retroactively. The Commission considers that in such cases, it may order the provisional recovery of unlawful aid (*recovery injunction*) pending the outcome of its examination, but, although it has announced its intention to use this instrument it has never done so.[24] The question whether the Commission has such a power has been the subject of much discussion. The jurisprudence of the Court is not directly relevant in clarifying this matter, because it deals with the power to take a final recovery decision. The Court ruled that the Commission could not take a recovery decision solely on the grounds of illegality without examining the compatibility of the aid.[25] However, it did not examine the possibility of a provisional recovery injunction.[26] The latter constitutes an interim measure which draws the consequences/inferences of the infringement of Art. 93(3), while the final recovery decision is based on Art. 93(2). As far as conservatory measures based on Art. 93(3) are concerned, it seems therefore that there are no legal grounds to deny the Commission the same powers as national judges in issuing a recovery injunction. This is especially necessary since at national level the interim protection of third parties against unlawful aid is often not sufficiently ensured.

In cases where the examination of unlawful aid results in a final negative decision, meaning the aid is not only unlawful on procedural grounds but also incompatible with the common market, definite recovery of the aid from the beneficiary is the only way to restore fair competition. Since the middle of the 1980s, the Commission, supported by the Court, has developed a policy of systematically ordering recovery. Negative decisions on unlawful aid include an article stating that the Member State concerned is required to reclaim the aid, including interest, from the beneficiary.[27] The Member State and the beneficiary may challenge the recovery decision pursuant to Art. 173, but the case law of the Court shows that, as recovery cannot be held to be disproportionate,[28] such actions for annulment of the recovery decision are unlikely to be successful.

Where Member States fail to comply with a recovery decision, the Commission can refer the matter directly to the Court of Justice, pursuant to Art. 93(2). The only argument a Member State can invoke for not fulfilling a recovery decision is the absolute impossibility of executing the decision.[29] However, until now the Court has systematically rejected arguments based on impossibility.[30] The Court has also held that where a Member State encounters unforeseen or unforeseeable difficulties, it should submit those problems to the Commission, together with proposals for suitable amendments. The Member State and the Commission should then, in accordance with the principle of cooperation laid down in Art. 5, work together in good faith with a view to overcoming the difficulties whilst fully observing Arts. 92 and 93.

Recovery is to be effected in accordance with national law.[31] As a consequence, beneficiaries are entitled to use the remedies existing under national law against the Member State's claim for reimbursement. However, according to consistent case law of the Court, provisions of national law, such as time limits for the revocation of an administrative act or provisions on legitimate expectations, cannot be invoked if they render recovery practically impossible.[32] The Court has consistently stated that aid recipients can normally not have any legitimate expectations where aid was granted in breach of Art. 93(3). A diligent businessman should be able to verify whether that procedure had been followed. As a result of this jurisprudence, several provisions of national law have had to be put aside in order to give full effect to the recovery decision.

4.2.3 Consequences of unlawful aid at the national level. Unlawful aid can also be the subject of action before national courts. Since Art. 93(3) is a provision with direct effect, any act implementing aid in breach of this article, is invalid and a final Commission decision cannot have the effect of regularising the infringement. The role foreseen for national courts in this context is to be distinguished from that of the Commission.[33] While the Commission always has to examine the compatibility of the aid, national courts must preserve until the final decision of the Commission the rights of individuals against infringements of Art. 93(3), draw all the consequences/ inferences [see e.g. OJ C – 254/90, ECR I – 5505, point 12.] of the illegality.[34] In particular, the Court has held that national courts may have to take interim measures, such as ordering the suspension or reimbursement of unlawful aid.[35] Hence, third parties have twin means of action when faced with unlawful aid to a competitor: they may complain to the Commission and they can take action before a national court. [36]

4.3 THE PROCEDURE FOR EXISTING AID

According to Art. 93(1), the Commission shall, in cooperation with the Member States, keep all existing aid schemes under constant review. Existing aid includes old or pre-accession aid[37] and authorised aid.[38]

The purpose of a procedure on existing aid is to provide the Commission with an instrument to secure the abolition or adaptation of schemes which are no longer compatible with the common market or which, in the case of pre-accession aid, might never have been compatible with the common market. It is used not only to review individual Member States' aid schemes, but also to carry a policy change through in all Member States at once as regards a particular sector or type of horizontal aid.

The Commission initiates the review procedure by writing for information to the Member State concerned. Where the Commission, in the light of the information and comments from the Member State on the Commission's preliminary view, concludes that the existing aid scheme is not compatible with the common market, it proposes appropriate measures in order to make the scheme compatible. Legally speaking, the proposals are simple recommendations. If the Member State declines to carry out the appropriate measures, the Commission will open the formal investigation procedure, which will then normally lead to a final negative or conditional decision. The Commission may thus finally require Member States to comply with the appropriate measures in the future through the formal investigation procedure.

4.4 JUDICIAL PROTECTION

All Commission decisions on the basis of Art. 93(2) and (3) may be subject to review by the European Courts. Member States may challenge the legality of a decision under Art. 173(2) within a period of two months. The action for annulment must be brought before the Court of Justice and does not have suspensive effect.

Natural and legal persons may bring an action to the Court of First Instance against a Commission decision. According to Art. 173(4), they only have standing if they meet the requirements of direct and individual concern. The beneficiaries of individual aid can be considered to fulfil these conditions.[39] In the case of schemes, however, the beneficiaries may not be identified sufficiently to be individually concerned,[40] except if the aid has already been illegally granted.[41] The Court also recognised the possible standing of associations in two sets of circumstances. The first is where the associations' own interests are affected, especially because they have negotiated on behalf of their members or they represent a sector and have been in close contact with the Commission.[42] The second is where the association has substituted itself for one or more of the members which it represents, on condition that the action of those members is also admissible.[43] Regional authorities, having granted aid, should challenge decisions under Art. 173(4) and not under 173(2) which only applies to Member States.[44]

As far as competitors are concerned, two distinctions have to be made. First, competitors will normally not have standing with regard to an aid scheme, but only with regard to decisions on individual aid.[45] Second an action against a decision not to raise objections under Art. 93(3) is to be distinguished from an action against a positive or conditional decision pursuant to Art. 93(2). In the case of the latter, the Court decided in the *Cofaz* judgement of 1986[46] that competitors have *locus standi* if their market position has been significantly affected by the aid and if they have participated in the procedure leading to the decision in question, e.g. by having submitted comments or having made a complaint.[47]

These conditions have not been transposed into actions for annulment of a decision not to raise objections. Since third parties have no role during the preliminary examination and may not even know about the aid project, they could not be required to have manifested themselves during this procedure. What is more surprising is that the Court did not mention the other condition, the need to establish the effect on the market position of the applicant.[48] The Court held that as third parties benefit from procedural guarantees, when the Art. 93(2) procedure is set in motion, they must have the right to bring an action for the annulment of the decision to approve aid without opening that procedure. It seems that at least in cases of individual aid, the interested party only has to show that it is a concerned party so that *locus standi* requirements to challenge a "no-objection" decision, in order to force the Commission to open a formal investigation, are much easier to fulfil. Competitors should, however, explicitly cite the infringement of the procedural safeguards of Art. 93(2) which they would have had if the Commission had opened proceedings. If they merely seek the annulment of the decision not to raise objections, the Court will apply the same admissibility tests as for final decisions.[49]

5. Conclusion

It appears from this general overview of state aid procedures that, although Art. 93 only sets out the outline of a procedural system, its principles have gradually been developed into a comprehensive body of rules. The driving forces behind this development are not only the Commission, but also the Court of justice. The latter laid down a procedural framework to deal with unlawful aid, also giving a role to national courts; it defined the rights of third parties and clarified a number of procedural issues.

Despite the useful clarification thus provided, the main critical comment one could make on the present system concerns precisely the fact that it is, to a large extent based on judge-made law. The Court's piecemeal creation of law on a case-by-case basis leads to an increasing fragmentation of rules and makes the system less transparent. In the absence of a clear and coherent legislative text which puts the different aspects of the procedures together, state aid control still lacks a basic instrument of modern law systems. The proposed Regulation on the basis of Art. 94 could fill this gap.[50]

NOTES

*   The views expressed in this Chapter are the author's own and should not be attributed to the EC Commission.

1. Regulation 17 was adopted as early as 1962, OJ 1962 13/204.
2. See K. Van Miert, XXVIIth Report on competition policy, EC Commission, Brussels, 1997, p. 3.
3. See Conclusions of the Ecofin Council Meeting on 1 December 1997 concerning taxation policy, OJ 1998 C 2/1.
4. See e.g. Case *Ianelli & Volpi* [1977] ECR 557; Case 78/76 *Steinike und Weinlig* [1977] ECR 595; Case C-17/91 *Lornoy* [1992] ECR I-6523.
5. Further categories of aid may be authorised by the Council under Art. 92(3)(e). So far this has only been done for aid to shipbuilding.
6. See Case 730/79 *Philip Morris* [1980] ECR 2671. See also A. Evans, *European Community Law of State Aid*, Oxford, Clarendon Press, 1997, p. 107-145.
7. See e.g. Case C-278/95 P *Siemens* [1997] ECR I-2507.
8. Legally speaking, they constitute "soft law" without any formal binding force. However, the Commission can be considered to have bound itself to respect the rules it has published. On the status of frameworks, see e.g. Case C-313/90 *CIRFS* [1993] ECR I-1125; Case T-214/95 *Het Vlaamse Gewest*, Judgement of 30.4.1998, not published yet. See also F. Rawlinson, "The Role of Policy Frameworks, Codes and Guidelines in the Control of State Aid", in I. Harden, *State Aid: Community Law and Policy*, Köln, Bundesanzeiger, 1993, p. 52 (59).
9. Cf. Chapter 11 on *State Aid Procedures: The Reform Project*.
10. Commission notice on the *de minimis* rule for state aid, OJ 1996 C 68/9.
11. However, individual notification may be required under some sectoral or horizontal frameworks (e.g. R&D framework, multisectoral framework on regional aid for large investment projects), or by the terms of the Commission's authorisation of a given programme.
12. See also A. Evans, op. cit, p. 27-106; L. Hancher, T. Ottervanger, P.J. Slot, EC State Aids, Chancery Law Publishing, 1993, p. 19-39.
13. A need for further clarification certainly exists with regard to the distinction between state aid and a general measure. The dividing line between both is particularly difficult to draw where measures, without being general, may be justified by the nature and general scheme of a system (see Case 173/73 *Italy v. Commission* [1974] ECR 709), for instance in the field of taxation or social security contributions.
14. See Commission letter to Member States SG (89) D/5521 of 27 April 1989 in: *European Commission, Competition law in the European Communities, Volume II A, Rules Applicable to State Aid*, Brussels, Luxembourg, 1995, p. 62.
15. Case 120/73 *Lorenz* [1973] ECR 1471.
16. See Case C-198/91 *Cook* [1993] ECR I-2487; Case 84/82 *Germany v. Commission* [1984] ECR 1451; Case T-49/93 *SIDE* [1995] ECR II-2501.
17. See Case 290/83 *Commission v. France* [1985] ECR 439.
18. Case 323/82 *Intermills* [1984] ECR 3809.

19. However, for an infringement of the right to be heard to result in annulment of the Commission's decision, it must be established that had it not been for that irregularity, the outcome of the procedure might have been different; see Case 259/85 *France v. Commission* [1987] ECR 4393.

20. See e.g. the different positions of the CFI and the Court in the *Sytraval* case (Case T-95/94 *Sytraval* [1995] ECR 2651 and Case C-367/95 P *Sytraval* of 2.4.1998, not published yet).

21. Number of negative decisions: 14 in 1990; 7 in 1991; 8 in 1992; 6 in 1993; 3 in 1994; 9 in 1995; 23 in 1996; and 9 in 1997.

22. In average the percentage lies between 14-20% of all registered cases. The figure for 1997 (ca. 21% of all registered cases) indicates that these high percentages are not decreasing.

23. Case C-301/87 *Boussac* [1990] ECR I-307; Case C-142/87 *Tubemeuse* [1990] ECR I-959.

24. Commission communication to the Member States, OJ C 156 of 22.6.1995, p. 5.

25. Case C-301/87 *Boussac* [1990] ECR I-307; Case C-142/87 *Tubemeuse* [1990] ECR I-959.

26. See, however, AG Tesauro in Case 142/87 *Tubemeuse* [1990] ECR I-959 and AG Jacobs in Case C-42/93 *Spain v. Commission* [1994] ECR I-4175.

27. Interests are calculated on the basis of the "reference rate" used to measure the grant equivalent of aid (see Commission notice on the method for setting the reference and discount rates, OJ 1997 C-273/3).

28. Case C-142/87 [1990] ECR I-959 *Tubemeuse*.

29. See e.g. Case 52/84 *Commission v. Belgium* [1986] ECR 89; Case 63/87 *Commission v. Greece*, [1988] ECR 2875; Case 94/87 *Commission v. Germany* [1989] ECR 175; Case C-183/91 *Commission v. Greece* [1993] I-3131; Case C-349/93 *Commission v. Italy* [1995] ECR I-343; Case C-280/95 *Commission v. Italy*, [1998] ECR I-259.

30. See e.g. the cases referred to in the previous footnote.

31. See e.g. Case C-94/87 *Alcan I* [1989] ECR I-175 and Case 5/89 *Alutechnik* [1990] ECR I-3437.

32. Case C-24/95 *Alcan II* [1997] ECR I-1591; Case 5/89 *Alutechnik* [1990] ECR I-3437.

33. Case C-354/90 *FNCE* [1991] ECR I-5505; Case C-39/94 *SFEI* [1996] ECR I-3547.

34. See also the Commission's Notice on cooperation between national courts and the Commission in the State aid field, OJ C 312 of 23.12.1995, p. 8.

35. See Case C-39/94 *SFEI* [1996] ECR I-3547.

36. On the role of national courts in state aid control, see M. Struys, Le rôle des juridictions nationales dans le contentieux communautaire des aides d'État, in: *Les aides d'État en droit communautaire et en droit national*, Rapports du 48e Séminaire, les 14-15 mai 1998, Faculté de Droit, Université de Liège.

37. i.e. aid schemes which existed prior to the entry into force of the Treaty in the respective Member State and are still applicable after the entry into force of the Treaty.

38. This covers aid which is authorised by a Commission or Council decision and aid which is authorised by default (Lorenz).
39. Case 730/79 *Philip Morris* [1980] ECR 2671.
40. Joint Cases 67, 68 and 70/85 *Van der Kooy* [1988] ECR 219.
41. The beneficiaries of an unlawful aid scheme can thus challenge the Commission's recovery decision; see e.g. the pending case T-298/97 *Alzetta Mauro*.
42. Joint Cases 67, 68 and 70/85 *Van der Kooy* [1988] ECR 219; Case C-313/90 *CIRFS* [1993] ECR I-1125; Case T-380/94 *AIUFFASS* [1996] ECR II-2169.
43. Joint Cases T-447, 448 and 449/93 *AITEC* [1995] ECR II-1971.
44. Case C-95/97 *Région Wallonne* [1997] ECR I-1787; Case C-180/97 *Regione Toscana* [1997] ECR I-5245; Case T-214/95 *Het Vlaamse Gewest,* Judgement of 30.4.1998, not published yet.
45. Since an aid scheme defines potential beneficiaries in a general and abstract manner, the existence of an actual beneficiary, and hence that of an active competitor of that beneficiary, presupposes the practical application of the aid scheme by the grant of individual aid. See Case T-398/94 *Kahn Scheepvaart* [1996] ECR II-477.
46. Case 169/84 *Cofaz I* [1986] ECR 391.
47. It is to be noted, however, that the CFI considered the significant effect on the market position of the competitors sufficient for their action to be admissible, in Case T-435/93 *ASPEC* [1995] ECR II-1281.
48. Case C-198/91 *Cook* [1993] ECR I-2487; Case C-225/91 *Matra* [1993] ECR I-3203. See also Case T-49/93 *SIDE* [1995] ECR II-2501.
49. Case T-266/94 *Skibsvaerftsforeningen* [1996] ECR II-1399.
50. Cf. Chapter 11 on *State Aid Procedures: The Reform Project.*

CHAPTER 2

STATE AID RULES:
DO THEY PROMOTE EFFICIENCY?

Phedon Nicolaides and Sanoussi Bilal*

1. The context of analysis

The policy of the European Community on state aid control is in a process of
evolution. New rules are being proposed by the Commission, which has
recently expressed its concern at the large amounts of aid still being offered
by central and regional governments in the Member States. This is an
opportune moment to take stock of Community practice and evaluate
Community rules. The purpose of this Chapter is to attempt to make such an
evaluation by asking whether the rules promote economic efficiency.

To assess whether EC state aid rules promote economic efficiency, we
first have to define the context in which we are making that assessment. An
issue that has to be clarified at the outset is whether governments should grant
state aid and whether the EC needs to have any rules at all on state aid. To put
it differently, before we even examine the efficiency of the existing rules, we
have to know why governments grant aid and why a regional grouping like
the EC needs to constrain what its members do.

Once we have established whether subsidies should be granted at all, and
whether groupings of countries should regulate the kind and amount of
subsidies given by their members, we can address the issue of whether
existing EC rules conform with what theory prescribes. To the extent that
practice deviates from theoretical prescription, we need to identify the causes
and effects of that discrepancy. If the EC has objectives other than the pursuit
of economic efficiency, are the prevailing rules and procedures the least
distortionary means of achieving those objectives?

S. Bilal and P. Nicolaides (eds.), Understanding State Aid Policy in the European Community, 29–46.
© 1999 *Kluwer Law International. Printed in the Netherlands.*

2. Why subsidies?

There is a large amount of literature on whether, when and how governments should aid their companies or industries. By and large, this literature concludes that, on efficiency grounds, aid may be justified when it is intended to correct market failure. The typical reasons cited for market failure are externalities (plus public goods), economies of scale and asymmetric information. Because of these reasons, it is thought necessary for a government to intervene and subsidise training, undertake part of the cost of research and other knowledge-generating activities, offer incentives for investment in environmentally friendly machinery and production processes, regulate entry into the utilities sector and define the obligations of producers towards consumers.

Note that market failure is a necessary but not a sufficient condition for providing public support to industry. The "first-best" policy would be to address market failure directly, instead of granting state aid to compensate for it. Only when direct measures are not feasible should aid be considered, as a "second-best" option. However, the appropriate amount and method of aid may still be too difficult to determine. Not only may the government have to rely on incomplete information about the state of the economy, but it may also suffer from asymmetric information. The private sector seeking to benefit from state aid possesses information not directly available to the government, which thus runs the risk of being misled when designing and implementing its aid policy. Besides, the aid-giving agency may be in danger of being "captured" by special interest groups. The "politicisation" of state aid is one of the major problems facing aid-granting agencies. Hence, the cost of getting the policy wrong may outweigh the benefits of intervention to correct market failure.

When should such intervention be classified as state aid? Here we follow the convention according to which a public measure is regarded as state aid if (i) it favours a particular firm or industry (i.e. it is a "specific" measure instead of a "general" one) and (ii) it results in financial cost to the government or its agencies (i.e. regulatory measures, even when they favour particular firms, are not considered to be state aid).

In the EC, much of the legal analysis in state aid cases focuses on whether a given state aid measure is specific or general. This legal issue has its economic counterpart. A specific measure would change the relative prices of goods and services nationally, while a general measure would leave them unchanged. Note, however, that this kind of neutrality prevails only under certain assumptions, which are unlikely to hold in practice. For example, a general measure such as an employment subsidy given to all sectors of the economy would still have a more pronounced impact on labour intensive sectors in labour-rich countries.

Given that countries trade goods for which they have a comparative advantage in their production, it is very doubtful whether there can be a general measure that has the same effect on all sectors of the economy. This does not mean that it is impossible to design measures that have a neutral impact. It only means that such measures are both difficult to design and unlikely to conform with what are normally presumed to be general measures (i.e. aid which is given on the basis of non-discriminatory criteria and through procedures which are automatically and unconditionally open to all sectors on the same terms). These are legal criteria which may not take into account the particularities of the various sectors of the economy.

A question that arises is whether general measures can also be efficient policy instruments. This is an interesting question in the context of this Chapter because a basic tenet of economic policy is that intervention should be as specific as possible to avoid unwanted side effects. We will return to this issue later on.

3. Why supranational rules on subsidies?

As argued above, measures that are not of a general nature have, by definition, an impact on relative prices and therefore on the allocation of resources among sectors. In an open economy, this implies that the terms of trade are affected. If the effect is significant enough it may shift the comparative advantage of the country. While this results in welfare losses when resources are reallocated to inefficient sectors, it may raise national welfare when aid policies are intended to correct market failures so as to shift resources to sectors where the true comparative advantage of a country lies. Note, once more, that for aid to be welfare improving, the efficiency gains derived from aid policies must be larger than the (direct and indirect) costs of state aid.

Assuming that state aid compensates for market distortions, we can turn to the question of why a group of countries, each of which is presumed (at least initially) to maximise efficiency, should need or tolerate any supranational constraints on their discretion to disburse subsidies or other forms of state aid? One answer is that rational, welfare-maximising behaviour does not preclude subsidy wars in pursuit of "beggar thy neighbour" objectives. Hence, supranational rules may be voluntarily adopted in order to prevent the emergence of predatory or rent-shifting national policies.

In this context it is worth noting that rent-shifting policies are normally implemented through the selection of "national champions" which have, or are expected to acquire, market power (as reflected in large market shares). Because they seek to be selective, they are, as a result, inherently discriminatory (and to a large extent, arbitrary). Given that the process of selection necessarily entails that (i) certain industries must be left out and (ii) those not favoured are penalised by not having access to public funds, it is not unreasonable to conclude that ultimately the ban on rent-shifting measures, intentionally or unintentionally, prevents governments from discriminating against "unfashionable" economic activities.

Economic policies, especially those that affect traded goods or mobile factors of production, generate cross-border spillovers. To the extent that these spillovers are positive (as, in some instances, with subsidies to an industry using imported goods as inputs), there is no need for supranational rules. Countries benefit from the state aid policy of their partners. In contrast, when a domestic aid policy generates negative spillover effects (i.e. it reduces the welfare of other countries), supranational rules may protect the interests of partner countries as well. Supranational rules may have the purpose of not only eliminating these negative spillovers, but also of introducing greater transparency and predictability in the partner countries' policy making. Greater policy transparency and predictability make it easier for companies to plan their investments and for other governments to formulate and implement their own policies.

Supranational rules may also prevent *tit-for-tat* strategies of the type "Since you give aid to your industry, I'll help my industry too". Governments often get caught in such "prisoner's dilemma" situations where domestic aid is granted to restore the "level playing field" with subsidised foreign industries. However, all countries would be better off with a cooperative outcome.

The need for supranational rules is further strengthened as the assumption of efficiency maximisation is relaxed. Such rules constrain the decision-making discretion of national governments and make them less vulnerable to domestic lobbying by special interest groups. This is not a farfetched supposition given the fact that external constraints are often sought for internal political reasons. In this context, supranational rules improve the fairness or objectivity of domestic decision-making. Even when supranational rules do not meet efficiency criteria, they may dilute national preferences for interventionist or discriminatory policies (which generally benefit small but organised, politically influential groups as they have to apply to (and accommodate) a larger number of entities. A national specific-interest group is therefore less likely to influence such rules or their application. Besides, supranational rules and institutions help to shield national decision-makers from domestic pressures as they can shift the blame for unpopular or politically difficult decisions not to support specific sectors (generally the so-called "national champions") to international institutions. The prevention of discriminatory measures or discouraging rent-seeking activities is in general welfare improving.

Finally, state aid may also serve non-economic objectives: self-sufficiency, protection of national interests (e.g. the defence sector), etc. In the context of the European Union, the integration of the internal market has been the main objective of Community policies and action. Hence, as discussed in the section on EC rules, state aid is subject to the requirement that it should not distort competition or intra-EU trade, at least in principle. However, the completion of the single market will not necessarily result in efficient (i.e. EU welfare-maximising) policies. It follows that the political objective of market integration may conflict with the economic prescription for efficiency. Supranational rules, however, may serve to clarify and rank these various objectives.

In summary, supranational rules serve several objectives. While we acknowledge this multiplicity of objectives, we are confining our analysis to the question of efficiency. Do EC rules permit only market-correcting intervention? This question has two facets. The first is whether *all* market-correcting interventions are allowed. The second is whether *only* market-correcting interventions are possible. That is, may interventions of a different sort (i.e. with different objectives) be permitted as well? To answer these two questions we have to examine in more detail the meaning and implications of market-correcting intervention.

4. Cross-border effects of state aid

Economic theory recognises that, in principle, the purpose of state aid is to correct or compensate for market failure, with the ultimate objective of improving economic welfare. Thus, it may seem that there should be no objection and, consequently, no supranational constraints on market-correcting measures. However, this may not hold true for at least two reasons.

First, it is well known from the theory of second-best that, in markets with multiple distortions, addressing only one source of distortion by intervening in the market creates its own distortion, which may have the apparently paradoxical effect of reducing welfare. For instance, R&D subsidies designed to stimulate technical innovation and productivity, if granted to an industry which operates in a protected sector and which causes environmental pollution, may result, respectively, in a greater misallocation of resources (away from the production of goods where the country has a natural comparative advantage) and to higher national negative externalities in terms of pollution, and thus have a negative welfare impact.

Second, as argued above, national policy may generate negative cross-border spillovers. This would happen for instance in the case of predatory or rent-shifting policies that are expressly intended to assist national firms in capturing market share from foreign firms. Obviously, rent-shifting policies often result in "negative-sum games" with the potential of making everyone worse off.

However, it cannot be generally argued that all strategic policies that seek to support particular industries necessarily worsen global welfare. One may wonder, therefore, whether such strategic state aid policies should be prohibited *per se* or only when the aid-providing government does not have the potential means to compensate for negative effects on third countries. In other words, should state aid which generates larger (domestic) gains than losses (abroad) be allowed? In such "positive-sum games" both national and global (i.e. all countries' aggregated) welfare increase, even if the welfare of some countries may be negatively affected. In this particular case, state aid is potentially Pareto-efficient, although it hurts some countries. EC rules, as they do not directly address the issue of efficiency, remain ambiguous in relation to such policies.

The argument for banning aid to particular industries is not only economic but also procedural. Who would evaluate whether global welfare has increased? There is only one supranational authority with that kind of power, and that is the Commission. Hence, it is not feasible to expect that countries outside the EU have the means to coordinate their actions so that only aid that is globally welfare improving is granted.

Apart from strategic aid to industry, there may be other forms of aid that also generate negative effects for some partner countries even in cases where global welfare increases. It becomes necessary to ask whether there are any market-correcting interventions that can result in cross-border spillovers? In open economies, internal policies virtually always have a direct or indirect external effect. Even intervention in a non-traded sector may have an indirect effect on a traded sector and thus on a foreign economy.

An example will help clarify this issue. Firms may choose to invest in a location where other similar firms already maintain production facilities or have an established business presence. They may make that investment in order to obtain access to raw materials, transport networks, factors of production or to benefit from external economies or agglomeration effects. The government may initiate and speed up the process of agglomeration by offering regional investment incentives. In case the government of another country attempts to follow precisely the same policy, the two countries may end up undermining each other's efforts even though both intend to pursue a first-best policy of basically correcting externalities. Both countries are trapped in a prisoner's dilemma situation. Should there be rules on investment incentives of this sort? Not only are there cross-border spillovers, but both countries may be better off by agreeing not to pursue those policies. However, if one country could compensate the other, a better option for both of them would be to agree for one to grant the subsidy while the other refrains from doing the same.

Consider a different example. A firm that proposes to build a new lean car engine asks the government for research subsidies. The firm wants to carry out research on new component materials, new fuels and new methods of fuel injection. Again there are extensive externalities and at the same time substantial commercial risks. Should the government subsidise this project? Even if subsidies are a first-best response to a market failure, should this kind of research still receive public support if governments in other countries intend to support similar projects submitted to them. Should they both subsidise or not?

Both examples illustrate a common prisoner's dilemma. All countries would be worse off without government intervention and yet there is a significant risk that public support could lead to too much intervention, with consequent excessive subsidies and waste of resources. Note that in neither example does the government explicitly intend to extract rent from other countries. We conclude that distortion-correcting aid is not necessarily free of negative cross-border effects, especially when it directly induces a shift in the location of production by influencing investment decisions.

When individual decisions lead to a sub-optimal collective outcome, ostensibly there is a need for coordination. The problem is how to define and measure this "collective interest" and how to coordinate national policies. In this context a blanket prohibition, as in the case, for example, of export subsidies, would not be appropriate. There is a need for a supranational mechanism or authority to coordinate national aid decisions. That authority needs to have discretion to judge each case on its own merits. Hence, within the context of a regional grouping like the EC, the pursuit of efficiency necessarily means some form of coordination which, in turn, means the exercise of policy discretion.

Without attempting to define the meaning of collective interest or other criteria that may guide coordination, on the basis of the discussion above we can derive a number of general but quite robust conclusions about the purpose of supranational rules on state aid. At a minimum state aid rules should ensure that:

(i) aid is given only when the market alone (before government intervention) leads to inefficient or sub-optimal outcome;

(ii) aid is capable of addressing the source of market failure directly (it should be as narrow or as wide as the extent of the failure);

(iii) market-corrective aid does not lead to a collective sub-optimal outcome.

As argued below, in the EC, the source and magnitude of market failure are not always identified and measured.

5. European Community state aid policy: The rules

Art. 92 declares as incompatible with the common market any form of aid that confers an advantage to a firm or undertaking and distorts intra-EC trade and competition. A few categories of aid, mostly of social character, are pronounced as compatible with the common market while a number of other categories may be found, under certain conditions (notably when it is in the Community interest), to be compatible with the common market. The Commission is, among other things, empowered with the task of establishing when aid falls in the latter categories. For more details, see Chapter 1 by Adinda Sinnaeve.

From a legal point of view, the construction and provisions of Art. 92 may be beyond reproach. The same, however, cannot be said from an economic point of view. On the one hand, the prohibition is too wide. It catches virtually all aid schemes because very few are found in practice not to have an actual or potential effect on intra-EC trade and competition. If a support measure is classified as a form of state aid, it is invariably found to affect trade and competition (which are often used interchangeably). On the other hand, the discretion enjoyed by the Commission to authorise aid is not bounded by precise operational criteria.

In determining the relevance of state aid, the Commission should assess the effects of the state aid scheme considered in relation to its presumed objectives: correction of market failure, social considerations, economic development, common interest, etc. Although the Commission considers the specific instruments and amounts it does not carry out an explicit cost-benefit analysis of the impact of state aid, nor does it examine whether the aid scheme represents an optimal (i.e. first-best) economic policy option. Besides, the nature of market failure is often not even clearly identified.

The examination of aid schemes is not normally done by considering what would happen in the absence of government support (although for certain schemes, such as those to support R&D, the Commission does require that governments show their necessity; i.e. that R&D would not be undertaken without state assistance). This is surprising because the European Court of Justice established early on in case law that public assistance should not replace market mechanisms. The Commission often asks how firms would behave without receiving state aid but, with a notable and admittedly significant exception, it does not attempt to quantify the magnitude of the distortion.

That exceptions are the permissible aid ceilings (or intensities) defined in the various guidelines with respect to certain aid schemes and industrial sectors. For example the permissible aid ceilings for regional development aid are set according to the perceived regional backwardness which may be assumed to correspond to the degree of market failure (if backwardness is market failure).

However, aid intensities or ceilings are defined more for the purpose of ensuring that aid is proportional to the objective sought. Even though the Commission always insists on proportionality and makes references to economic factors such as "regional handicaps", it does not appear to relate aid to what is necessary to offset underlying market distortions.

While aid intensities may be construed in some loose manner as the Commission's way of relating allowable aid to the magnitude of market failure, it is puzzling why similar reasoning has not been used to evaluate direct involvement of the state in companies through injections of public capital (i.e. situations where the state becomes a shareholder).

The Commission has pioneered the "private investor" principle according to which governments should behave like any other private investor by expecting to receive a reasonable financial return on their investments. Although the private investor principle can probably be considered as a bold initiative, given that the Treaty does not exclude the state from ownership of factors of production (Art. 222), the Commission should be asking why certain companies have difficulty attracting private capital. Even if the state receives the same return as a private investor would expect to earn, it cannot be considered to be equivalent to a private investor (otherwise, why could a company not attract private capital? Participation by the state should be either presumed to correct an imperfection (and therefore the return can be justifiably lower) or otherwise it should be expected to earn a higher rate of return because of the advantages it carries. This means that under normal conditions, investment by the state should carry a "handicap", rather than be considered as equivalent to investment by private firms.

The absence of sufficient analysis of the need for public support is most obvious in aid schemes for the rescue or restructuring of ailing companies. The main criteria used by the Commission are that aid should be transitory and should make the recipient companies commercially viable again. It is not always clear what kind of imperfection such state aid schemes seek to redress (apart from the imperfections and failures of the management of those firms).

Admittedly, aid is frequently sought in these situations in order to offset charges related to the dismissal of workers and the rationalisation of operations (e.g. compensation, pension liabilities, etc.). It is presumably in the broader national interest to facilitate industrial adjustment. The problem is that aid in cases of rescue and restructuring is not exclusively granted for those purposes.

More puzzling is the fact that aid is approved when it is demonstrated that the beneficiaries will be able to function profitably without it. But if they can live without public handouts, why do they need any at all? Why is private capital not able to bring that kind of change? Why are those companies not able to attract private capital if indeed they can demonstrate the feasibility of their long-term profitability?

The closest that the Commission comes to coordinating national aid schemes is when it defines ceilings for regional aid and imposes "compensatory" conditions on other schemes it approves. This conditional authorisation aims to prevent the recipient of aid from using public handouts to strengthen its commercial position at the expense of firms in other member states. For example, aid to national airlines such as Air France, Alitalia, Olympic, Iberia and Sabena has been approved on condition that these airlines do not attempt to expand their market share by reducing prices or acquiring other airlines. In this context, it would not be inaccurate to say that coordination in practice means prevention of a disturbance of the status quo. Clearly, there is an element of "strategic" policy in this kind of aid schemes, with the difference that the intent is not to capture rents, but rather to defend (i.e. prevent the shifting abroad of) rents. Arguably, such schemes, by maintaining the status quo and existing level of trade and degree of competition in the EU, effectively prevent the competitive effects derived from integration of the internal market from being realised.

If aid is authorised explicitly for the purpose of correcting market failure, it ought not to make any difference that the status quo is disturbed. By definition, the current market conditions are not those that would have prevailed had the distortion not existed. And, after all, economic integration and the removal of obstacles to trade, movement and investment are market-correcting schemes on a larger scale.

Under certain conditions, the Treaty in Art. 92(3)(c) enables the Commission to authorise aid intended to promote the development of particular regions or economic activities, provided that it is not contrary to Community interest. Such aid goes beyond what is necessary to offset regional backwardness or severe unemployment and which is already permitted under Art. 92(3)(a). There is no definition of Community interest in the Treaty. Over the years it has been asserted that the interest of the Community has been advanced by aid such as that to attract ships back to EU registries or to provide financial services to Central and East European countries. The Treaty expresses so many different objectives that it is fairly easy for the Member States and the Commission to claim that a certain project is not contrary to the Community interest.

The Commission admittedly applies stricter criteria and lower ceilings to aid schemes authorised under 92(3)(c) than under 92(3)(a). But the question is whether it should authorise aid at all, given that it is not clear that the market has failed in those cases.

The EC has a number of non-economic objectives and some of those inevitably creep into the Court's rulings on state aid and into the Commission's evaluations of notified or non-notified schemes. Although certain policy objectives are non-economic, policy makers should still quantify and take into account their costs in terms of forgone efficiency and, therefore, welfare. The fact that those objectives are not explicitly economic does not make them costless. More importantly, policy makers should always favour first-best policies when available. State aid may often prove to be an inefficient instrument to address non-economic objectives.

6. European Community state aid policy: Practice and facts[1]

The Commission has been increasingly active in monitoring state aid over the last 15 years. The total annual number of decisions taken by the Commission was more than two and a half times higher in 1997 than in 1985, with 835 decisions compared to 317. However, the amount of aid granted by Member States remains high. The overall annual amount of state aid, excluding agriculture for which no comprehensive data are available, is estimated at about ECU 87 billion (in 1996 prices) for the period 1994-1996, which corresponds on average to 1.4% of EU GDP (excluding the value added for the agricultural sector). This is a massive amount of money, equivalent to almost one and a half times the total annual contribution of Member States to the EU budget. Were state aid granted according to a sound economic rationale, this would suggest that market failure is a major problem in the EU.

When excluding agriculture, fisheries, coal and transport (sectors traditionally heavily supported by the state and benefiting from special regimes), state aid to industry reached, on annual average, about ECU 39 billion for the period 1994-1996 (in 1996 prices), or on average 0.63% of the GDP of the EU-12. In terms of control at the European level, state aid to industry represented more than 60% of all decisions taken by the Commission for the period 1985-1997. This suggests that either the Commission has paid more attention to state aid to industry than to the traditional sectors that enjoy strong political support, or that aid schemes in the agriculture, fisheries, coal and transport sectors is relatively larger than for the rest of the industry. In any case, control of these special sectors by the Commission appears rather weak in view of the lack of transparency of these aid schemes, data for most countries being either unavailable or incomplete. For this reason, the remainder of the discussion will focus solely on state aid to industry for which data are publicly available.

A declining trend can be identified in the granting of state aid for the period 1986-1996 (for which the Commission has published aggregated data). The biggest "spenders" on state aid (ranked in decreasing order of importance) are Germany, Italy, France, Spain and the United Kingdom. Not surprisingly, large countries account for most of state aid granted in the EU.

However, in relative terms (i.e. taking the size of the economy into account), the main traditional providers of state aid are Greece, Italy and Ireland, as well as Germany since the reunification.

The relative importance of state aid varies considerably among Member States. In Denmark, France, Luxembourg, the Netherlands and the UK, state aid has attracted relatively lower resources. We can also see that Portugal and Belgium have heavily relied on state aid at times, although in a more erratic way. It is worth noting that Greece, Spain and the UK have drastically reduced their aid programme since 1986, cutting their spending by more than four-fold in real terms (respectively by 6.4, 2.7 and 3 times). In 1986, aid amounted to about ECU 5.1 billion in Greece, ECU 7.4 billion in Spain and ECU 5.4 billion in the UK, while in 1996 the figures dropped to ECU 0.8, 2.7 and 1.8 billion, respectively (in 1996 prices). Meanwhile, the level of aid granted by the German Government has doubled, from ECU 9 to 20.7 billion in 1994, but decreased again to 12.9 billion in 1996; the bulk of this increase represented aid to the new *Länder*.

The breakdown of state aid objectives for each country reveals sharp contrasts in aid policy between Member States. The majority (56%) of state aid to industry was granted for regional development, with 74% of aid in Germany, 66% in Greece, 65% in Luxembourg and 58% in Italy being spent on regional objectives for the period 1994-1996. Although sectoral state aid accounted for only 13% of all aid in the EU for this period, the level reached 63% and 52% in Spain and Portugal, respectively. In contrast, most aid was granted under horizontal objectives in Denmark (84%), Austria (74%), the Netherlands (74%), and Finland (74%).

Although further investigation would be required, it appears than no general pattern of state aid policy emerges when comparing situations in the Member States. Or, to put it in another way, state aid does not seem to be systematically related to specific macroeconomic features in a similar way in all Member States. This could perhaps suggest that state aid is not of a general nature or designed to address global economic problems, but rather of a specific nature tailored to address particular situations. Another explanation could be that national traditions and political systems remain a major factor in the shaping of state aid policy. Indeed, Member States reveal distinct preferences for different forms of state aid (regional, sectoral, horizontal, etc.).

Looking at the activity of the Commission in controlling state aid to industry, it is worth mentioning that while the overall number of Commission decisions on state aid to industry increased from 195 in 1983 to 502 in 1997, 21 negative final decisions were taken in 1983 (accounting for 11% of all decisions that year) for only 9 in 1997 (2% of all decisions). The Commission raised no objection in relation to 52% of its decisions in 1983 and to 77% in

1997. Similarly, while the overall number of decisions more than doubled over this period, the share of procedures initiated by the Commission was cut by half. It is hard to believe that the level of compliance with EC state aid rules has improved to such an extent that the Commission does not have to flex its muscles apart from on rare occasions.

The Commission is not above reproach either. It appears to be difficult to obtain information and explanations on how data on state aid are collected and aggregated by the Commission services. For instance, when we add up all the Commission decisions on individual schemes as itemised in the annexes of the various annual reports on Competition Policy, we find a consistently lower total number of decisions than the aggregated numbers. The size and consistency of the sign of these discrepancies rule out the possibility of any marginal or random errors.

More fundamentally, the Commission does not provide sufficiently detailed reasoning and specific economic analysis to justify its decisions on aid schemes. Yet, discretionary power has to be accompanied by clarity and transparency to guarantee a credible and consistent mechanism to control state aid.

Finally, as specific annual data on the amount of state aid granted are not published at the European level, information on the main sectors benefiting from state aid has to be derived from the individual decisions taken by the Commission. A detailed investigation would go beyond the scope of this Chapter. Here, it is sufficient to mention that most of the decisions on state aid to industry concern mainly shipbuilding, steel, information technology, consumer electronics, motor vehicles, mechanical engineering and the chemical industry. Since the 1990s, some sectors such as energy and tourism have also attracted more attention from the Commission. Aid to SMEs and for employment has also been on the increase. Apart from regional aid which remains one of the principal objectives of state aid, financial measures, R&D projects, (industrial) investment aid and to some extent environmental aid represent increasingly common justifications of aid schemes.

This evolution suggests that while some traditional sectors remain the focus of most state aid activities, the type and nature of aid schemes has shifted over time. It remains to be seen whether this corresponds to an improvement of state aid control by the Commission. Yet, while regional and horizontal schemes could conceivably aim to improve the functioning of the market, it is very hard to believe that sectoral aid has the same objectives or that the recipient industries have been suffering from sector-specific distortions for so many years. The same goes for individual awards of aid to particular firms.

7. How can the rules be improved?

It would be completely unrealistic, if not naive, to expect that EC rules could be changed in such a way as to prohibit absolutely any state aid scheme that is not intended to correct market failure. Indeed, if a proposal along these lines were ever discussed, there would be interminable debates on the definition of market failure. It is doubtful that politicians would ever reach a consensus on the meaning of market failure or, even if they did, that they would be able to define it in an operationally meaningful manner that would not be open to creative interpretation and abuse.

Hence, it is unavoidable that the Member States would want to assist particular firms, industries or regions for reasons other than economic ones. In this case the Commission has an important role to play in ensuring that aid does not distort intra-EC trade to an extent unwarranted by the objective sought. It is impossible to define *a priori* the magnitude of aid that is appropriate for each of those objectives. Despite this inherent difficulty, the Commission should attempt to make explicit the non-economic objectives for which aid may be authorised. That would improve decision-making transparency in an important policy area.

But instead of focusing on what is not possible, it would be more productive to examine what is possible. Can market-correcting aid be meaningfully defined and then exempted all together? That would reduce the workload of the Commission and allow it to concentrate its resources on serious cases of state aid.

As mentioned earlier, a basic tenet of the theory of economic policy is that intervention should go to the heart of the distortion. This is normally understood that corrective measures should be as specific as possible so that they do not generate unwanted side-effects. But going to the heart of the distortion also means that the scope of the corrective measures should cover the (full) extent of the distortion itself, implying that no affected activities or areas are left outside. For example, governments should not grant loans or inject capital to the manufacturing industry at subsidised interest rates in an attempt to offset imperfectly functioning capital markets. It would be more efficient to intervene directly in the capital markets so that the manufacturing industry does not receive more favourable treatment than the service sector.

Also if the government, for example, proposes to give aid to an industry for the training of workers, it should explain why it does not offer similar assistance to other industries with similar training needs. If available resources are limited or if the identified industry is perceived to have more urgent needs, there can be defined objective criteria for selecting the neediest industry or the training programme that generates the highest value or return. Such objective (i.e. non-discriminatory) criteria in effect "generalise" the scope of application of the particular state aid scheme and prevent public assistance from flowing to politically favoured industries.

As already mentioned, alleged market failures can justify government interventions in areas such as training, R&D, investment, industrial production, the environment, consumer protection, etc. This is not an exhaustive list of what governments should or actually do. It is rather an indicative list that suggests that market failure is very unlikely to be confined to a single firm or even a single industry. As its name suggests, if the failure of the market is generic, it is likely to be market-wide. That is, when voluntary exchange and transactions do not lead to a socially optimal outcome, it is reasonable to expect that the cause is not confined to a particular firm or industry.

This is an important conclusion. Market correcting intervention should seek to address particular causes of market failure in all the industries or sectors they appear. Consequently, correcting measures should be of a more general than specific nature. This would conform with EC rules on state aid that allow general aid schemes. Therefore, if governments claim that their schemes seek to correct market failure, the presumption should be that corrective measures are general and that they are automatically exempt from the prohibition of Art. 92.

Carrying the argument to its logical conclusion, suggests, on the other hand, that aid to individual firms or industries is very unlikely to be the optimum method of correcting generic market failure. It should, as a rule, be prohibited even if the granting agencies show that the recipients can eventually operate without aid. The burden of proof should be on governments to show that their proposed schemes deal with a firm-specific or industry-specific failure. Moreover, if they can demonstrate that the recipients can become commercially viable, it is *prima facie* evidence that the market has not failed. Ironically, this reasoning itself undermines the case for aid.

Indeed, the question why firms cannot attract funds from capital markets should also be raised in cases of public injection of capital and acquisition of private shareholdings. The question should not be whether the state behaves like a private investor. This is a fiction because the state cannot default. The relevant question is why the recipient firms cannot attract 100% private funding. Where is the market failure that discourages that kind of funding?

The Commission must be more explicit about the criteria it uses to determine when aid is compatible with the common or Community interest. Presumably, the common interest dictates eligible aid schemes when they cause significant cross-border effects so as to induce relocation of production or investment. But how much aid is too much? How much aid is sufficient to correct market distortions and how much should be permitted for each Member State? Concepts of the common interest as they are used at present are incapable of providing answers to these questions, especially when not all

Member States would gain if all granted aid.

In conclusion, it is not possible to define in precise detail acceptable and unacceptable categories of state aid (even though the WTO agreement on subsidies attempted to do just that) because a simple prohibition against all schemes that have cross-border effects would be too wide, while a narrower ban on all schemes that do not or cannot improve efficiency would be too vague and politically unacceptable. Member States may want to subsidise particular economic activities and particular regions for social or political reasons. However, current practice as regards this kind of aid could still be improved by stricter application of the requirement that it is not contrary to a well-defined concept of Community interest.

Where aid has an implicit economic objective, the Commission should seek to rigorously establish the nature and magnitude of market failure. Permitted aid should be solely what is necessary to correct that failure. When aid schemes have the potential to shift economic activity from one location to another, then the Commission should also impose additional limits on the amount of aid or other compensatory requirements.

Finally, one may ask whether these suggestions can be implemented under current Treaty provisions on state aid. We do not see any major obstacles here. Art. 92(3) identifies certain policy objectives for which Member States *may* grant aid in order to attain them. It is up to the Commission to determine the conditions under which aid is compatible with the common market. Such compatibility need not be in conflict with the correction of market failure.

8. Conclusion

EC state aid rules are both too restrictive and too permissive. They prohibit all forms of aid that may affect intra-EC trade or competition. We argue that, in principle, aid intended to correct market failure should be allowed even if it has cross-border effects. On the other hand, authorised aid schemes are hardly confined to the correction of market failure. They have much broader objectives. The problem is that it is not obvious how much distortion of competition is tolerated in the pursuit of those broader objectives.

The control of state aid would be improved and aligned to efficiency considerations if the Commission analysed whether market failure is the centrepiece of its evaluation of aid cases and whether the proposed modalities and amount of aid are both necessary and proportional to the task of correcting the failure.

The presumption should be that specific schemes that benefit particular firms or industries are incompatible with the common market because market failure is unlikely to be confined to a single firm or even a single industry. Moreover, the injection of public capital and acquisition of shares by a government should also be presumed to be a form of aid even if the state purports to behave as a private investor. The burden of proof should be on governments to demonstrate the need for their involvement and the reason why private investment is not forthcoming.

NOTES

*   We are grateful to Roel Polmans for his extensive assistance in the preparation
     of the statistical section of this Chapter. We also would like to thank Jean-Marie
     Grether for his helpful comments and the Foundation BBV for its financial
     support.
1.   For a more comprehensive account and systematic analysis, see Chapter 3 by
     Bilal and Polmans.

CHAPTER 3

IS STATE AID IN DECLINE? TRENDS OF STATE AID
TO INDUSTRY IN THE MEMBER STATES OF THE
EUROPEAN UNION

Sanoussi Bilal and Roel Polmans*

1. Introduction

Public support for industry is a prevalent and persistent phenomenon in most
developed countries, including those of the European Union (EU).[1] Between
1986 and 1996, the state aid granted by the then 12 Member States of the EU
to industry alone (i.e. excluding agriculture, fisheries, coal and transport)
amounted to an average of over ECU 45 billion per year (in 1996 prices).[2]
This is a significant level of support which amounted to 0.76% of the EU-12
GDP on average and corresponds to about two thirds of the total budget of the
EU.

It is important to remember that state aid to industry amounts to only a
fraction of the overall aid provided by the Member States and that a complete
picture on state aid practices cannot be drawn due to lack of data. In particular,
information on national aid to agriculture is often non-existent or incomplete.
However, the European Commission in its latest survey on state aid estimated
that, excluding the agricultural sector, the overall amount of state aid granted
by the Member State was on average about ECU 87 billion per year from 1994
to 1996 (compared to more than ECU 90 billion from 1992 to 1994).[3]

As can be seen from Table 1, state aid to the manufacturing sector
accounts for less than half of the total amount of aid granted by the Member
States (excluding agriculture). It is worth noting the increasing magnitude of
state aid to the service sector, which has become almost as important as the
manufacturing sector was in the 1994-1996 period.

S. Bilal and P. Nicolaides (eds.), Understanding State Aid Policy in the European Community, 47–80.
© 1999 *Kluwer Law International. Printed in the Netherlands.*

Table 1:
EU aggregated aid to main sectors as a share of overall state aid
excluding agriculture (in percent)

	1992-1994	1994-1996
Manufacturing sector	**47.1**	**45.8**
Shipbuilding development aid*	0.1	0.2
Steel	n.a.	1.8
Motor vehicles**	1.5	0.7
Services	**36.8**	**43.7**
Financial services	0.4	1.5
Air transport	0.8	1.6
Coal	**15.7**	**10.1**
Fisheries	**0.4**	**0.4**
Overall national aid****	**100**	**100**

Data source: Calculations from the European Commission's Sixth Survey on State Aid.
Notes: * State aid granted to European shipyards for the construction of ships for developing countries; ** In 1992, one case in Italy amounted to ECU 3,056 million; *** The totals do not include figures on aid given to the agricultural sector.

However, due to the unavailability of data on non-manufacturing sectors, this Chapter focuses solely on state aid to industry in the Member States. In particular, it attempts to identify some general trends and patterns in the allocation of national aid in the EU for the period from 1986 to 1996 (see Table 2). In particular, Section 2 presents the general trends in the Member States and attempts to identify some macroeconomic factors associated with the granting of state aid. Among other things, it reveals that while in the EU as a whole state aid to industry has been in decline over the last few years, this evolution masks significant disparities between the Member States. Section 3 offers a critical analysis of some of the main patterns in the official objectives of aid schemes in the Member States, whereas Section 4 discusses the activity of the Commission in controlling and monitoring state aid granted by the Member States. Finally, Section 5 brings the discussion to a close by summarising some of the main findings.

Table 2: *Amount of state aid to industry in million ECU for 1986-1996 in constant (1996) prices*

	1986	1987	1988	1989	1990	1991	1992	1993	1994	1995	1996
Belgium	1,211	1,248	1,523	1,344	1,694	3,239	657	872	1,126	1,044	1,277
Denmark	304	367	437	415	350	328	359	621	604	682	746
Germany	9,292	9,228	9,791	9,779	1,1687	13,731	16,029	20,846	20,786	15,961	12,889
Greece	5,149	6,289	4,404	2,555	2,281	1,642	1,713	639	431	937	798
Spain	7,473	5,144	6,393	2,153	2,944	1,521	1,214	1,641	1,639	2,159	2,794
France	7,262	6,315	9,017	6,551	5,808	4,954	5,104	5,426	4,194	3,441	3,767
Ireland	541	574	471	418	426	293	225	227	193	200	279
Italy	17,182	13,450	14,130	10,053	20,227	14,957	14,189	13,789	10,923	11,290	10,265
Luxembourg	34	49	48	64	56	62	67	43	44	48	46
Netherlands	1,234	1,219	1,361	1,218	1,378	883	684	670	674	733	649
Austria	n.a.	n.a.	n.a.	n.a.	n.a.	n.a.	n.a.	n.a.	n.a.	503	390
Portugal	549	299	338	1,391	1,074	567	392	447	631	287	254
Finland	n.a.	n.a.	n.a.	n.a.	n.a.	n.a.	n.a.	n.a.	n.a.	405	327
Sweden	n.a.	n.a.	n.a.	n.a.	n.a.	n.a.	n.a.	n.a.	n.a.	313	361
UK	5,445	5,334	5,636	4,259	3,392	3,043	2,185	1,247	1,405	1,525	1,863
EU-15										39528	36705
EU-12	55,674	49,516	53,548	40,199	51,317	45,221	42,817	46,469	42,649	38,307	35,628

Data source: Amounts of aid from European Commission's Third to Sixth Surveys on State Aid; price indices from Eurostat.

2. General trends in the Member States

2.1 THE MAIN TENDENCIES

In nominal terms, the amount of state aid to industry in the EU-12 remained stable over the ten-year period, with ECU 35,580 million in 1986 and ECU 35,628 million in 1996. However, in real terms (at 1996 prices), the overall amount of state aid to industry granted by Member States dropped by 36% (from ECU 55,674 million in 1986 to ECU 35,628 million in 1996), which amounts to a fall of 43% in terms of EU-12 GDP (from 1% of EU-12 GDP in 1986 to 0.57% in 1996). From 1993 to 1996 alone, state aid to the manufacturing sector fell by 23%. Such figures might indicate that, over the last decade, the European economy has relied more on market forces and less of public support. Yet, this global picture masks large fluctuations over time and notable disparities between Member States.

As illustrated by Table A1 (see Appendix), the annual growth rate of state aid to industry in the EU is generally negative, although positive at times (i.e. in 1988, 1990 and 1993), and ranged, in absolute terms, from 5.3% in 1988 to 27.7% in 1990. The evolution of state aid measures in the EU suggests that although a declining long-term trend can clearly be identified, it is marked by important annual swings which do not appear to follow any specific pattern. Between 1987 to 1996, the average annual growth rate of aid in the EU was 12.3% in absolute values.

The overall picture at the EU level regroups a variety of independent national policy patterns, though. Indeed, the evolution of state aid measures differs widely among Member States. For instance, for the period 1986-1996, the amount, in real terms, of state aid granted to manufacturing more than doubled in Denmark (from ECU 304 million in 1986 to ECU 746 million in 1996) and increased by 39% in Germany (from ECU 9,292 million to ECU 12,889 million). It remained roughly constant in Belgium (with ECU 1,211 million in 1986 and ECU 1,277 million in 1996). In contrast, over the same period, it dropped by 84% in Greece, 66% in the United Kingdom, 62% in Spain, 54% in Portugal, 48% in France and Ireland, 47% in the Netherlands and 40% in Italy.

One could be tempted to conclude that, with few exceptions, state aid to industry has become less significant in most Member States, perhaps suggesting that governments have been successful in resisting domestic pressures to support industry. However, recent national trends in state aid reveal a more complex pattern.

Consider the period from 1993 to 1996. State aid to the manufacturing sector within the EU fell by more than ECU 10 billion (in 1996 prices), of which about ECU 8 billion was due to a reduction of state aid in Germany and over ECU 1.5 billion to a decrease in state aid in France. Hence, while state aid to manufacturing declined in five countries (by 43% in Portugal, 38% in Germany, 31% in France, 26% in Italy and 3% in the Netherlands), it increased in the seven other EU-12 Member States (by 6% in Luxembourg, 20% in Denmark, 23% in Ireland, 25% in Greece, 46% in Belgium, 49% in the United Kingdom and 70% in Spain). It would thus seem premature to assume that state aid is well under control in most of the Member States.

The surge of state aid in Germany (an increase of 97% from 1986 to 1994) can be largely explained by the reunification in 1990. The real growth rate in the amount of aid for the period from 1986 to 1990 was 26% (which amounts to an annual growth rate of 5.9%), compared to 78% for the period 1990-1994 (i.e. 15.5% annually) and minus 38% from 1994 to 1996 (i.e. minus 21.3% annually).

In absolute terms, the biggest spenders of state aid in 1986 where, in decreasing order: Italy, Germany, Spain, France and the United Kingdom. By 1996, this ranking was broadly similar, with the only difference being that Germany had overtaken Italy, and France had overtaken Spain. Incidentally, it is worth noting that while aid provided by Germany and Italy accounted for 48% of all aid granted by Member States in 1986, it reached 65% of all state aid in the EU-12 in 1996. This relative increase cannot be explained by a growth of these two economies (due to factors such as the German reunification), as they accounted for 42.6% of EU-12 GDP in 1986 and 44.6% in 1996.[4] However, Germany was pouring large amounts of state aid in the former East German *Länder* to assist companies to re-equip or close down.

2.2 THE RELATIVE IMPORTANCE OF STATE AID

The fact that, in absolute terms, large countries spend more on state aid than small ones is no surprise. To the extent that state aid to industry is proportional to the size of the domestic industry, the larger the economy, the larger the amount of aid granted. Indeed, there is an almost perfect correlation (around 0.98) each year across Member States between the amount of aid granted and the level of GDP, suggesting that the amount of aid is roughly proportionate to the size of the economy (see Table A2 in the Appendix).

In relative terms, however, there is no *a priori* reason to expect this to be the case. Indeed, no (cross-section) correlation between the relative amount of state aid granted by Member States (in terms of share of GDP) and the level of GDP can be identified (see Table A2 in the Appendix).

So, taking into account the size of the economy (as captured by the level of GDP), the Member States devoting the largest amount of resources, in relative terms, to state aid were, in 1986, Greece, Spain, Italy and Ireland, all spending above 1.5% of their GDP on state aid to industry (see Table 3). The lowest spenders were Denmark (with 0.28% of its GDP), the Netherlands (0.56%) and the UK (0.61%). By 1996, the disparity in the relative importance of state aid between Member States (as measured by this variance) was significantly reduced, ranging from 0.21% of GDP in the UK and the Netherlands and 0.31% in France and Portugal, to 0.70% of GDP in Germany, 0.82% in Greece and 1.07% in Italy.

Table 3 also reveals that, at the aggregate EU level, there is a downward trend in the relative amount of state aid granted which could, however, reflect the decline in manufacturing. For this reason, a better indicator might be the amount of state aid to industry expressed as a percentage of the gross added value of manufactured products, building and construction. As a share of GDP, gross value added of manufacturing, building and construction fell from 26.5% in 1986 to 24.3% in 1995. Over this period, however, there was a very high correlation between the trends of GDP and this measure of gross value added. Hence, the relative decline of state aid is confirmed. State aid to industry amounted to 3.4% of the gross value added of manufactured products, building and construction in 1986, it dropped to a low of 2.3% in 1989 and reached 2.5% in 1995 (see Table A3 in the Appendix for more details).[5]

To better compare the relative importance (in terms of GDP) of state aid between Member States, an index has been constructed, which indicates the relative share of a country in EU-aggregated aid over its relative share of EU GDP. Hence, a country granting proportionally more (less) aid than the relative size of its economy would imply an index higher (lower) than one. Values are reported in Table 4. For instance, in 1986, the Table indicates that Belgium gave only 84% (0.84) of the relative average amount of state aid given by the EU Member States (the EU average being equal to 1 by definition).

It can be seen that, in 1986, Spain supported its industry, relative to its size, twice as much (i.e. 1.9) as the EU average. In contrast, in 1994, the amount of state aid granted to Spanish industry dropped to a third (i.e. 0.33) of the relative EU-12 average, to settle around the EU-12 average (i.e. 1.07) in 1996. It follows from Table 4 that, looking at the changes in index values (as captured by the variance) from 1986 to 1996, the country that most drastically modified its support to industry, compared to other Member States, was Greece, followed by Portugal, Spain and Belgium. In contrast, the Member States that experienced the smallest modifications in the relative amount of state aid granted to their industry are the Netherlands, France and the United Kingdom. Table 4 also confirms that the disparity between Member States tended to diminish over this period.

However, while it appears that there was some kind of convergence in the level of state aid to industry between the various Member States over the

Table 3: Amount of state aid to industry as a share of GDP, 1986-1996

	1986	1987	1988	1989	1990	1991	1992	1993	1994	1995	1996
Belgium	0.84	0.82	0.96	0.81	0.97	1.81	0.35	0.46	0.56	0.50	0.61
Denmark	0.28	0.33	0.39	0.38	0.31	0.29	0.30	0.51	0.47	0.51	0.54
Germany	0.81	0.76	0.78	0.75	0.84	0.87	0.96	1.21	1.17	0.85	0.70
Greece	2.86	4.07	2.84	1.68	1.69	1.31	1.51	0.62	0.44	0.99	0.82
Spain	1.90	1.27	1.44	0.44	0.57	0.28	0.23	0.35	0.37	0.49	0.60
France	0.75	0.66	0.91	0.63	0.54	0.46	0.46	0.48	0.36	0.29	0.31
Ireland	1.55	1.66	1.28	1.06	1.03	0.70	0.51	0.51	0.40	0.40	0.50
Italy	1.69	1.30	1.33	0.90	1.77	1.29	1.27	1.44	1.17	1.31	1.07
Luxembourg	0.47	0.65	0.58	0.71	0.59	0.63	0.62	0.37	0.34	0.36	0.33
Netherlands	0.56	0.53	0.57	0.49	0.53	0.33	0.25	0.24	0.23	0.24	0.21
Austria	n.a.	n.a.	n.a.	n.a.	n.a.	n.a.	n.a.	n.a.	n.a.	0.29	0.22
Portugal	0.72	0.40	0.45	1.79	1.39	0.70	0.46	0.57	0.82	0.36	0.31
Finland	n.a.	n.a.	n.a.	n.a.	n.a.	n.a.	n.a.	n.a.	n.a.	0.42	0.33
Sweden	n.a.	n.a.	n.a.	n.a.	n.a.	n.a.	n.a.	n.a.	n.a.	0.18	0.18
UK	0.61	0.59	0.56	0.42	0.35	0.32	0.24	0.14	0.15	0.18	0.21
EU-15										0.60	0.54
EU-12	1.00	0.87	0.92	0.68	0.84	0.73	0.69	0.77	0.70	0.62	0.57

Data source: Calculations from European Commission's Third to Sixth Surveys on State Aid; Eurostat.

Table 4: Index of the relative importance of state aid to industry

	1986	1987	1988	1989	1990	1991	1992	1993	1994	1995	1996
Belgium	0.84	0.95	1.04	1.19	1.15	2.49	0.51	0.59	0.80	0.80	1.08
Denmark	0.28	0.38	0.43	0.55	0.36	0.39	0.44	0.66	0.67	0.81	0.96
Germany	0.81	0.88	0.84	1.10	0.99	1.19	1.39	1.56	1.67	1.37	1.23
Greece	2.87	4.69	3.08	2.47	2.01	1.80	2.20	0.80	0.63	1.59	1.46
Spain	1.90	1.46	1.56	0.64	0.68	0.39	0.33	0.46	0.53	0.78	1.07
France	0.76	0.75	0.98	0.93	0.64	0.63	0.67	0.62	0.51	0.46	0.55
Ireland	1.56	1.91	1.39	1.56	1.22	0.95	0.74	0.66	0.58	0.64	0.89
Italy	1.70	1.49	1.44	1.32	2.10	1.76	1.84	1.86	1.67	2.09	1.90
Luxembourg	0.47	0.75	0.63	1.04	0.70	0.86	0.90	0.48	0.49	0.57	0.59
Netherlands	0.56	0.61	0.62	0.72	0.63	0.46	0.37	0.30	0.33	0.38	0.37
Portugal	0.72	0.47	0.48	2.63	1.66	0.96	0.67	0.73	1.17	0.58	0.55
UK	0.61	0.68	0.60	0.62	0.42	0.45	0.36	0.18	0.22	0.28	0.36

Data source: Calculations from European Commission's Second to Sixth Survey on State Aid to Industry; Eurostat.

Note: The index is calculated as follows: Index = $\dfrac{\text{(country's aid)/(EU-12 aid)}}{\text{(country's GDP)/(EU-12 GDP)}}$

1986-1996 period, great national disparities remained. Besides, while the level of state aid seems to exhibit trends in some Member States (an upward trend in Denmark, downwards in the Netherlands, as well as in Greece and the UK until 1994), it remained highly volatile in other Member States like Portugal and Belgium. Data also show that even in countries where a trend can be identified, such as the declining reliance on state aid in Spain (at least until 1992), huge variations can be identified.

One may wonder therefore whether some countries experience higher variability in the granting of state aid because they are more prone to economic shocks or whether they are more willing to grant aid to assist companies in financial difficulty.

Yet, aggregate values at the EU level are partially misleading to the extent that they mask significant differences in the recourse to state aid between Member States.

The considerable variations in the level of state aid over time and among Member States suggest that, in spite of the Commission's efforts to control state aid, the determination of state aid policy remains mainly a national prerogative. Governments decide, within the EC regulatory framework, to what extent they want to support their industry.

2.3 FACTORS AFFECTING THE LEVEL OF STATE AID

The purpose of this Chapter is not to explain the evolution of state aid in each Member State, but rather to identify and describe some general trends. In this respect, one may wonder whether changes in the level of state aid interventions could be explained by some broad macroeconomic indicators.

This Section focuses only on four main variables which represent the state of the economy: [1] national income (i.e. GDP), as a standard measure of the absolute level of welfare of an economy; [2] GDP per capita, which provides an indication of the relative welfare of a society; [3] the unemployment rate, as an implicit measure of the state of the industrial sector; and finally [4] the level of deficit or surplus of the budget of the central government (expressed in percentage of GDP), which reflects the financial capacity of the state to support its industry.

Simple correlation measures between the level of state aid and each of these four variables are presented in Table 5. Note that for the relationship over time, the degree of correlation with a one-year lag is probably the most relevant. The justification is that state aid policy is assumed to come as a response to changes in macroeconomic conditions, hence with a time delay. Besides, it is important to remember that results related to the degree correlation should be considered with caution. They do not reflect causal links and should be viewed as indicative only.

Table 5: Correlations by Member State between levels of state aid to industry and economic indicators

	Amount of aid and GDP (1996 prices)		Amount of aid as a share of GDP and GDP per capita (1996 prices)		Amount of aid as a share of GDP and unemployment rate		Amount of aid and deficit or surplus of central government, as a share of GDP	
	current	lagged	current	lagged	current	lagged	current	lagged
Belgium	-0.17	-0.19	-0.38	-0.37	-0.47	-0.23	-0.31	-0.23
Denmark	0.91	0.90	0.83	0.81	0.18	0.37	0.37	0.10
Germany	0.80	0.73	0.31	0.21	0.59	0.55	-0.37	-0.42
Spain	-0.70	-0.78	-0.74	-0.81	0.10	0.30	-0.16	-0.02
Greece	0.89	0.89	0.84	0.87	-0.72	-0.64	-0.03	0.19
France	-0.87	-0.88	-0.91	-0.91	-0.63	-0.46	-0.54	-0.34
Ireland	-0.82	-0.83	-0.87	-0.88	0.67	0.64	-0.67	-0.60
Italy	0.51	0.63	0.11	0.40	-0.46	-0.27	-0.30	-0.14
Luxembourg	-0.04	-0.39	-0.74	-0.87	-0.88	-0.65	-0.63	-0.33
Netherlands	-0.83	-0.85	-0.90	-0.90	0.58	0.72	-0.65	-0.50
Portugal	-0.20	-0.19	-0.23	-0.21	-0.38	-0.36	-0.38	-0.23
UK	0.53	0.28	0.43	0.23	0.20	0.24	0.11	0.33
EU-12	-0.73	-0.54	-0.63	-0.41	n.a.	n.a.	n.a.	n.a.

Data source: European Commission's Third to Sixth Survey on State Aid; Eurostat.

As already mentioned, although larger Member States spend more in absolute terms on state aid than smaller ones, they do not provide more support to their industry in relative terms (as measured by the amount of aid as a share of GDP). In short, size does not seem to matter in determining the intensity of state aid to industry.[6]

It is sometimes argued that rich countries give more aid to their industry. This hypothesis does not seem to be supported, as there is no apparent (cross-section) correlation between national aid as a share of GDP and GDP per capita (see Table A2 in the Appendix). This suggests that, contrary to common belief, there is no systematic bias whereby richer Member States support their industry more heavily than poorer ones.

The situation is slightly different when looking at the national trends in state aid over time. Consider first, for each Member State, the link over time between, on the one hand, amounts of aid and the level of GDP, and, on the other hand, the amount of aid as a percentage of GDP and GDP per capita, as shown by Table 5. With regard to the former relationship, state aid seems to decrease (increase) as the economy grows (declines) in several Member States. This is the case in France, the Netherlands, Ireland, Spain and to a lesser extent in Luxembourg, as well as for aid at the EU aggregated level. In contrast, in Denmark, Greece, Germany, Italy (and perhaps the United Kingdom), the coefficients of correlation are positive. Finally, in Belgium and Portugal changes in amounts of state aid do not seem to be significantly related to the evolution of GDP.

The relationship between changes in the relative intensity of state aid and the prosperity of a Member State is also country specific. In Greece, state aid has become less important as the economic condition has worsened and in Denmark a higher GDP per capita is associated with more state aid. A weak positive link between state aid as a share of GDP and GDP per capita also appears in Italy and at the aggregated EU level. In contrast, in France, the Netherlands, Ireland, Luxembourg and Spain economic hardship seems to be accompanied by a larger share of GDP devoted to helping the manufacturing sector, whereas in Portugal, the United Kingdom and Germany no significant relationship can be identified.

To summarise, it appears that, broadly speaking, two categories of Member States can be identified, depending on whether their level of state aid is positively or negatively related to their level of income, measured either in absolute or relative terms. In most Member States, larger state support to industry is associated with economic decline (although to various degrees), excepted in Denmark, Germany, Greece, Italy and the United Kingdom.

Finally, Table 5 also reports the degree of correlation, for each Member State, between state aid measures and both the level of unemployment and the budget balance of the central government. No significant relationship seems to emerge. Yet, in Ireland and the Netherlands, relatively more (less) aid is granted as unemployment and the budget deficit increases (falls). The same links seem also present to some extent in Germany. In contrast, changes in state aid support appear to be negatively correlated to unemployment in Greece and Luxembourg. Besides, it is interesting to note that while Member States experiencing a budget deficit (surplus) seem to have granted more (less) aid during the period from 1986 to 1992 (with a coefficient of correlation averaging at around 0.6), the connection disappeared after 1992 (and even seemed to be reversed in 1995-1996, as shown in Table A2).

3. Patterns in the allocation of state aid

3.1 THE DATA

There is a serious lack of transparency in the specific allocation of state aid in the Member States. So, although the overall amount of state aid to manufacturing granted by Member States is rather well documented, the patterns of national support to industry remain more obscure. Specific data on the allocation of aid by sectors, types of measures and instruments are not readily available at the EU level. Yet, in its surveys on state aid[7], the European Commission has published three-year-average breakdowns by main objectives of state aid to manufacturing in the Member States, for the periods 1988-1990, 1990-1992, 1992-1994 and 1994-1996. The data are reported in Table 6.

In this "refined" information, three objectives are identified: horizontal, sectoral (i.e. particular sectors) and regional objectives. The Commission also purports to publish more detailed state aid data according to sectors and functions. Table A4 in the Appendix presents the latest data available for the 1994-1996 period. However, the more specific breakdown seems unreliable. Several reasons for this can be identified. First, the classification of state aid is partly arbitrary. As mentioned by the surveys:

"The classification of aid is, in many cases, somewhat arbitrary because it is necessary to decide which of the objectives declared by a Member State is to be considered as the primary objective. In some Member States, aid for research and development is administered through sector specific R&D programmes, in others aid to particular sectors is limited to small and medium-sized enterprises, etc. Furthermore, primary objectives cannot give a true picture of the final beneficiaries: a large part of regional aid is in fact paid to small and medium-sized enterprises, aid for research and development goes to particular sectors, and so on."[8]

Table 6: State aid to Industry 1988-1996: Breakdown by main objectives (in percent)

	Horizontal Objectives				Particular Sectors				Regional Objectives			
	88-90	90-92	92-94	94-96	88-90	90-92	92-94	94-96	88-90	90-92	92-94	94-96
Belgium	77	62	56	46	3	29	19	29	21	9	26	25
Denmark	61	67	73	84	36	31	26	14	3	2	1	2
Germany	26	16	14	19	10	3	6	7	64	81	80	74
Greece	71	61	53	31	4	10	20	3	25	29	27	66
Spain	26	39	38	24	69	49	43	63	5	12	19	13
France	66	66	70	51	25	17	11	15	9	17	19	34
Ireland	49	31	36	37	0	0	0	7	51	69	63	56
Italy	30	25	35	31	15	18	12	11	55	57	53	58
Luxembourg	39	30	29	33	0	0	0	2	60	70	70	65
Netherlands	76	73	76	74	11	10	5	10	14	17	19	17
Austria	n.a.	n.a.	n.a.	74	n.a.	n.a.	n.a.	13	n.a.	n.a.	n.a.	13
Portugal	14	57	23	24	81	33	36	52	5	10	41	24
Finland	n.a.	n.a.	n.a.	74	n.a.	n.a.	n.a.	2	n.a.	n.a.	n.a.	23
Sweden	n.a.	n.a.	n.a.	34	n.a.	n.a.	n.a.	4	n.a.	n.a.	n.a.	61
UK	42	50	32	22	28	18	16	19	30	31	53	59
Total EU-12	40	35	31	n.a.	21	15	11	n.a.	39	50	58	n.a.
Total EU-15				30				13				56
Average EU-12	48	48	45	40	24	18	16	19	29	34	39	41
Average EU-15				44				17				39

Data source: Averages for 1988-1990 are from the Fourth Survey, 1990-1992 from the Fifth Survey, and 1992-1994, 1994-1996 from the Sixth Survey on State Aid.

So, discrepancies between Member States in the allocation of state aid may not only reflect different policy patterns, but may simply result from different administrative practices.

Second, and perhaps even more disturbing, the specific breakdowns of data published by the Commission (for example, those reported in Table A4 in the Appendix) do not always seem reliable. The main problem is that state aid data are significantly revised by the Commission (generally in cooperation with the Member States). For instance, in its Sixth Survey, the Commission acknowledges that "the amounts for the last year reported on (1996) are to a non-negligible extent provisional and ... will certainly be modified by the Member States in future."[9] Table 7 reveals the differences between the last three surveys in terms of percentage points for the breakdown by main objectives. It appears that adjustments, even on the three-year averages (which, according to the Commission, should smooth out discrepancies over time), are significant. Hence, although the Commission claims in its latest survey that its "procedure ensures that a relatively high degree of reliance can be placed in the data",[10] recent data should be considered with caution.

No one will blame the Commission and the Member Sates for revising and updating data on state aid so as to increase accuracy. The issue here, however, is a question of transparency. The Commission publishes detailed information on the allocation of state aid in its surveys. The breakdown of the share of aid is provided in the main section of the surveys,[11] whereas numerous tables in the surveys' annexes[12] contain breakdown of data on amounts of aid. Yet, each survey provides this detailed breakdown of averages for the latest three-year period only (i.e. 1988-1990 in the Third Survey, 1990-1992 in the Fourth Survey, 1992-1994 in the Fifth Survey and 1994-1996 in the Sixth Survey), while the figures have to be updated later on. It follows that reliable (i.e. revised) figures for the amount of state aid by sector and function are never released. One may thus wonder what the point of publishing these (incomplete and hence incorrect) data is in the first place.

Furthermore, the Sixth Survey claims to introduce greater transparency, compared to the previous surveys, by "highlighting" state aid to financial services and air transport sectors which were formerly classified under the manufacturing sector.[13] However, the immediate consequence of this change is to render straightforward comparisons between the amounts of aid to industry before and after 1992 impossible, as no distinct (and desegregated) data on state aid to air transport and financial services sectors are provided. Paradoxically, in this case alleged greater transparency has led to more opaque statistics.

Indeed, were state aid to financial services and air transport sectors insignificant, as was the case prior to 1992, its exclusion from global figures on state aid to industry would not matter. However, state aid to these sectors

Table 7: *Differences in percentage points between the shares of state aid to industry by main objectives as reported by the different European Commission's Surveys*

	Horizontal Objectives			Particular Sectors			Regional Objectives		
	3rd-4th Surveys 1988-1990	4th-5th Surveys 1990-1992	5th-6th Surveys 1992-1994	3rd-4th Surveys 1988-1990	4th-5th Surveys 1990-1992	5th-6th Surveys 1992-1994	3rd-4th Surveys 1988-1990	4th-5th Surveys 1990-1992	5th-6th Surveys 1992-1994
Belgium	1	-20	-26	-1	27	16	0	-7	11
Denmark	2	-1	1	-2	1	1	0	0	-2
Germany	-3	-5	-1	-1	-5	1	3	9	0
Greece	-10	-3	-7	-1	4	1	10	-1	6
Spain	-2	-11	-2	2	15	0	0	-4	3
France	0	-5	26	0	-1	-27	0	6	1
Ireland	-1	0	21	-9	0	-11	9	0	-10
Italy	0	-5	8	0	10	-10	0	-5	3
Luxembourg	0	-4	-1	0	0	0	-1	4	0
Netherlands	-1	1	2	0	0	-6	2	-1	4
Portugal	-3	23	-6	3	-22	-9	0	-1	15
UK	-3	5	-3	8	-7	-1	-4	1	5
EU-12	-2	-3	n.a.	1	3	n.a.	1	0	n.a.

Data source: Calculations from European Commission's Third to Sixth Survey on State Aid.

(mainly granted on ad hoc basis) amounted to a total yearly average of ECU 2,756 million for the whole EU for the 1994-1996 period (compared to ECU 1,045 million for 1992-1994), which accounted for around 7% (2% for 1992-1994) of the aid granted to the manufactured factor (see also Table 1). Disregarding these figures would distort the extent to which the manufacturing sector is supported by Member States, and would suggest a lower degree of state aid intervention than the one experienced.

3.2 MAIN TENDENCIES

Based on the information reported in Table 6, it appears that the allocation of state aid varies greatly over time and from one Member State to another. First, looking at the overlapping three-year averages from 1988 to 1996, some Member States reveal significant shifts in their allocation of aid to manufacturing, as shown by the breakdown by main objectives (i.e. horizontal, sectoral and regional objectives) in Table 6. For instance, in Belgium, the average share of aid with a horizontal objective dropped from 77% in the 1988-1990 period to 46% between 1994 and 1996, whereas in the same time state aid to particular sectors rose from 3% to 29%. Similarly, in Portugal, aid granted for horizontal objectives accounted for 14% of all state aid to the manufacturing sector in 1988-1990, peaked to 57% between 1990 and 1992 and settled around a yearly average of 24% for the period 1992-1996. In the meantime, aid to particular manufacturing sectors in Portugal plunged, from 81% between 1988 and 1990 to 33% between 1990 and 1992, to reach 52% of total aid to manufacturing between 1994 and 1996. More generally, countries like Denmark, France, Greece, Spain and the United Kingdom also experience significant fluctuations over time in their shares of state aid given to manufacturing by main objectives.

At the EU level, though, a rather clear pattern seems to emerge with regards to the breakdown of aid to manufacturing according to the main objectives. Most aid is traditionally labelled as regional aid, and increasingly so, with 39% for the period 1988-1990 and around 57% for the 1992-1996 period. Horizontal objectives come second, although to a decreasing degree, with 40% in 1988-1990 and 30% in 1994-1996. Lastly, state aid explicitly assigned to particular sectors amounted to 13% of all aid to manufacturing in 1994-1996.[14]

However, this overall stability in the patterns of allocation of state aid to the manufacturing sector at the EU level masks large disparities between Member States. For instance, while Spain allocated 69% of its aid to particular sectors in 1988-1990 (and Portugal 81%) and 63% in 1994-1996, sectorial aid in Luxembourg and Ireland was non-existent between 1988 and 1990 and represented, respectively, only 2% and 7% of aid to manufacturing between 1994 and 1996.

Broadly speaking, Member States can be separated in three groups according to their priority objective. Most state aid to the manufacturing sector is provided under regional objectives in Germany, Greece, Sweden, Luxembourg, the United Kingdom, Ireland and Italy.[15] Horizontal aid is a primary objective in Denmark, the Netherlands, Austria, Finland, France and Belgium. Finally, certain sectors obtain the most state aid in Spain (with 20% of aid going to shipbuilding alone in 1994-1996, as shown by Table A4 in the Appendix) and Portugal.

Note that the aggregate breakdown of state aid to industry by main objectives at EU level can be somewhat misleading as it reflects the heavier weight of some large countries like Germany and Italy, which have traditionally granted a majority of their aid to manufacturing under regional objectives.

Assuming an equal weight for each Member State, the EU averages by objectives show that horizontal objectives are a predominant justification for granting state aid, accounting on average for 46% of state aid to manufacturing from 1988 to 1996, compared to 35% and 19%, respectively, for regional and sectoral objectives.

4. The activity of the Commission

Although state aid schemes are initiated by Member States, they have to be approved by the Commission, according to Art. 93 of the Treaty of Rome, before being implemented.[16] It is, therefore, of particular interest to look at the Commission's activity in monitoring state aid to be granted by the Member States.

4.1 OVERALL TRENDS

Table 8 shows, from 1983 to 1997, the annual number of decisions taken by the Commission. These are divided into six categories: [1] cases where the Commission raised no objection; [2] decisions to initiate the procedure (under Art. 93(2) or Art. 8(3) of decision 2320/81 ECSC); [3] decisions to close (terminate) the procedure; [4] negative final decisions; [5] conditional decisions; and [6] other decisions (to re-open a procedure or related to changes in cases, for instance). Note that for each procedure initiated the Commission has to take two decisions: to open the procedure and then a final decision terminating it. Hence, the total number of decisions taken each year does not correspond to the number of proposals notified mainly because of the nature and the length of the procedure. Another factor is that some proposals for state aid notified by the Member States are later withdrawn,

Table 8: Activity in the control of state aid 1983-1997, decisions taken by the Commission (excluding aid to agriculture, fisheries, coal and transport)*

	Number of schemes notified	No objection	Initiation of the procedure	Decisions to close (terminate) the procedure	Final negative decisions	Conditional decisions	Other decisions	Total number of decisions**
83	173	101 (52)	55 (28)	18 (9)	21 (11)	-	-	195
84	162	201 (64)	58 (18)	34 (11)	21 (7)	1 (-)	-	315
85	133	102 (57)	38 (21)	31 (17)	7 (4)	-	-	178
86	124	98 (54)	47 (26)	26 (14)	10 (6)	-	-	181
87	326	205 (74)	27 (10)	32 (12)	10 (4)	2 (1)	-	276
88	375	303 (74)	36 (9)	20 (5)	14 (3)	9 (2)	28 (7)	410
89	296	259 (76)	36 (10)	21 (6)	16 (5)	-	11 (3)	343
90	429	415 (84)	34 (7)	20 (4)	14 (3)	-	9 (2)	492
91	472	493 (83)	54 (9)	28 (5)	7 (1)	2 (-)	13 (2)	597
92	459	473 (86)	30 (5)	25 (5)	8 (1)	7 (1)	9 (2)	552
93	475	399 (85)	32 (7)	19 (4)	6 (1)	1 (-)	10 (2)	467
94	510	440 (83)	40 (8)	15 (3)	3 (1)	2 (-)	27 (5)	527
95	493	504 (81)	57 (9)	22 (4)	9 (1)	5 (1)	22 (4)	619
96	366	373 (79)	43 (9)	14 (3)	23 (5)	3 (1)	18 (4)	474
97	515	385 (77)	68 (14)	21 (4)	9 (2)	5 (1)	14 (3)	502

Data source: European Commission's XIIIth to XXVIIth Reports on Competition Policy.
Notes: * Percentages of total number of decisions are given in parenthesis; ** Total of summary statistics from the European Commission Reports on Competition Policy.

before the Commission makes a formal decision.

Clearly, the number of state aid schemes notified to the Commission has increased over the last 15 years, from 173 cases in 1983 to a high of 515 cases in 1997.[17] Naturally, the annual total number of decisions taken by the Commission has also increased in the same proportion, from 195 decisions in 1983 to 502 in 1997. In most cases, though, the Commission raised no objection. Interestingly, while in the mid-1980s less than two thirds of the schemes generated no objection, this increased to more than three quarters of the decisions during the 1990s. So, it appears that in most instances the Commission considers that state aid schemes unambiguously comply with Arts. 92 and 93. On average, since 1987, the decision to initiate an investigation procedure has represented less than 10% of the total annual number of decisions.

Somewhat surprisingly, the absolute number of final negative decisions from the Commission remained rather stable, with an average of 12 negative decisions per year (from an annual average of 14 decisions for the period 1983-1990, to 9 decisions from 1991 to 1997). In view of the increase in the overall number of decisions, this implies that the share of negative decisions fell drastically, from an annual average of 5.4% from 1983 to 1990 to 1.7% from 1991 to 1997.

The Commission sees this evolution as a sign that the European state aid policy framework has become increasingly well known and accepted by the Member States. One also suspects that Member States only notify aid schemes which are in line with the criteria established in the state aid frameworks and guidelines. Besides, Member States also tend to withdraw their notification when it becomes clear that no approval can be obtained.

Another possible explanation could be that Member States only provide as much information as needed to obtain approval from the Commission. Controversial information on a state aid scheme could be hidden to somewhat mislead the Commission. This would also suggest that the investigative power of the Commission and its monitoring of state aid activities are rather limited and/or inefficient.

Figure 1, where all decisions including those on agriculture, coal, fisheries and transport are presented, also shows a significant increase in the number of decisions. Over the last 13 years, the overall number of Commission decisions was increased by a factor of 2.6, from 317 decisions in 1985 to 835 decisions in 1997.

In spite of the call for clarity and transparency from the Commission, it is obvious that information on the decisions and practices concerning state aid remains elusive. This is exemplified by the information contained in Table 9. Since 1990, the cases of non-notified aid identified by the Commission has accounted for over 20% of all state aid proposals officially notified to the

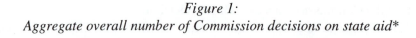

Figure 1:
Aggregate overall number of Commission decisions on state aid*

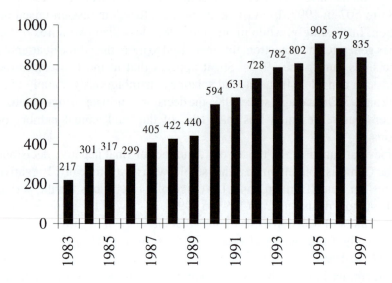

Data source: European Commission's XIIIth to XXVIIth Report on Competition Policy.

Note: *Data for 1983 and 1984 do not include decisions on agriculture, fisheries, coal and transport.

Commission by the Member States. Unfortunately, this is probably only the tip of the iceberg. How many more aid schemes are concealed by the Member States? The question then arises of whether governments try to play by the rules.

The Commission is not above reproach either. It appears to be difficult to obtain information on and explanations of how data on state aid are collected and aggregated by the Commission services. For instance, when adding up all the Commission decisions on individual schemes as itemised in the annexes of the various annual reports on Competition Policy, the total obtained is consistently lower than the aggregated numbers shown in the general tables of these reports (see Table 9). The size and consistency of the sign of these discrepancies rule out the possibility of any marginal or random errors.[18]

Table 9: *Number of (non-)notified cases and discrepancies in the number of decisions taken by the Commission, 1983-1997 (excluding aid to agriculture, fisheries, coal and transport)*

Year	Non-notified aid	(%)*	Number of Proposals notified	Total number of decisions: Summary**	Total number of decisions: Aggregated ***	Discrepancies (%)
1983	n.a.		173	195	195	0
1984	n.a.		162	315	280	12.5
1985	n.a.		133	178	175	1.7
1986	n.a.		124	181	170	6.5
1987	n.a.		326	276	265	4.2
1988	n.a.		375	410	278	47.5
1989	n.a.		296	343	298	15.1
1990	105	(24.5)	429	492	393	25.2
1991	105	(22.2)	472	597	426	40.1
1992	102	(22.2)	459	552	521	6.0
1993	85	(17.9)	475	467	445	4.9
1994	68	(13.3)	510	527	509	3.5
1995	113	(22.9)	493	619	595	4.0
1996	91	(24.9)	366	474	444	6.8
1997	140	(27.2)	515	502	484	3.7

Data source: European Commission's XIIIth to XXVIIth Reports on Competition Policy.

Notes: *Non-notified aid in percentage of number of proposals notified are given in parenthesis; **Total of summary statistics Reports on Competition Policy; ***Aggregation of individually mentioned decisions in the Annexes of the XIIIth-XXVIIth Reports on Competition Policy.

4.2 COMMISSION DECISIONS BY SECTORS AND TYPES OF AID

Trying to identify the breakdown of Commission decisions according to the type of aid or sector concerned for aid schemes is not an easy task, as no aggregate information is published by the Commission. In Tables 10 and 11, all state aid schemes listed in the Commission Reports on Competition Policy[19] are categorised according to sectors and types of aid, respectively. For instance, a scheme officially referred to as regional aid to agriculture is accounted for as both regional aid and aid to agriculture. Hence, the classification in Tables 10 and 11 reflects only the official nomenclature of state aid schemes, which is to some extent arbitrary, and does not necessarily correspond to the effective allocation of state aid.[20] Besides, the large number of schemes which are not labelled according to a particular sector or type of aid are excluded from the Tables. Finally, it should be noted that, in an attempt to provide more detailed information, this classification differs from the one adopted by the Commission surveys on state aid, where aid schemes are divided by main objectives (see Tables 6 and A4).

Table 10 clearly shows that the majority of Commission decisions concern agriculture. This is interesting because although the agricultural sector traditionally enjoys strong public support, agricultural policy is supposed to fall within the exclusive domain of the Community. Most decisions in this sector concerns aid schemes in Spain, Austria and Germany (principally the new *Länder*). The majority of Commission decisions for Finland and Denmark concern the agricultural sector, although in absolute terms they only account for a small share of the number of decisions in this sector aggregated at the EU level.

A large number of Commission decisions relate to steel, fisheries, shipbuilding, information technology, consumer electronics, motor vehicles, mechanical engineering and more recently the energy sector. Many of the decisions on state aid to the steel sectors affect Belgium, Ireland and Italy.

Table 10 also reveals that while a declining number of decisions concern the textile, clothing, leather, and footwear sectors, the number of decisions on aid to the tourism sector increased from two decisions in 1983 to 19 decisions in 1997. Most decisions on tourism involve aid schemes in Portugal, Italy and Spain. On the whole, however, traditional sectors (such as steel, shipbuilding, cars, chemicals, textiles) continue to attract a lot of attention from the state.

Finally, an overview of the breakdown of Commission decisions on state aid by type of aid is provided in Table 11. It confirms that most of state aid schemes are labelled as regional aid, and increasingly so. This is mainly due to schemes in Germany (in particular the new *Länder*), but also in Italy, Spain and the United Kingdom. Financial measures also account for a large and

Table 10:

Overall state aid: Annual average number of decisions by sector

Sectors	1983-1987	1988-1992	1993-1997
Agriculture	133	178	278
Steel	31	17	44
Fisheries	20	34	36
Shipbuilding	17	29	36
Information technology and consumer electronics	19	31	26
Motor vehicles and mechanical engineering	24	15	25
Energy	2	13	22
Chemicals	11	8	18
Tourism	2	13	19
Textiles, clothing, leather, footwear	16	10	7
Glass, wood, paper	9	8	10
Fibres	5	4	6
Financial services	1	1	5
Pharmaceuticals	2	3	1
Aluminium	3	1	2
Food, drink and tobacco	3	1	1

Data source: Compilation from European Commission's XIIIth to XXVIIth Reports on Competition Policy.

Table 11:

Overall state aid: Annual average number of decisions by type of aid

Types of aid	1983-1987	1988-1992	1993-1997
Regional aid	57	157	111
R&D	17	48	45
SMEs	10	27	39
Employment aid	6	16	26
Environmental aid	5	18	24
Restructuring aid	8	10	13
Export in intra-community trade	2	2	4

Data source: Compilation from European Commission's XVIth to XXIVth Reports on Competition Policy.

growing share of decisions taken by the Commission, in particular in France and the Netherlands. While the number of decisions relating to research and development (R&D) aid remains fairly constant over time, there has been a surge of decisions concerning aid schemes addressed to small and medium-size enterprises (SMEs). Commission decisions on environmental and employment aid schemes have also become more common in different Member States. Finally, at least officially, very few aid schemes are labelled as restructuring aid.

To summarise, Tables 10 and 11 show that there are a few sectors and types of aid which account for the majority of decisions taken by the Commission. These sectors are agriculture, fisheries, steel and shipbuilding. Most aid schemes concern regional, R&D, SMEs and investment aid. While traditional sectors remain the focus of most state aid activities, the time and nature of aid schemes has shifted over time.

Two factors come to mind to explain the predominance of traditional sectors in attracting state aid. First, these sectors amount to an important share of economic activity and employment. Perhaps even more relevant is the fact that these sectors share a common feature: in general, they have traditionally been labour intensive activities which have had to face significant restructuring. This might suggest that in spite of the proclaimed official objectives (e.g. regional development, R&D, etc.), aid provided to these sectors is rather part of an effort to rescue (or protect) declining industries and to ease often painful structural adjustments.

It should be remembered that, while looking at the activity of the Commission in terms of the number of decisions concerning national aid is instructive as to the way state aid is conducted in the Member States and its monitoring by the Commission, it should not be seen as an indicator of the amounts of aid granted. A decision may concern a large as well as a small aid scheme. Hence, the number of decisions may be seen as a rough indicator of the number of state aid schemes, but not of the size of the schemes.

Indeed, except perhaps in the case of Germany, Denmark and Ireland, Table A5 in the Appendix reveals that an increase (reduction) in state support aid is not associated with more (less) decisions by the Commission. In several Member States (in particular Spain, the United Kingdom, the Netherlands and Luxembourg), as well as at the aggregated EU level, there is even a negative correlation over time between the amount of aid (in constant prices) and the number of decisions. However, it is true that large Member States are subject to more decisions by the Commission than smaller ones (see Table A6 in the Appendix).

5. Conclusion

Although declining, state aid remains a predominant feature of economic policy in the Member States of the EU. A careful analysis of the information provided by the European Commission *Surveys on State Aid in the European Community in the Manufacturing and Certain Other Sectors*, covering the period 1986 to 1996, reveals that global figures at the EU level mask significant differences between Member States in the trends and patterns of state aid.

The absolute amount of state aid granted by a Member State is roughly proportional to the size of its economy. In relative terms, however, the main providers of state aid to industry are Italy, Greece, Germany, Spain and Belgium. At the other end of the scale, the United Kingdom, the Netherlands, Austria and Sweden are the Member States whose industry benefit least from state aid measures.

The intensity of state aid differs not only between Member States, but also over time. While there is a general tendency towards greater convergence in the degree of support to the manufacturing sector among Member States, country specific characteristics continue to prevail in determining state aid policy, in spite the Commission's activity to control state aid. The Member States which experienced the greatest fluctuations in the intensity of government support to industry are Greece, Portugal, Spain and Belgium.

There is no evidence indicating that richer Member States grant systematically more aid than less favoured ones. In many Member States, greater support to industry even seems to be associated with economic downturns.

As for patterns in the allocation of state aid, most schemes appear to be labelled as regional aid or fall under horizontal objectives. Aid under sectoral objectives does not seem to be very popular in the EU. It remains to be proved whether this official classification reflects actual practices or is simply mere rhetoric by Member States willing to disguise sector specific aid measures under general (horizontal or regional) schemes. Indeed, some sectors appear to attract a lot of state aid. These include steel, motor vehicles, shipbuilding and more recently financial services and air transport sectors.

In spite of the commendable effort by the Commission (in its surveys on state aid and its competition reports), the information available on state aid practices by the Member States remains scarce, incomplete and opaque, if not misleading. It follows that a proper detailed assessment of state aid measures in the EU remains a difficult task.

Nonetheless, from a global perspective, the analysis presented in this Chapter suggests that at a time when governments generally profess their belief in market forces and the virtues of competition, and express their willingness to restrict direct state intervention in the economy, Member States in the EU have on the whole failed to significantly curb state aid.

APPENDIX

A.I. Methodological Appendix

All the data on the amount of state aid are derived from the European Commission's Third to Sixth Surveys on State Aid in the European Community in the Manufacturing and Certain Other Sectors (see EC 1992, 1995, 1997, 1998), and are shown in ECU. To facilitate comparisons over time, amounts are expressed in 1996 prices. In the Annexes of its surveys, the Commission publishes annual amounts of state aid to the manufacturing sector and are in ECU in current prices. Each survey covers a five-year period. As the Commission revises and adjusts data on state aid, data available from the most recent surveys are used in all cases. That is, amounts of aid to manufacturing in current prices for the periods 1986-1987, 1988-1989, 1990-1991 and 1992-1996 are taken from the Third, Fourth, Fifth and Sixth Survey, respectively. To obtain amounts of aid in constant prices, the consumer price index for each Member State from 1986 to 1996, as published by Eurostat, is used, adopting 1996 as the base year.

Arguably, this is not the most appropriate index, as state aid (to industry) is not directly related to consumer prices. For this reasons, according to officials at DG IV, the GDP deflator has been adopted since 1992 for use in the Commission's surveys to express amounts of aid in constant prices, instead of the consumer price index. (Incidentally, note that there is no indication as to which price index is used in the surveys themselves). However, as no GDP deflators can be obtained for the Member States prior to 1990, such an index could not be employed in this Chapter to compare amounts of aid from 1986 to 1996.

An alternative would have been to rely on the (manufacturing) producer price index to express amounts of aid to the manufacturing sector in constant prices. The problem is that this index is not published by Eurostat or the OECD for Portugal and for Luxembourg prior to 1988.

Hence, the only index available covering all the Member States for the entire period concerned is the consumer price index. Note, however, that the amounts of aid expressed in 1996 consumer prices and in 1996 producer prices are always highly correlated (with correlation coefficients above 0.9), perhaps suggesting that providing amounts in constant consumer prices does not introduce any significant distortion to state aid trends.

Information on the definition of state aid and the specific methodology adopted by the Commission can be found in each survey (in particular in their Technical Annex).

Sanoussi Bilal and Roel Polmans

A.II. Tables

Table A1: Annual growth rate of state aid to industry (1996 prices)

	1987	1988	1989	1990	1991	1992	1993	1994	1995	1996
Belgium	3.1	22.0	-11.8	26.0	91.2	-79.7	32.7	29.1	-7.3	22.3
Denmark	20.7	19.1	-5.0	-15.7	-6.3	9.5	73.0	-2.7	12.9	9.4
Germany	-0.7	6.1	-0.1	19.5	17.5	16.7	30.1	-0.3	-23.2	-19.2
Greece	22.1	-30.0	-42.0	-10.7	-28.0	4.3	-62.7	-32.6	117.4	-14.8
Spain	-31.2	24.3	-66.3	36.7	-48.3	-20.2	35.2	-0.1	31.7	29.4
France	-13.0	42.8	-27.3	-11.3	-14.7	3.0	6.3	-22.7	-18.0	9.5
Ireland	6.1	-17.9	-11.3	1.9	-31.2	-23.2	0.9	-15.0	3.6	39.5
Italy	-21.7	5.1	-28.9	101.2	-26.1	-5.1	-2.8	-20.8	3.4	-9.1
Luxembourg	44.1	-2.0	33.3	-12.5	10.7	8.1	-35.8	2.3	9.1	-4.2
Netherlands	-1.2	11.6	-10.5	13.1	-35.9	-22.5	-2.0	0.6	8.8	-11.5
Austria	n.a.	n.a.	n.a.	n.a.	n.a.	n.a.	n.a.	n.a.	n.a.	-22.5
Portugal	-45.5	13.0	311.5	-22.8	-47.2	-30.9	14.0	41.2	-54.5	-11.5
Finland	n.a.	n.a.	n.a.	n.a.	n.a.	n.a.	n.a.	n.a.	n.a.	-19.3
Sweden	n.a.	n.a.	n.a.	n.a.	n.a.	n.a.	n.a.	n.a.	n.a.	15.3
UK	-2.0	5.7	-24.4	-20.4	-10.3	-28.2	-42.9	12.7	8.5	22.2
EU-15										-7.1
EU-12	-11.1	8.1	-24.9	27.7	-11.9	-5.3	8.5	-8.2	-10.2	-7.0

Data source: Calculated from European Commission's Third to Sixth Surveys on State Aid.

Table A2: Cross-section correlations for all Member States between levels of state aid to industry and some economic indicators, 1986-1996

	Amount of aid and GDP	Amount of aid as a share of GDP and GDP (in 1996 prices)	Amount of aid as a share of GDP and GDP per capita	Amount of aid as a share of GDP and unemployment rate	Amount of aid as a share of GDP and central gov. deficit or surplus as a share of GDP
1986	0.98	-0.04	-0.18	0.36	-0.53
1987	0.99	-0.1	-0.16	0.11	-0.32
1988	0.99	-0.06	-0.21	0.31	-0.63
1989	0.99	-0.19	-0.58	-0.2	-0.77
1990	0.97	-0.03	-0.39	-0.04	-0.82
1991	0.98	-0.02	-0.05	-0.21	-0.48
1992	0.97	0.13	-0.05	-0.06	-0.62
1993	0.97	0.31	0.02	0.13	-0.18
1994	0.96	0.28	-0.07	0.13	-0.15
1995	0.98	0.2	-0.23	0.23	0.25
1996	0.99	0.19	-0.26	0.41	0.38

Table A3: Amounts of state aid to industry as a share of gross value added of manufactured products, building and construction, 1986-1996

	1986	1987	1988	1989	1990	1991	1992	1993	1994	1995
Belgium	3.2	3.2	3.6	3.0	3.6	7.3	1.4	1.9	2.4	2.0
Denmark	1.2	1.4	1.7	1.7	1.4	1.3	1.4	2.3	2.1	2.2
Germany	2.3	2.2	2.3	2.2	2.5	2.8	3.3	4.5	4.5	3.4
Greece	11.8	18.1	12.7	7.6	7.9	6.6	7.9	3.2	2.4	5.7
Spain	6.4	4.3	4.9	1.5	1.9	1.0	0.8	1.4	1.4	1.8
France	2.9	2.6	3.5	2.5	2.1	1.9	1.9	2.1	1.6	1.3
Ireland	4.8	5.2	4.0	3.3	3.2	2.1	1.6	1.6	1.2	1.2
Italy	5.7	4.4	4.5	3.1	6.3	4.8	4.8	5.6	4.6	5.1
Luxembourg	1.5	2.2	2.0	2.3	2.0	2.3	2.4	1.6	1.5	1.6
Netherlands	2.5	2.4	2.5	2.1	2.3	1.5	1.2	1.1	1.1	1.1
Portugal	2.2	1.3	1.4	5.5	4.4	2.3	1.6	1.9	2.6	1.1
UK	2.1	2.1	1.9	1.4	1.3	1.3	1.0	0.6	0.6	0.7
EU-12	3.4	3.0	3.1	2.3	2.9	2.7	2.6	3.2	2.8	2.5

Data source: European Commission's Third to Sixth Survey on State Aid; Eurostat.

Table A4: State aid to the manufacturing sector 1994-1996: Breakdown of aid according to sector and function

SECTORS / FUNCTION	B	DK	D	GR	E	F	IRL	I	L	NL	A	P	FIN	S	UK	EU-15
Horizontal Objectives	**46**	**84**	**19**	**31**	**24**	**51**	**37**	**31**	**33**	**74**	**74**	**24**	**74**	**34**	**22**	**30**
Research & Development	10	29	7	2	7	28	6	3	7	20	19	4	35	11	12	9
Environment	0	10	1	0	1	1	0	0	5	10	16	0	2	5	0	1
SME	21	5	5	2	10	6	17	6	21	8	13	0	21	16	4	7
Trade	4	7	0	15	0	11	3	9	1	3	0	0	10	0	5	3
Energy saving	0	34	2	0	1	1	1	1	0	31	1	2	4	3	0	2
General Investment	0	0	0	2	0	0	0	0	0	0	0	0	0	0	0	0
Other Objectives	11	0	4	12	4	5	10	12	0	3	24	19	2	0	1	7
Particular Sectors	**29**	**14**	**7**	**3**	**63**	**15**	**7**	**11**	**2**	**10**	**13**	**52**	**2**	**4**	**19**	**13**
Shipbuilding	2	10	4	0	20	1	0	2	0	7	0	4	0	0	1	4
Other sectors	27	4	3	3	43	14	7	9	2	3	13	48	2	4	18	10
Regional Objectives	**25**	**2**	**74**	**66**	**13**	**34**	**56**	**58**	**65**	**17**	**13**	**24**	**23**	**61**	**59**	**56**
Regions under 92(3)c	25	2	3	0	9	22	0	1	65	17	10	0	23	61	36	7
Regions under 92(3)a	0	0	69	66	4	12	56	57	0	0	3	24	0	0	23	48
Germany:Berlin/Zonenrand	0	0	2	0	0	0	0	0	0	0	0	0	0	0	0	1
TOTAL	**100**	**100**	**100**	**100**	**100**	**100**	**100**	**100**	**100**	**100**	**100**	**100**	**100**	**100**	**100**	**100**

Data source: European Commission (1998) Sixth Survey on State Aid, Table 6.

Table A5:
Correlation over time between the amounts of state aid (in 1996 prices)
and the number of decisions on aid schemes taken by the Commission,
1986-1996

Aid (in 96 prices) and number of decisions		
	Current	**lagged**
Belgium	0.02	-0.09
Denmark	0.67	0.66
Germany	0.93	0.95
Greece	0.04	-0.20
Spain	-0.90	-0.80
France	-0.01	0.11
Ireland	0.55	0.44
Italy	0.14	-0.17
Luxembourg	0.25	-0.61
Netherlands	-0.76	-0.68
Portugal	-0.19	0.27
UK	-0.60	-0.77
EU-12	-0.66	-0.44

Table A6:
Cross-section correlation for all Member States between amounts of state
aid (in 1996 prices) and number of decisions taken by the Commission

Year	1986	1987	1988	1989	1990	1991	1992	1993	1994
Correlation	0.96	0.96	0.98	0.99	0.94	0.95	0.95	0.96	0.97

NOTES

* We would like to thank Phedon Nicolaides for his helpful comments and the Foundation BBV for its financial support.
1. See the 1996 OECD report on Public Support to Industry.
2. Unless it is explicitly mentioned otherwise, all amounts in this Chapter are expressed in 1996 prices.
3. See European Commission (1998), *Sixth Surveys on State Aid in the European Community in the Manufacturing and Certain Other Sectors*, COM (98) 417.
4. For Germany alone, its GDP accounted for 25.4% of EU-12 GDP in 1986 compared to 29.4% of EU-12 GDP in 1996.
5. Note that a standard measure of state aid is in percentage of gross value added of manufactured goods. This is the approach adopted by the OECD (1996) and by the Commission Surveys. Expressed in these terms, state aid accounted for an annual average of 3.6% of gross value added of market products for the period from 1986 to 1995 (from 4.2% in 1986 to 3.2% in 1995).
6. See correlation coefficients reported for each year in Table A4 in the Appendix.
7. See European Commission's Third to Sixth Surveys on State Aid in the European Community in the Manufacturing and Certain Other Sectors.
8. See Fifth Survey (COM 97/170, para.21, page 14) and Sixth Survey (COM 98/417, para.25, page 20).
9. See Sixth Survey (COM 98/417, para.6, page 3).
10. See Sixth Survey (COM 98/417, para.8, page 4).
11. See Table 6 in the Fourth and Fifth Survey and Table 8 in the Sixth Survey.
12. See Tables A5 in the Fourth Survey and Tables A4 in the Fifth and Sixth Surveys.
13. See Sixth Survey (COM 98/417, para.7, page 4).
14. This excludes ad hoc aid, which is also mostly directed at particular sectors.
15. In the case of Greece and the United Kingdom, the emphasis shifted away from horizontal towards regional objectives.
16. See Chapter 1 by Sinnaeve and Chapter 2 by Nicolaides and Bilal for a short description.
17. Note that the number of Member States increased from 10 in 1983 to 15 in 1997.
18. To date, no explanation has been obtained from the Commission for the reason for these discrepancies.
19. See European Commission, XIIIth to XXVIIth Reports on Competition Policy.
20. Note that counting decisions can be difficult as illustrated by the case of Portugal. No explanation could be obtained from the Commission on whether an aid scheme which provides aid to different sectors should be counted as one decisions or several decisions (corresponding to the number of sectors covered). This problem was encountered with several aid schemes in Portugal, for instance.

REFERENCES

European Commission (1992), *Third Survey on State Aid in the European Community in the Manufacturing and Certain Other Sectors*, Luxembourg: Office for Official Publications of the European Communities.

European Commission (1995), *Fourth Survey on State Aid in the European Union in the Manufacturing and Certain Other Sectors*, COM 564/95, Luxembourg: Office for Official Publications of the European Communities.

European Commission (1997), *Fifth Survey on State Aid in the European Union in the Manufacturing and Certain Other Sectors*, COM 97/170. (http://europa.eu.int/en/comm/dg04/aid/en/rap5.htm)

European Commission (1998), *Sixth Survey on State Aid in the European Union in the Manufacturing and Certain Other Sectors*, COM 98/417. (http://europa.eu.int/en/comm/dg04/aid/en/rap6.pdf)

OECD (1996), *Public Support to Industry*, Report by the Industry Committee to the Council at Ministerial Level, OECD/GD (96)82, Paris: Organisation for Economic Co-operation and Development.

CHAPTER 4

EC POLICY ON STATE AID: ARE THE PROCEDURES "USER-FRIENDLY"? THE RIGHTS OF THIRD PARTIES

Piet Jan Slot

1. Introduction

This Chapter will look at the procedures of EC state aid law from the perspective of the user. The above mentioned title suggests that the need for user-friendliness is particularly relevant for the rights of third parties. It is therefore necessary to agree first of all to who the third parties are. As the procedural rules on state aid are designed for the two main parties involved – the Member States who wish to grant aid and the EC Commission who has to assess the aid – all others involved are considered to be third parties. Thus both the intended beneficiaries of the aid and their competitors are third parties.

In reality this may represent a rather simplified view of the sometimes complex relations between the governments involved and the intended beneficiaries. The latter will of course often play an active role in drafting the actual aid plans. Nevertheless, it is for the government concerned to notify the aid, to assume the full responsibility for its approval, and subsequently to effect the implementation of the Commission's decision approving or disapproving the proposed aid. As we shall see it is precisely this situation – where both the government and the beneficiary are for practical purposes equally involved yet it is only the government that is responsible vis-à-vis the Commission – which causes some of the user-unfriendly features of the procedural law of state aid. This is particularly striking when the procedural rules concerning state aid are compared with those of competition.

I just note in passing that it would also have been possible to include the governments in the category of users. After all it is they who employ the instrument of state aid to achieve goals of national economic policy. In order to limit the scope of this presentation, I will, however, only refer to the

S. Bilal and P. Nicolaides (eds.), Understanding State Aid Policy in the European Community, 81–97.
© 1999 *Kluwer Law International. Printed in the Netherlands.*

position of governments when this is relevant for the overall assessment of
the procedures.

It is also necessary to define what we mean by user-friendly in relation to
the procedural law of state aid. In discussing the notion of user-friendly
competition law, Diane P. Wood noted that such a system should ideally have
the following four characteristics:

(1) Transparency
(2) Efficiency
(3) Consistency
(4) Substantive Soundness[1]

Transparency means that the user is able to know at all times the content
of the laws and regulations, both substantive and procedural, to which he or
she will be subject. Goyder adds that it is important that there is a fair
procedure allowing complete access to the relevant documents.[2] Efficiency
refers to both the speed and accuracy of the procedures. Goyder notes that
timetables for the completion of a procedure are not only good for the parties
but also for the regulators. A system can be considered consistent if it delivers
rules which can be predicted with a reasonable degree of certainty. In other
words, if it does not change without clear and prior indication and, I would
like to stress, is not subject to political pressure. The last criterion refers to
the acceptability of the rules by those who are subject to them. The rules must
be understood and respected.

In addition Goyder mentions that decisions must not be either totally
discretionary or opaque. They must give sufficient reasons. He adds that
decisions must be given as legal cases decided on legal principles. Finally, he
notes that a related element is the question of whether the authority is or is not
authorised to act. For example, the US Department of Justice is authorised to
enter into a consent decree concerning the settlement of antitrust cases.

Before embarking on any analysis of the position of third parties as
defined above, it is necessary to recall that there is no secondary legislation
on the rules of procedures as there is in the field of competition law in the form
of regulation No. 17/62. Even though Art. 94 EC gives the Council the power
to adopt such rules the Commission has only recently forwarded a proposal.[3]
This absence of proper legislation has had an enormous influence on the way
the rights of third parties have gradually been defined in the case law of the
Court of Justice and, more recently, by the Court of First Instance. Where
necessary for the proper understanding of the rules I will discuss these
jurisprudential rules.

In this Chapter, I will first look at the position of the intended beneficiary
and its position in the successive stages of the procedure for the approval of
state aid. I will then proceed to assess the position of a third party competitor,
who may also be a complainant, in the respective procedures. These sections

will serve as a brief overview of the possibilities third parties have of making their views known throughout the procedure and of defending their rights accordingly. I will conclude with an assessment of the results of the previous sections against the standards laid down in the above section and by identifying the bottlenecks in the system. It will appear that some principles outlined here are only developed to a rudimentary form in the procedural law of state aid. A clear example is the principle of access to the files. In comparison with the rules under Arts. 85 and 86 there is still a long way to go. Similarly, the position of the intended beneficiary is particularly weak when it comes to the imposition of conditions and obligations. Third parties have hardly any say in the matter except for the possibilities given to them by the government involved. Surprisingly, the position of the complainant has, after the recent judgement of Court of Justice in the *Sytraval* appeal,[4] received recognition, although not as clearly as under the rules of Arts. 85, 86 and regulation No. 17.

It will appear that the whole of the first stage of the approval procedure for state aid under Art. 93(3) can hardly be called user-friendly. There is virtually no possibility of getting information about what is going on and consequently there is no officially recognised way of exerting any influence.

2. The position of the intended beneficiary

The starting point for an analysis of the position of the intended beneficiary is that there are no specific procedural rules for companies involved in state aid cases to bring their interests to bear. But it is worth observing that such a company often has the option of teaming up with its government in trying to expedite matters to the maximum possible extent. As an alternative it can bring a complaint to the Commission explaining its, normally precarious, position and ask the Commission to do its utmost to clear the planned aid as soon as possible. Of course, ultimately, there are various possibilities of exerting political pressure as the *Vilvoorde* case clearly demonstrated.

At this point it may be useful to give a brief outline of the procedures for the approval of state aid plans under Art. 93 of the EC Treaty. Art. 93 provides for three distinctly different procedures. Art. 93(1) lays down rules for the supervision of existing aid, this is aid which has at one point been implemented in conformity with the rules for new aid, or aid which existed prior to the accession of the Member States concerned. Existing aid is reviewed by the Commission, which may take action if the aid is no longer compatible with the Common Market. If Member States do not follow the Commission's proposed amendments the later can take action under Art. 93(2). The second and third procedures both concern new aid, the preliminary procedure of Art.

93(3) and the contentious procedure of Art. 93(2).

For new aid the starting point is the obligation of the last sentence of Art. 93(3) for governments to notify all new aid to the Commission with a view to obtaining its approval. Non-observance of this obligation may be enforced in national courts, as the notification obligation has direct effect. This means that aid that is implemented before the Commission has given its approval can be blocked through actions in national courts. This remedy is also available if the aid is subsequently approved by the Commission.[5] I will omit a further discussion of the complications that can arise in national court procedures. The Commission or competitors can claim that interest be paid for the period that the aid was illegally implemented.

Under the Art. 93(3) procedure the Commission has two months to decide whether or not it can approve the aid. If it does approve it, it may do so by imposing obligations and conditions, but it is unlikely that it will impose such conditions and obligations under the preliminary procedure of Art. 93(3). If it does not approve it decides accordingly. If it finds that the matter is too complicated to be resolved within the rather short time limit of two months, it must open the contentious procedure of Art. 93(2). This procedure provides for more procedural guarantees. A summary of the aid plan is then published in the Official Journal C series and interested parties are invited to comment, as are the governments of the other Member States who have been informed directly. For all three categories, the intended beneficiary can appeal against the Commission's decision.[6] The beneficiary will only be happy if the aid is straightforwardly and unconditionally approved. In all other cases it may have to wait until further procedures clarify matters. A Commission veto of the aid, a conditional approval or a decision to prolong the investigation under the procedural regime of Art. 93(2) can all be challenged by the intended beneficiary in a procedure before the Court of First Instance and in urgent cases interim measures may be asked for.

Except for the procedure for interim measures, all procedures take a long time. Court cases can take up to two years and even longer if there is an appeal against the judgement of the Court of First Instance which takes the case to the Court of Justice. During that whole period the company potentially benefiting from the aid is left uncertain as to the legality of the aid. Similarly, the Commission's approval under the aegis of Art. 93(2) may take a long time. Under the case law of the Court there is no time limit for this procedure although the Court once ruled that a period of 26 month was too long.[7] The conclusion of the Art. 93(2) procedure is in the form of a decision, which again can be positive, conditionally positive or negative, and can also be appealed against, adding another period of uncertainty for the company involved.

Is there anything the intended beneficiary can do to shorten the long waiting period? Actually there is very little it can do other than assisting the government in preparing the case as thoroughly as possible with a view to its expeditious approval. As I indicated above, matters may get worse for the beneficiary if complaints by competitors slow the procedures down further. This will be discussed in the next paragraph.

It transpires from this brief survey of the approval procedures for state aid that beneficiary companies are exposed to long and uncertain approval procedures. There are basically two ways to remedy this situation. The first is that the aid is implemented without awaiting the Commission's approval. This solution has the risk that even if the aid is subsequently approved, the company may still have to pay interest covering the period when the aid was implemented illegally.[8] There is also a risk that competitors can claim damages if they can prove that they incurred losses as a result of the non-observance of the standstill provision of Art. 93(3). This solution has an additional risk that national courts may order the government not to implement the aid or to freeze its effects. The second solution may be found in the setting up of a framework for future aid and the seeking of the prior approval of the Commission for such a general aid plan. This method has only limited use. The Commission does not give blanket approval for general aid schemes, especially not if they involve substantial amounts of aid. In such cases the Commission insists that any new aid under such schemes is also notified.[9] Thus this method is only of use in cases which involve insubstantial amounts of aid.

The rules of procedure also provide that aid implemented illegally has to be recovered. The general principle governing the recovery is that beneficiaries should be aware of the fact that illegally implemented aid will be recovered. This was also clearly spelt out in 1983 Commission communication to the Member States.[10] Since then the Commission has consistently repeated this message in summary publications of new aid plans under the procedure of Art. 93(2). There is no possibility for the undertakings concerned to rely on the legal principle of legitimate expectations.[11] The only possibility of challenging recovery is to challenge the Commission's decision. As the *RSV* judgement shows the Commission's decision may be invalidated if it takes too long to conclude the Art. 93(2) procedure.[12] It may, of course, also be invalidated for other reasons. If companies fail to challenge the decision they are not in a position to challenge the validity of the national measures Member States may use in conforming with an order to recover the aid.[13] In itself the instrument of recovery cannot be viewed as being "user-unfriendly" as recovery goes to the heart of the supervisory rules on state aid. Nor can the rules relating to recovery be considered user unfriendly, in view of Commission's practice, at least from the point of view of the beneficiary. From the perspective of the competitor, recovery is not always carried out in a satisfactory manner i.e. they sometimes have to wait rather a long time before governments implement such an order. During which period the beneficiary will, of course, continue to enjoy an unfair competitive advantage. Furthermore, it is not clear to whether and to what extent the Commission monitors these obligations.

3. The position of the third party competitor

3.1 INTRODUCTION

Like the position of the intended beneficiary, there is no specific procedural rule for the protection of the interests of a third party competitor. It is also useful to point out that this third party may have lodged a complaint with the Commission or have only expressed its views in response to the Commission's publication under Art. 93(2) or have only taken action once that procedure was concluded by a decision. This may have a bearing on the possibilities the competitor has to challenge the Commission's decision. It should be pointed out in this context that Commission actions can only be challenged if they are qualified as decisions.[14] Thus it was an important step when the Court of Justice in the *Cook* case ruled that the Commission's decision not to open the Art. 93(2) procedure is an act which can be reviewed.[15]

In this section I will start with the assumption that the competitor has actually brought a complaint and analyse its position to challenge the Commission's decisions on state aid. I will then look at a situation where a competitor has not brought a complaint but tries to protect its interests once it discovers that its interests are affected. Finally, I will briefly discuss the possibilities competitors have to protect their interests through proceedings in national courts.

3.2 A COMPLAINANT HAS THE RIGHT TO BRING AN ART. 175 ACTION

Unlike Art. 3(2) of Regulation 17/62, implementing Arts. 85 and 86, there is no provision for lodging complaints under the rules of procedure for state aid. Nor is there such a provision under general EC law. Nevertheless, the Commission appears to examine complaints, especially from those who are directly concerned, such as competitors, and it recognises that they are entitled to a response.[16] The absence of an officially recognised possibility for bringing complaints raises the question of whether a complainant can bring an Art. 175 action against the Commission. Under that article, natural or legal persons can bring actions before the Court of Justice against a Community institution if it has failed to address an action to it. However, that right was only thought to exist if the Community has an obligation to act vis-à-vis the person concerned.[17] It is this article that allows complainants in competition cases to put pressure on the Commission and even if the "Automec" doctrine allows the Commission to set its administrative priorities and consequently not to actually pursue the case, it does provide a rather effective form of legal protection.[18]

In a judgement of 15 September 1998 the Court of First Instance ruled that a complainant has the right to bring an Art. 175 action.[19] This judgement constitutes a significant step towards the judicial protection of the complainant. From now on a complainant will be able to spur the Commission into action. The Commission will have to define a position on the complaint. The next question then is whether this reaction by the Commission will also constitute a decision which can be appealed against. This would seem to be the logical consequence of the Court's judgement.[20]

3.3 THE *SYTRAVAL* JUDGEMENT

The right to a decision rejecting a complaint was discussed in the very recent judgement of the Court in the appeal of the Court of First Instance judgement in the *Sytraval* case.[21] The Commission, in its submissions in this case, denied that the right to obtain a decision for the complainant exists, as Community law now stands. The Court did not directly rule on that question but rather it observed that decisions concerning state aid are necessarily addressed to governments, even if they result from a complaint. Nevertheless, according to the Court:

> "Where the Commission adopts such a decision and proceeds, in accordance with its duty of sound administration, to inform the complainants of its decision, it is the decision addressed to the Member State which must form the subject matter of any action for annulment which the complainant may bring, and not the letter to that complainant informing him of the decision.

> "Consequently, whilst it may be regrettable that the Commission did not inform the complainants of its position by sending them a copy of a properly reasoned decision addressed to the Member State concerned, the Court of First Instance erred in law when it found that the contested decision constituted a decision addressed not to that State but to the complainants, rejecting their application for a declaration by the Commission that the French Republic had infringed Arts. 92 and 93 of the Treaty by granting aid to Sécuripost.

"The error of law thus committed by the Court of First Instance does not, however, invalidate its judgement, since, as the Commission has conceded, the decision in question was of direct and individual concern to the complainants. In finding in its decision that the investigation had revealed no grounds for concluding that state aid existed within the meaning of Art. 92 of the Treaty, the Commission implicitly refused to initiate procedure under Art. 93(2). It follows from the judgements of the Court cited in paras. 40 and 41 above that, in such a situation, the persons intended to benefit from the procedural guarantees afforded by Art. 93(2) may secure compliance with it only if they are able to challenge the decision in question before the Community judicature under the fourth paragraph of Art. 173 of the Treaty. That principle is of equal application, whether the grounds on which the decision is taken is that the Commission regards the aid as compatible with the common market or that, in its view, the very existence of aid must be discounted.

"Since the complainants undeniably qualify as persons entitled to the benefit of the procedural guarantees in question, they must, as such, be regarded as directly and individually concerned by the contested decision. Consequently, they were entitled to seek its annulment (*Cook v Commission*, paras. 25 and 26)."

It is interesting to observe that the result of this ruling of the Court is that complainants, if and when they have legitimate interest,[22] are in a position to challenge the Commission decision which addresses the contested aid. It should also be remembered that the Commission is expected to give an opinion on the proposed aid under Art. 93.[23] It can be stated that for practical purposes the Commission is under an obligation to give a decision which will then automatically serve to protect the interests of the complainant. In comparison with the position of the complainant in competition cases it may be observed that the complainant in state aid cases is in a stronger position because the "Automec" doctrine gives the Commission the right to set priorities, the right not to pursue a complaint, and to open proceedings in competition cases, whereas in the area of state aid it must give a substantive decision. In other words, due to the fact that the actions of Member States on aid necessarily have to be addressed by the Commission, the complainant is also in a position to protect its interests.

Of course, the legal protection available for the complainant is subject to the well-known test of Art. 173 para. 4, that the decision addressed to the Member State has to be of direct and individual concern to the undertaking. Proving direct and individual concern is at times quite a formidable hurdle for third parties as is demonstrated in the case law of the Court and the Court of First Instance.[24] However, companies that can clearly demonstrate that they are active in the same market – both the product as well as the geographical market – as the proposed beneficiary will normally have standing. It helps if they manifest themselves clearly throughout the whole procedure i.e. both the Art. 93(3) as well as the Art. 93(2) procedure. In the latter procedure it will be particularly relevant if the complainant makes his view known in the Art. 93(2) procedure pursuant to the publication of the summary of the aid plan in the Official Journal. Such comments are, however, neither a prerequisite for Art. 173 para. 4 to apply nor is such a representation a sufficient condition for the subsequent qualification under Art. 173 para. 4. Furthermore, it is not possible as a rule to bring class actions. However, following the case law of the Court of First Instance in competition cases it may be thought that associations who are entitled to represent their members in commercial negotiations meet the Art. 173 para. 4 tests.[25] It should be noted that the Court of Justice in the *Sytraval* judgement also indicated that associations whose interests might be affected, may have standing to bring actions against Commission decisions on state aid.[26]

The second part of the *Sytraval* judgement, combining the second and the third plea, deals with the question what the obligations of the Commission are towards the complainant as far as the statement of reasons and the investigation of the complaint are concerned. It should be recalled that the Court of First Instance had formulated some rather stringent requirements in this respect. It put the burden of collecting the relevant evidence upon the shoulders of the Commission once the complainant had sufficiently established that there was good reason to assume that aid was involved. It also imposed an obligation on the Commission to conduct a contradictory procedure under Art. 93(3), very much along the lines of the procedure of Art. 93(2).

The Court summarises the Commission's position in para. 51:

"Whilst acknowledging that, regardless of the addressee, it is obliged to provide a statement of reasons permitting the legality of the decision to be reviewed, and that, as regards the complainants, it was bound to examine all the facts and points of law which they brought to its notice, the Commission submits that the Court of First Instance was wrong in assessing the scope of the obligation to state reasons as if the complainants were the addressees of its decisions."

The Court answered these arguments in paras. 58, 59, 60, 62, 64 and 75.

"As regards, first, the proposition that the Commission is under an obligation in certain circumstances to conduct an exchange of views and arguments with the complainant, flowing, according to the contested judgement, from the Commission's obligation to state reasons for its decisions, it must be stated that there exists no basis for the imposition of such an obligation on the Commission."

As the Advocate General notes at point 83 of his Opinion, such an obligation cannot be founded solely on Art. 190 of the Treaty. Moreover, as the Commission and the interveners have observed, it follows from the judgements cited in paras. 38 and 39 of this judgement that the Commission is not obliged to give the complainants an opportunity to state their views at the stage of the initial review provided for by Art. 93(3) of the Treaty. Furthermore, those judgements show that, in the context of an examination under Art. 93(2), the Commission is required merely to give notice to the parties concerned to submit their comments. Consequently, as observed by the interveners and by the Advocate General at point 91 of this Opinion, the imposition on the Commission of an obligation requiring it to conduct an exchange of views and arguments with the complainant in the context of the initial review provided for by Art. 93(3) of the Treaty could lead to conflict between the procedural regime established by that provision and that laid down by Art. 93(2).

Next, as regards the statement that the Commission is obliged to examine certain objections of its own actions, it must be stated, contrary to the opinion held by the Court of First Instance, that the Commission is under no obligation to examine any objections to its actions which the complainant would certainly have raised had it been given the opportunity of taking cognisance of the information obtained by the Commission in the course of its investigation.

However, this finding does not mean that the Commission is not obliged, where necessary, to extend its investigations beyond a mere examination of the facts and points of law brought to its notice by the complainant. The Commission is required, in the interest of the sound administration of the fundamental rules of the Treaty relating to state aid, to conduct a diligent and impartial examination of the complaint, which may make it necessary for it to examine matters not expressly raised by the complainant.

As regards, more particularly, a Commission decision finding that no state aid as alleged by a complainant exists, the Commission must at least – contrary to the submission of the German Government – provide the complainant with an adequate explanation of the reasons why the facts and points of law put forward in the complaint have failed to demonstrate the existence of state aid. The Commission is not required, however, to define its position on matters which are manifestly irrelevant, insignificant or plainly of secondary importance.

"The Court of First Instance was correct in finding that the reasoning contained in the contested decision was inadequate in that regard, since the Commission had not responded to that objection. That objection, which had been expressly raised in the complaint, could not be regarded as a secondary aspect of the objections concerning the total or partial payment by the State of the remuneration of the staff of Sécuripost. Even if the remuneration of all staff seconded by the post office had been paid by Sécuripost, the latter would still have enjoyed the potential benefit of not having to pay any compensation in the event of their redundancy or dismissal".[21]

It may be useful to summarise the position of the complainant and the Commission's corresponding obligations when dealing with a state aid case.

First, as Community law, i.e. the case law of the Courts, now stands the complainant might be entitled to a Commission decision stating its position on the complaint. Second, the Commission has to investigate complaints with due care which may entail examining certain objections even if they have not been brought by the complainant. The Commission must at least provide the complainant with an adequate explanation of the reasons why the facts and the points of law that have been put forward by him have failed to demonstrate the existence of aid. Third, the Commission is not obliged to engage in a contradictory procedure under Art. 93(3).

As can be deduced from this summary, the position of complainant is rather well protected and it may well be that the Court will in future judgements rule that the complainant also has a right to a decision addressed to him. The Judgement of the Court in para. 64 comes very close to accepting that the complainant has a right to such a decision. This summary shows quite clearly the importance of bringing a complaint. However, the complainant does not, during the preliminary procedure, have a right to be heard nor is there an obligation to invite him to come forward with comments. The weak point in the position of the complainant in the Art. 93(3) procedure is, of course, that he may not know about the aid plan and hence may not be in a position to bring a complaint. This may, however, in practice not be a very serious problem in most cases. Most companies will know what the financial position of their competitors is and will follow rumours about aid plans closely. It should also be pointed out that the absence of a contradictory procedure under Art. 93(3) is not a major handicap since the Commission may only take decisions under the procedure of this provision if it is sufficiently informed, otherwise it must open the procedure of Art. 93(2). If it nevertheless proceeds without sufficient information its decision may be challenged and annulled by the Community courts.

Competitors that have not brought a complaint may still manifest themselves in the Art. 93(2) procedure and submit comments pursuant to the notice in the Official Journal. Such a competitor will then be in very similar position as the complainant and have similar rights as those that have been summarised above. Conversely, the Commission will have similar obligations towards such competitors, always assuming that the competitor meets the standards of Art. 173 para. 4.

Competitors who also fail to manifest themselves through the Art. 93(2) procedure may still have standing to challenge the final Commission decision approving the aid or the conditions to which the approval is subject, provided that they meet the test of Art. 173 para. 4.

Any competitor has the right to bring proceedings in national courts on the basis of the direct effect of the notification obligation of Art. 93(3). As the Court's judgement in the earlier French *La Poste* state aid case demonstrated, this right is not *disallowed* by the fact that the aid plan is under the scrutiny of the Commission.[27] The Commission has also issued a notice on the cooperation between national courts and the Commission in the state aid field outlining the possibilities for national courts and competitors.[28] I know of at least one instance where this remedy was employed and although the plaintiffs did not succeed in obtaining an order to stop the aid, the procedure nevertheless clearly demonstrated its effectiveness.[29]

4. Evaluation

The two sections above have shown that there is now, after many judgements of the Court of Justice, a rather well-developed system of legal protection of the procedural rights of third parties. The recent Commission proposal for a regulation does not add much to this. As there is no specific provision for the rights of third parties be they intended beneficiaries, complainants or otherwise interested competitors. There is only an obligation in Art. 25 of the draft for the Commission to send a copy of its decisions to interested parties who have submitted comments during the formal, Art. 93(2) procedure. However, there is no mention of a similar obligation towards interested parties who have given uninvited comments during the preliminary procedure. Even though there is clear language in the *Sytraval* judgement of the Court suggesting this. It may well be wise for the Commission to supplement its proposal after the *Sytraval* judgement otherwise it risks being corrected by the Community Courts.

A subject which has not been addressed in state aid procedures so far, is the question of access to the files.[30] This subject is now well developed in the area of competition law.[31] The Commission has also published a notice dealing with this topic.[32] There are obviously important differences in the position of parties in competition cases and third parties in state aid cases. The former may the subject of "administrative" procedures which may lead to serious fines. On the other hand third parties in state aid cases may well be greatly affected by decisions on state aid. The protection of their interests may justify some form of protection through access to the file. A parallel may be drawn with the judgement of the Court in the Dutch courier services case which was adjudicated on the basis of Art. 90(3).[33] In this Judgement the Court found that the failure of the Commission to hear the Dutch PTT in the procedure under Art. 90(3), which lead to the Commission declaring the exclusive right of the Dutch Postal Service company to be contrary to Art. 90(1), constituted an infringement of the latter's procedural rights. Like the state aid procedures the Art. 90(3) procedure is directed towards the Member State and not the company concerned. I submit that a similar reasoning may be forwarded to argue for a right of access to the files. The right for undertakings involved in the state aid procedure to be heard, has been discussed above.

The overall assessment of the procedures available for third parties turns out to be rather positive. There are ample means to protect their interest and these are also adequate in many situations. It should also be stressed that the existence of these procedural rights, the fact that they have been used extensively and their review, in particular by the Court of First Instance, have greatly contributed to the development of the substantive rules on state aid. The bottlenecks of the rules are the lack of openness of the Art. 93(3) procedure and the absence of a right of access to the files.

So far only the procedural aspects of the "user-friendliness" have been discussed, it is now time to devote some attention to matters of substantive law. As might be expected in a system based on general norms, the substantive rules on state aid had to be clarified considerably through the Court of Justice's interpretation. Like the rules on competition, state aid rules are largely judge made law. Almost all the concepts of Art. 92 have now been the subject of rulings of the Court and as such they can be considered reasonably transparent. A major difference with the substantive competition rules is the relative absence of legislation. Apart from successive directives on aid in the shipbuilding sector, a Commission directive on financial transfers to public enterprises, regulations in the inland transport sector and decisions on the coal and steel sector, there has been no legislation. The numerous Commission communications, notices, codes, frameworks, guidelines as well as other forms of rules not foreseen as binding categories of acts under Art. 189, cannot be considered to be legislation.[34] They do not have the same legal status as for example block exemptions in the field of competition law. Their legal effect is still subject to an assessment by the Community Courts. Until now the Court has assumed that some of these rules have been accepted by the Member States and therefore declared them binding.[35] The situation for other Commission notices, etc. to this effect is not yet clear. It is hoped that the new regulation on block exemptions in the field of state aid will settle this uncertainty. It should also be noted that some Commission notices do not formulate hard and fast rules. Thus the guidelines for state aid in the air transport sector start from the presumption that aid can only be approved if it is the last aid, yet the Commission also makes it clear that it considers that the principle cannot be enforced.[36]

What applies to the legal nature of the various Commission notices applies even more to the individual Commission decisions. These decisions usually provide clear guidance for future decisions. Occasionally a number of decisions in a particular section will be used as the basis to draft guidelines. This was the case in the air transport sector. Normally one gets the feeling that the decisions are drafted to produce a pre-determined result. This impression is further strengthened by the lack of sufficient supporting data. In several cases the Commission has used the services of external experts such as Coopers & Lybrand. However, the reader does not get to see the reports of these experts. On the whole the Commission decisions do not always inspire great confidence as to their consistency and substantive soundness. This impression is further strengthened by the relatively loose nature of the notices. This lack of substantive soundness and coherence is to some extent counterbalanced by the possibility of interventions by the governments of other Member States and competitors. These interventions enforce the Commission's hand considerably.

The efficiency of the system is largely measured by the time-frame within which decisions are taken. Although many minor cases are dealt with rather speedily, many major cases take a long time. Whether this contributes to the "user-friendliness" or not, depends of course from which point of view one looks at it. For the competitor this may a good thing. However, the intended beneficiary will not accept this with glee.

NOTES

1. Diane P. Wood, "User-friendly Competition Law in the United States", in P.J. Slot and A. McDonnell, *Procedure and Enforcement in E.C. and U.S. Competition Law*, Chapter 2, p.7, London 1993, Sweet & Maxwell.

2. Dan Goyder, " User-friendly Competition Law", *ibidem,* Chapter 1, p. 3. In EC Competition law the rights of access to the files has recently been given an important boost in the Judgment of the Court of First Instance in the *Solvay* case. Case T-30/91, *Solvay v. Commission*, [1995] ECR II-1779; 33 CML Rev. 1996, 355 with annotation by S. Moore.

3. Recently, it has introduced such a proposal, OJ 1998, C 116/13, which is presently being discussed in the Council, *Agence Europe* No. 7218, 9 May 1998. The debate reveals radical divergences between the Commission and the Member States. The later want to introduce a maximum time period for the conclusion of the Art. 93(2) period. On the same day the Council adopted a regulation on the control of certain categories of aid, introducing the principle of block exemptions.

4. Case C-367/95 P, *Commission appellant*, [1998] ECR I-1719, Judgment of 2 April 1998.

5. Case C-39/94, *SFEI v. La Poste*, [1996] ECR I-3547.

6. Case 730/79, *Philip Morris v. Commission*. [1980] ECR 2671. In this judgment the Court had no difficulty in finding that Philip Morris met the test of Art. 173 para. 4 i.e. that it was directly and individually concerned by the Commission's decision.

7. Case 223/85, *RSV v. Commission*, [1987] ECR 4617, actually the Court ruled that 26 months after notification the Commission was by the principle legitimate expectations, barred from ordering the recovery of the aid.

8. Since the Court's judgment in the Boussac case C-301/87, *France v. Commission*, [1990] ECR I-307, it is clear that non-notification does not automatically lead to incompatibility of the aid with the common market. Thus non-notified aid may nevertheless subsequently be approved by the Commission but there is the risk that the Commission will order repayment of interest for the period that the aid was implemented illegally, i.e. without its approval.

9. This was the case with the SIR investment aid in the Netherlands. The aid plan that eventually lead to the *Philip Morris* case was such a type of aid.

10. OJ 1983, C 318.

11. Case C-5/89, *Germany v. Commission*, [1990] ECR I-3437.

12. Case 223/85, *RSV v. Commission*, [1987] ECR 4617.

13. Case C-188/92, *TWD Textilwerke Deggendorf*, [1994] ECR I-833 and even more explicitly Case C-24/95, *Land Rheinland-Pfalz v. Alcan*, [1997] ECR I-1591.

14. Cf. Case T-277/94, *AITEC v. Commission*, [1996] ECR II-351. Where a letter from the head of unit on state aid cases, Mr. Petersen, expressing an opinion about the desirability of referring a non-executed Commission decision by the Greek Government to the Court of Justice under Art. 93(2), was found not to be

reviewable act.
15. Case C-198/91, *Cook v. Commission*, [1993] ECR I-2487.
16. There exists a form for complaints against Member States for failure to comply with their Treaty obligations, OJ 1989, C 26/6. In 1997, the Commission announced that would publish a new complaints form, *Fourteenth Annual Report on Monitoring the Application of Community law* (1996) COM (97) 299 final, OJ 1997, C 332/1. See also Jacob Soderman, The European Ombudsman: "The citizen, the administration and community law" *General Report for the 1998 FIDE Congres.*
17. Case 246/81, *Lord Bethell*, [1982] ECR 2277. See also case T-227/94, *AITEC v. Commission*, [1996] ECR II-351. See A. Albors-Llorens, in her annotation to case C-68/95, *T. Port*, [1996] ECR I-6065, 35 *CML. Rev.* 1998, 227-245.
18. A good summary can be found in C.S. Kerse, "The complainant in competition cases: a progress report", 34 *CMLRev.* 1997, 213-265.
19. Case T-95/96, *Gestevision Telecinco SS v. Commission*, [1998] ECR II 15 September 1998, can be found at http://www.curia.eu.int/jurisp/cgi-bin/form.pl?lang=en&Submit=Submit&docrequire=judgements&numaff=T-95%2F96
20. The English text of the dictum of the judgment uses the words "failing to adopt a decision".
21. Case C-367/95 P, see note 4.
22. C.S. Kerse argues that this means that: "any person who can show that he is suffering, or likely to suffer, injury or loss directly from the illegal infringement, should be regarded as having such an interest for the purpose of Art. 3(2)of regulation 17, C.S. Kerse: *EC Antitrust Procedure,* 3rd ed. (Sweet & Maxwell, 1994) para. 2.29.
23. If the Commission does not pronounce itself on the proposed aid under Art. 93(3) within two months, the Member State concerned is allowed, after giving notice to the Commission, to implement the aid. The Court has not yet had an occasion to lay down a comparable rule under the procedure of Art. 93(2).
24. Cf. J. Soderman, *op. cit.*, at para. 2.7 writes: "that attempts by complainants to bring proceedings against the Commission under Art. 173 and 175 will remain inadmissible."
25. Case T- 114/92, *BENIM v. Commission*, [1995] ECR II-147.
26. In para. 41.
27. Case C-39/94, *SFEI v. La Poste*, [1996] ECR I-3547. This judgment follows a similar pattern as the *Delimitis* judgment C-234/89, [1991] ECR I-935.
28. OJ 1995, C 312/11.
29. NJ 1997, No. 303 Frima.
30. There was a case before the Court, C-97/92, OJ 1992, C 121/11, where the applicants sought access to correspondence between the Commission and the Member State concerning the imposition of conditions. Apparently, the case has been withdrawn.
31. Cf. M. Levitt, "Access to the file: The Commission's administrative procedures in cases under Arts. 85 and 86", 34, *CML Rev.* 1997, 1413-1444.

32. OJ 1997, C 23/3.
33. Joint cases C-48/90 and C-66/90, *Netherlands and PTT v. Commission*, [1992] ECR I-565.
34. An enumeration of these different forms of rules on state aid can be found in: *"Competition law in the European Communities, Volume IIA Rules applicable to State aid. Situation at 31 December 1994*, EC Commission DG IV Brussels 1995. It should be noted that the terminology is, to say the least, not very consistent, this in itself is a source of confusion and the Commission would do well to streamline the terminology.
35. Case C-313/90, CIRFS, [1993] ECR I-1125.
36. OJ 1994, C 350/5.

PART II:

THE "GUIDELINE" MECHANISM: HORIZONTAL, SECTORAL AND REGIONAL GUIDELINES

CHAPTER 5

THE COMMUNITY FRAMEWORK FOR STATE AID FOR RESEARCH AND DEVELOPMENT: THE RECENT PRACTICE OF THE COURT AND THE COMMISSION

Marco Núñez Müller

1. Introduction

Although, during the 1990s, the European Commission has become increasingly critical of the level of state aid granted each year by the Member States, and of the frequent infringements of Community law in that regard, the Commission has maintained its generally favourable attitude to state aid for research and development (R&D aid).

The reason is to be found primarily in the EC Treaty: pursuant to Art. 3m of the Treaty,[1] the activities of the Community shall include, *inter alia*, the "promotion of research and technological development". Art. 130f *et seq.* of the Treaty states the EC's objectives and policies in that field, with Art. 130f(1) ruling that "the Community shall have the objective of strengthening the scientific and technological bases of the Community's industry and of encouraging it to become more competitive at international level". By virtue of Art. 130f(3), *all* Community activities related to research and development, i.e. irrespective of the Commission's enforcement of competition and state aid rules, are decided on and implemented in accordance with the overall Community objectives as regards research and development.

However, whereas state aid for R&D projects may strengthen the international competitiveness of the Community's industry, thereby promoting economic growth and structural adjustments in relation to the ever-changing requirements of the markets, such aid also brings severe risks to the internal market. Given that smaller, or financially weaker, Member States often lack the means to finance large-scale R&D projects, larger Member States may be prompted to initiate an "R&D race", thereby guaranteeing their national industry a long-term competitive advantage *vis-à-vis* the other Member States. Moreover, since the Commission has tightened its enforcement of the

S. Bilal and P. Nicolaides (eds.), Understanding State Aid Policy in the European Community, 101–118.
© 1999 *Kluwer Law International. Printed in the Netherlands.*

Treaty's state aid rules, many Member States are tempted to disguise operational aid (which is rarely authorised by the Commission) by declaring such financial aid to be part of a research and development programme.

Nevertheless, of the 120 or so R&D cases which the Commission investigated in 1997 all but four were finally approved by the Commission.[2]

2. Legislative background of R&D aid investigation

Most R&D aid cases are reviewed under the EC Treaty. If they come under the very broad scope of Art. 92(1) Member States seek their authorisation mostly under Art. 92(3) b and c. Under 92(3) b, the Commission may authorise "aid to promote the execution of an important project of common European interest"; pursuant to 92(3) c, it may approve "aid to facilitate the development of certain economic activities ... where such aid does not adversely affect trading conditions to an extent contrary to the Community interest". Both rules are to be construed restrictively and provide the Commission with a broad margin of discretion.

However, quite a few R&D cases have recently related to the coal and steel industries and have had to be investigated under the even stricter rules of the ECSC Treaty. Pursuant to Art. 4c of the ECSC Treaty, all state aid in that market is prohibited and to be abolished. The criteria for its exceptional authorisation are set out in several Commission Decisions, most notably the Sixth Steel Aid Code[3] and the Coal Aid Code.[4]

Under the EC Treaty, the Commission has recently been granted the right to adopt a group exemption regulation for, *inter alia,* aid in favour of research and development.[5] Such a regulation will exempt entire categories of state aid from the application of Art. 92 and, consequently, from the notification requirement under Art. 93(3) of the Treaty. The Commission expects that the concept of group exemption (imported from competition law into state aid law) will provide the public with greater legal certainty while reducing the Commission's administrative burden. The Commission is expected to develop and publish a draft R&D group exemption regulation early in 1999.

At the sub-statutory level, in 1996 the Commission published the new "Community Framework for State Aid for Research and Development" (the "Framework").[6] This Framework, which is subject to revision in 2001 and which has already been amended in order to also cover agricultural R&D aid,[7] replaces the 1986 R&D aid Framework.[8]

Finally, as regards competition and trade relations with third countries, the Agreement on Subsidies and Countervailing Measures (SCM Agreement), which is part of the 1994 WTO Agreement,[9] explicitly refers to R&D aid. Art. 8(2) a of the SCM Agreement deems all "assistance for research activities conducted by firms or by higher education or research establishments on a contract basis with firms" non-actionable, provided that the aid is limited to certain cost categories and does not cover more than 75% of the costs of industrial research or 50% of the costs of precompetitive development activity.

3.　The 1996 Framework on R&D state aid

The Framework confirms the Commission's favourable view of R&D aid.[10] Compared to the 1986 Framework, the 1996 Framework contains adjustments to the recommendations of the Commission's "White Paper on Growth" and to the SCM Agreement. The Framework now allows, *inter alia*, for aid cumulation within the limits of the SCM Agreement and obliges Member States to notify any significant amounts they wish to grant under general R&D aid programmes already authorised by the Commission.

3.1　THE FRAMEWORK'S APPROACH AND SCOPE

The Framework generally judges R&D aid according to its proximity to the market. The closer the subsidised research and development is to the market, the more significant the distortive effect on competition and the lower the allowable aid limits are, if any.

In this context, the Framework strictly distinguishes between three different categories of research and development, i.e. fundamental research, industrial research and precompetitive development activities, which are explicitly defined.[11]

While the Framework now also covers research and development related to agricultural products,[12] it does not, in principle, specifically address individual industries but applies to all R&D aid covered by the EC Treaty. Moreover, its scope of application is significantly extended by references in the Coal Aid Code,[13] and in the Sixth Steel Aid Code,[14] explicitly stating that all R&D aid in the Coal and Steel industry is to be examined according to the Framework.[15]

On the other hand, the R&D Framework is also applicable in economic sectors normally subject to specific aid guidelines. Most notably, all R&D aid granted to the car manufacturing industry and/or to small- and medium-sized enterprises is to be examined according to the criteria laid out in the Framework.[16]

3.2 THE FRAMEWORK'S CONTENTS

The structure of the Framework largely reflects the structure of Art. 92 and 93 of the EC Treaty for obvious reasons: the Framework's main chapters deal with the applicability of the state aid rules to R&D aid (Chapter 2); the compatibility of R&D aid with the Common Market (Chapter 3); the notification of R&D aid to the Commission (Chapter 4); the allowable intensity and the required incentive effect of R&D aid, which are among the principle criteria when assessing the aid's compatibility with the Common Market (Chapters 5 and 6).

3.2.1 Aid not covered by Art. 92(1) of the EC Treaty. Under the Framework, some kinds of R&D aid are normally not covered by Art. 92(1) of the EC Treaty and do not therefore need any approval by the Commission[17] :

– public financing of R&D activities undertaken by public non-profit-making higher education or research establishments;

– R&D aid of the above kind if the results are made available to the Community industry, i.e. including competing companies abroad, on a non-discriminatory basis;

– aid for R&D by the above public establishments together with the industry, if the public establishment acts like a commercial firm, e.g. doing R&D in return for payment at market level; or if the industry bears all R&D costs; or if the results are widely disseminated and any intellectual property rights remain with, or are sold by, the public non-profit organisation at a market price.

If a Member State commissions R&D by, or buys the results from, industry Art. 92(1) does not normally apply providing the pertinent contracts between the public body and the private company are concluded under market conditions. Such market conditions are deemed to have been applied, if the contract was awarded following an open tender procedure.[18]

3.2.2 Approval under Art. 92(3) b and c of the EC Treaty. An R&D project is deemed to be in the common European interest, so that any state aid involved may be authorised pursuant to Art. 92(3) b, if, for example, that national project either aims at achieving specific Community objectives or is obviously better than any R&D programme which the Community has established in that field. This has been assumed to be the case in relation to certain major transnational projects such as Eureka.[19]

When examining whether R&D aid may be authorised under Art. 92(3) c, the Commission pays special attention to, inter alia, the following criteria: the type of research carried out; its beneficiaries; the aid intensity; and the access to the R&D results.

(1) The Commission determines the allowable aid intensity on a case-by-case basis, thereby also considering overall policy considerations and the overall negative effects on competition or intra-Community trade.

However, it has allocated maximum aid intensities to specific kinds of R&D:

- aid for fundamental research by private entities may amount to 100%;
- aid for industrial research may amount to 50% of certain eligible costs;[20]
- aid for pre-competitve development activities may amount to 25% of certain eligible costs;[21]

The Framework also states maximum aid intensities for "mixed situations" such as aid for R&D carried out together by public non-profit and by private entities, aid for R&D covering two of the above aid categories, and combined aid granted by the Community and a Member State.[22]

Moreover, subject always to a maximum level of 75% for industrial research, and 50% for precompetitive development activities, the Framework allows for the following aid bonuses to be added to the above maximum aid intensities: 10 percentage points, for instance, for SMEs, regions under Art. 92(3) a, and effective cross-border R&D cooperation.[23]

Finally, R&D in the agricultural sector may, under certain conditions, be subsidised 100%, even if the R&D is undertaken by private companies.[24]

(2) When evaluating R&D aid, the Commission considers in particular whether the aid has an "incentive effect", i.e. whether it will induce firms to pursue R&D which they would not otherwise have pursued. While such an effect is assumed if the beneficiary is a SME, the lack of such effect is assumed if a large proportion of the aid has been granted prior to its notification. Besides that, the "incentive effect" has to be demonstrated by the Member State concerned on the basis of figures showing significant changes in R&D spending and R&D staff.[25]

3.3 NOTIFICATION REQUIREMENTS UNDER THE FRAMEWORK

3.3.1 Aid to be Notified. New R&D aid must always be notified, unless the amount does not exceed ECU 100,000 in which case the aid would be considered *"de minimis"*.[26]

Existing R&D aid schemes must be notified, if their budget is more than doubled or if their duration is extended by more than 5 years or if, due to such an extension, they are no longer in line with the 1996 Framework.[27]

Moreover, the Commission now requests that Member States even notify individual aid granted under an existing scheme, if the aid amounts to more than ECU 5 million and if it is spent on a project costing more than ECU 25 million.[28] However, Member States are bound by this "appropriate measure" only to the extent they have agreed to it.[29]

3.3.2 Information to be Provided in the Notification. The notification should be made according to the standard form which the Commission informed the Member States of in its letters dated 22 February 1994 and 2 August 1995,[30] although as regards R&D aid this has been significantly amended by the Framework.[31]

Apart from giving detailed information as to the donor, the beneficiary, the amount and form of the aid and any relation to an existing aid scheme, the Member State concerned must now provide details regarding the R&D phases and cost items to be subsidised, the intensity of aid, national and international cooperation and the distribution of the R&D results, etc.

3.4 THE FRAMEWORK'S LEGAL VALUE

Frameworks and guidelines are measures not provided for in the EC or ECSC Treaties. In particular, they do not constitute binding legal acts such as regulations, directives or decisions under the EC Treaty or decisions and recommendations under the ECSC Treaty. Nevertheless, the Commission regularly and openly applies such "soft law" measures when investigating and deciding on R&D aid. Therefore, the question arises as to what the legal value, or binding force, of these frameworks and guidelines is.

3.4.1 New versus Existing Aid Schemes. Art. 93(1) of the EC Treaty distinguishes between "new" and "existing" aid schemes. Existing aid schemes are those which (1) were either in force in 1958 (or at the time of the respective Member State's accession to the EC) or (2) have since been authorised by the Commission. Existing aid schemes are privileged in that the Member States, in principle, are exempt from notifying them according to Art. 93(3) and that the Commission is, in principle, barred from examining them again under Art. 92. When specific aid is granted under a general and existing aid scheme, the Commission is limited to examining whether that specific aid complies with the (national) requirements of the existing aid scheme. However, under Art. 93(1) of the Treaty, the Commission constantly reviews the existing aid schemes. Moreover, it may propose "appropriate measures" in order to adjust existing aid schemes to the Common Market.

On the other hand, "new" (i.e. not pre-existing) aid – as well as significant alterations to existing aid schemes – must, in principle, be notified by the Member States under Art. 93(3). It is examined by the Commission pursuant to Art. 92 of the EC Treaty.

For reasons of transparency, the Commission tries, at least in the English versions, to reflect the above distinction in the names of the respective "soft laws": "Frameworks" apply to both new and existing aid schemes and as far as the latter are concerned, they are "appropriate measures" within the meaning of Art. 93(1) of the EC Treaty. "Guidelines", on the other hand, in principle apply only to new aid schemes.[32]

The R&D Framework therefore covers both new and existing schemes. It expressly introduces, as an "appropriate measure" the Member States' obligation to notify all individual aid which, although granted under an authorised R&D aid scheme, both amounts to more than ECU 5 million and is granted for a project costing more than ECU 25 million.[33] However, as shown below, its binding force depends on whether it is applied to new or existing aid.

3.4.2   Enforceability of the Framework against the Commission. A framework is, first of all, a description of the criteria which the Commission wishes to apply, and announces, when deciding on whether to authorise state aid. These criteria often refer to preceding court judgements and Commission decisions, if any, as regards the type of aid at issue.

Even if a framework remains in force for several years, the Commission is not prevented from amending, or even cancelling, it if the framework expressly provides for such amendments.[34] However, such a framework may only be amended by way of the same proceedings which were used when adopting it. In other words, if the Commission has, when introducing a framework, requested the Member States' consent it must submit any draft amendment to the Member States prior to adopting the changes.[35]

However, the principles of legal certainty and protection of legitimate expectations request that, as long as a framework remains in force, the Commission is forced to apply it when investigating state aid.

3.4.3   Enforceability of the Framework against the Member States. As already mentioned, a framework, to the extent it is applied to *existing* aid, merely constitutes an "appropriate measure" within the meaning of Art. 93(1) of the EC Treaty. Hence, it constitutes a proposal, the enforceability of which *vis-à-vis* a Member State depends on whether that Member State has agreed to it. In other words, if a Member State has consented to such a measure, or if a Member State has been obliged, by a Commission Decision, to adjust its practice to such a measure, a framework binds that Member State *de jure* also as to existing aid schemes.[36] If, however, a Member State has neither agreed, nor been obliged to agree, to such an appropriate measure, the latter is not legally enforceable against that Member State.

As to *new* aid schemes, the situation is different. Here the Commission may act unilaterally without seeking the consent of the Member States. However, frameworks which have been adopted unilaterally, do not bind Member States *de jure*, but *de facto*: as far as they establish a duty of notification and such duty already results from Art. 93(3). Moreover, frameworks are not listed among the legal acts enumerated in Art. 189 and they normally do not expressly name a legal basis. However, frameworks do bind Member States *de facto* for the simple reasons that the Commission is bound by them and that Member States will not receive the authorisation for such aid unless they apply the criteria which the Commission establishes in these frameworks.

3.4.4 Enforceability of the Framework in National Courts. National courts do not have the competence to decide whether aid is compatible with the Common Market, pursuant to Art. 92(2) and (3) of the EC Treaty. However, to the extent a framework is *de jure* binding upon a Member State it is also enforceable in national courts. If, therefore, a Member State has agreed to adapt its existing aid scheme to a framework, which thereby becomes binding, the issue of whether this adjustment obligation has been complied with may, in principle, be invoked and decided by national courts.

3.4.5 Result. The R&D Framework binds, and is enforceable against, the Commission.

The R&D Framework binds, and is enforceable against, Member States, to the extent it refers to existing aid and it has been approved by these Member States.

As to new aid schemes, the R&D Framework binds Member States *de facto*, since their grant of aid will not be authorised unless they comply with the Framework's criteria.

The R&D Framework may be invoked by, and must be enforced by, national courts to the extent it is legally binding on the pertinent Member State.

4. The recent practice of the Court and the Commission under the Framework

Whereas the Court of First Instance has rendered very few judgements on R&D aid since 1990,[37] the Commission has adopted quite a number of formal decisions in that context during the same period.[38]

Since the structure of these decisions, unsurprisingly, follows the structure of the 1986 and 1996 Frameworks they are analysed here in the same way.

4.1 APPLICABILITY OF ART. 92(1) OF THE EC-TREATY

4.1.1 Research by Public Non-profit-making Entities. In two cases, i.e. Commission Decisions 91/500/EEC *Friuli* and 96/615/EC *IFP*, the

Commission has recently confirmed that aid to research is not caught by Art. 92(1) of the Treaty if it concerns only fundamental research not carried out by an enterprise but by a public non-profit-making establishment.[39] Although the "Institut Français du Pétrole" (IFP), which statutorily is a public non-profit-making body, probably violated its own statutes by selling its research findings at market prices the Commission, quite remarkably, still considered the IFP to be non-profit-making. Therefore the R&D aid for the IFP did not come under Art. 92(1) of the Treaty, because the R&D aid was not sufficient to finance *all* its R&D activities.[40]

As a consequence, it must be assumed that the privilege which public non-profit-making bodies enjoy under the R&D aid rules remains unaffected, even if these entities are partially funding their R&D activities by selling their R&D results at a profit.

4.1.1 Parafiscal Charges for Financing R&D Aid. However, the IFP decision is mainly interesting because it deals with two main R&D aid issues, i.e. the financing of R&D activities by means of a parafiscal charge and the way the R&D results are distributed among private companies.

IFP is a non-profit-making scientific and technical institute which was founded in 1944 and which is engaged primarily in R&D projects in the petrochemical field. The IFP is mainly financed from the proceeds of a parafiscal charge on certain oil products (amounting to approximately ECU 155 million per year) which is imposed on both domestic and imported oil products. The Commission considered both the financing of the IFP's R&D activities from the proceeds of that parafiscal charge and the transfer of IFP's R&D results to companies as not constituting aid within the meaning of Art. 92(1) of the Treaty.

The Commission has continuously held that parafiscal charges introduced by a Member State for the purpose of financing a research establishment constitute, in general, state aid within the meaning of Art. 92(1) of the Treaty. The obvious reason is that such parafiscal charges normally provide greater advantages to firms from the Member State introducing them than to their foreign EC competitors. This specific benefit for domestic firms relates to the fact that: (1) the subsidised R&D activities mainly benefit domestic companies whereas the charge is disproportionately financed by companies from other Member States, and (2) such charges are imposed on sales in the pertinent Member State, while exports from that Member State remain exempt, the result being that exports are promoted while imports and sales in the domestic market are put at a disadvantage. This, however, clearly affects intra-Community trade. This principle was confirmed by the Court of Justice in its 1970 ruling on parafiscal charges for the benefit of the Institut Textile de France.[41]

As a consequence, the Commission has constantly considered such parafiscal charges financing R&D activities to not only constitute state aid but also to not qualify for the exemption provided for in Art. 92(3) c of the Treaty, to the extent that such charges were also imposed on products imported from other Member States.[42]

However, in the IFP case, the Commission held that these parafiscal charges did not constitute state aid, but it obliged France to also levy them on export products.[43] The main reason is to be found in the way IFP distributed its R&D results.

France maintained that the results of IFP's research were accessible both to French and foreign companies without any discrimination. On the basis of a detailed examination of IFP's R&D expenditure and client structure, the Commission concluded that, although the two leading French companies in the oil and automobile industries were among IFP's most important customers, IFP generated most of its turnover from foreign companies. Therefore, the Commission assumed that French firms were not the chief beneficiaries of the findings of R&D carried out by the IFP and that these findings were available both to domestic and foreign firms without discrimination.[44]

However, given IFP's profitable sales policy, the Commission should have considered that the parafiscal charge constituted state aid and should have continued its examination as to whether that aid could be exempt under Art. 92(3) of the Treaty. Instead, the Commission mixed two levels of examination by taking IFP's allegedly non-discriminatory sales policy as an issue capable of "cleaning" the parafiscal charge from its state aid *"odeur"*.

4.1.3 Structural R&D Aid. R&D state aid may also be found in a state-controlled price policy, as the Commission stated in its decision on Belgian pharmaceutical programme contracts.[45] Maximum prices for pharmaceutical products were frozen in Belgium and although exemptions were possible they were, *de facto*, only granted by way of so-called programme contracts concluded between Belgium and producers, importers or packagers of pharmaceuticals. These programme contracts were designed to promote investment and basic research, by allowing the other party to increase the price of those products covered by a programme contract and by granting a preferential arrangement as regards eligibility for reimbursement.

The Commission considered these price increases authorised by programme contracts as constituting state aid since they enabled the beneficiaries to carry out research without having to bear the normal costs. Given that the pharmaceutical market is highly competitive and that the programme contracts mainly favoured Belgian producers, the Commission also refused to grant an exemption under Art. 92(3), since the fact that the prices were frozen at a very low level in Belgium had severe impacts on EC competitors, which were not able to recover their proportional research costs in Belgium.

4.1.4 Aid for Modernisation and Ancillary Measures. In two decisions, the Commission had the opportunity to clarify the notion of R&D aid.

In *Halyvourgia*, the Commission held that investment aid aimed at the modernisation of existing production facilities does not come under the rules for R&D aid.[46]

On the other hand, in its decision on aid to the French coal industry,[47] the Commission held that aid aimed at supporting activities which are merely ancillary to R&D activities may still be judged according to the R&D aid rules.

4.2 AUTHORISATION UNDER ART. 92(3) OF THE EC TREATY

Whereas none of the formal decisions adopted during the 1990s has exempt aid for promoting an important project of common European interest (Art. 92(3) b of the EC Treaty), most of them have analysed R&D aid as to its possible exemption under Art. 92(3) c of the Treaty. In that regard, the most significant criteria have been the aid intensity and the so-called incentive effect.

4.2.1 Aid Intensity. In its decision on French R&D aid to the coal industry,[48] the Commission concluded that the R&D aid amounted to less than 20% of all expenditure earmarked by the beneficiary for mining research and development. The Commission thus found the aid in question to be compatible with its R&D aid rules.

However, in *Georgsmarienhütte,*[49] the Commission had to decide on the R&D character of the project, the eligibility of the investment costs at issue for R&D aid proposed and on the intensity of the aid. On the basis of Art. 2 of the Steel Aid Code together with the Framework, the Commission repeated the principle that basic industrial research may qualify for higher levels of aid than applied research, which is closer to the market. Furthermore, aid for basic industrial research may amount to up to 50% of the project's gross costs, whereas applied R&D may be subsidised up to only 25% of the costs.[50]

As a consequence, the Commission admitted only those costs which were a direct result of the R&D project and which were in direct relation to the project eligible for R&D state aid. Moreover, it rejected Germany's request to allow aid for applied R&D with an intensity of 30% or more, although it permitted an intensity of 25% gross.

4.2.2 Incentive Effect. In *Olivetti*, the Commission decided to initiate the proceedings under Art. 93(2) of the Treaty – the proceedings which later resulted in the withdrawal of the aid scheme at issue – because Italy and Olivetti were not capable of demonstrating the required "incentive effect". Given that the pertinent project (i.e. the development of portable multimedia personal computers) had already been started prior to the notification of the planned aid, the Commission decided that apparently the project was embarked upon because of future market opportunities, and that the receipt of R&D aid was not indispensable for the project.[51]

In *SGS-Thomson*, the Commission held the incentive effect to be non-existent since the main parts of the aided R&D activities closely matched the day-to-day activities of the beneficiary.[52]

4.3 NOTIFICATION

Several Commission decisions have dealt with the notification requirement under Art. 93(3) of the Treaty and under the Framework.

In *IFP*, France argued that both the R&D activities of the IFP and its financing by way of a parafiscal charge were introduced in 1944, thus constituting existing aid not subject to the notification requirement under Art. 93(3) of the Treaty. The Commission rejected that argument apparently on the basis of the amount of that charge (ECU 155 million per year) and the fact that this charge was to be renewed, under the corresponding French law, for another 5-year-period.

In *SGS*,[53] the Commission insisted on proper notification of the R&D aid at issue since the research project cost more than ECU 25 million and the proposed aid was to amount to more than ECU 5 million, thus exceeding the limits set by para. 4.7 of the Framework.

Several decisions also related to wrong or incomplete notifications. Thus, in *Valtellina*, the Commission obliged Italy, by way of a formal decision, to provide additional information on the proposed R&D aid and project and, in the meantime, strictly limited the amounts Italy was allowed to spend for R&D.[54] In *Hoffmann-La Roche*, the Commission initiated proceedings under Art. 93(2) of the Treaty mainly because Austria withheld necessary detailed information which would have allowed the Commission to evaluate the R&D project and aid in question.[55]

5. Conclusion

Frameworks provide both the Commission and the "customers" of state aid law – i.e. potential beneficiaries and donors of state aid, and potential competitors of the aid recipients – with several advantages. Frameworks allow the Commission to state, in much more detail than in legislative acts, the criteria which are relevant when assessing, and eventually authorising, a given type of state aid. They thus promote transparency and legal certainty in this rather complex area of EC law. Moreover, since the adoption of frameworks is not subject to the – sometimes lengthy – legislative proceedings provided for under the EC Treaty, they are a tool allowing the Commission to react relatively quickly to specific developments in the relevant markets.

On the other hand, however, frameworks sometimes lack the clarity, both in structure and in wording, which is mostly found in legislative acts. Moreover, their legal value – i.e. their binding force on Member States – may sometimes be doubtful if Member States refuse to accept a framework as to existing aid schemes.

The above conclusions also apply to the R&D Framework. Whereas the R&D Framework is most useful as regards the description of the criteria for aid evaluation, such as the aid intensity and the incentive effect, it is surprisingly vague in defining the basic principles. The definitions of "fundamental research", "industrial research", and "precompetitive development activity", as given in Annex I of the Framework, are far too short and abstract as to permit a clear and foreseeable distinction of a given R&D activity. This is all the more true, since the Framework, quite contrary to other frameworks and guidelines, does not refer to pertinent court judgements and Commission decisions which would provide examples for the Commission's practice in categorising R&D measures. The Framework thus leaves the aforementioned "customers" of state aid law with quite some uncertainty, in particular as to the maximum allowable aid intensity which, under para. 5 of the Framework, obviously depends on whether a given R&D measure is to be considered fundamental, industrial research or a precompetitive development activity.

Unfortunately, the Commission's practice has added to this uncertainty. In exempting IFP from the application of Art. 92(1) of the EC Treaty, despite IFP's commercial behaviour in the market, the Commission blurred to some extent the distinction between public non-profit-making research entities, which are rightly privileged under the Framework, and private entities which regularly make the results of their research commercially available and which are therefore not privileged under the state aid rules. Moreover, IFP also opened an exception to the general rule according to which Member States may not impose parafiscal charges in order to finance the R&D activities of their national industries, since these charges discriminate against competitors from other Member States in that these competitors are subjected to the parafiscal charges without benefiting from them.

ANNEX

I. Recent Commission Decisions approving R&D aid

- Commission Decision 91/500/EEC, *Friuli region*, OJ 1991 L 262/29
- Commission Decision 95/519/EC, *French coal industry*, OJ 1995 L 299/18
- Commission Decision 96/76/EC, *DAF*, OJ 1996 L 15/37
- Commission Decision 96/458/ECSC, *French coal industry*, OJ 1996 L 191/45
- Commission Decision 96/575/ECSC, *Spanish coal industry*, OJ 1996 L 253/15
- Commission Decision 96/591/ECSC, *Spanish coal industry*, OJ 1996 L 259/14
- Commission Decision 96/615/EC, *IFP*, OJ 1996 L 272/53

II. Recent Commission Decisions (partially) not authorising R&D aid

- Commission Decision 90/188/EEC, *Dutch parafiscal charges I*, OJ 1990 L 101/35
- Commission Decision 90/189/EEC, *Dutch parafiscal charges II*, OJ 1990 L 101/38
- Commission Decision 91/547/ECSC, *Sardinian Steel*, OJ 1991 L 298/1
- Commission Decision 92/327/EEC, *Belgian programme contracts*, OJ 1992 L 182/89
- Commission Decision 93/134/EEC, *Brussels regional aid*, OJ 1993 L 55/61
- Commission Decision 94/172/EEC, *Valtellina*, OJ 1994 L 79/24
- Commission Decision 95/437/ECSC, *Georgsmarienhütte*, OJ 1995 L 257/37
- Commission Decision 95/456/EC, *Greek pharma*, OJ 1995 L 265/30
- Commission Decision 96/573/ECSC, *Halyvourgia*, OJ 1996 L 252/19

III. Some Recent Authorisations (cases where Commission raised no objections)

- Case N 388/94 (aid to the new Länder for research of new products), OJ 1994 C 385/34
- Case NN 34/94 (Dutch aircraft research programme), ibid
- Case N 334/94 (UK Vaccines Research Institute), ibid
- Cases N 562/93 and N 584/93 (research in the seeds sector), ibid at p. 41
- Case N 847/95 (aid for research of Spanish SMEs), OJ 1996 C 114/ 6
- Case N 1014/95 (aid for research of French public bodies and enterprises), ibid
- Case NN 136/95 (French aid for Sagem, Bull SA, Océ, Nipson and Siab related to research on the design of new peripherals for personal computers), ibid
- Case NN 127/95 (*Renault and Sollac* – Eureka Programme), OJ 1996 C 150/11

- Case N 175/B/94 (R&D on magnetic levitation trains – *Transrapid* – comprising DM 560 million at an aid intensity from 35-100%), OJ 1996 C 300/ 4, cf. also *Competition Report 1996*, p. 248
- Case N 222/96 (research of Spanish SMEs), E 4/96 (Austrian Industrial Research Promotion Fund), ibid
- Case N 233/97 (*Eurocopter* – comprising 36 million ECU), OJ 1997 C 395/12
- Case N 349/97 (MEDEA – Eureka 1535 – comprising 112 million ECU), ibid
- Case N 336/97 (Austrian ERP programme, section R&D), ibid.

NOTES

1. The Treaty provisions hereinafter cited are those in force in November 1998. However, under the Treaty of Amsterdam, which was signed on 2 October 1997 and which – subject to ratification by all Member States – is supposed to enter into force in 1999, the numbering of the EC Treaty provisions will be changed as follows: Art. 3m, 92, 93, 130f of the EC Treaty shall, respectively, become Art. 3n, 87, 88, 163 of the EC Treaty.
2. Cf. European Commission, Competition Report 1997, at para. 289.
3. Commission Decision 2496/96/ECSC, establishing Community Rules for State Aid to the Steel Industry, OJ 1996 L 338/42; the Sixth Steel Aid Code is valid from 1 January 1997 until 22 July 2002.
4. Commission Decision 3632/93/ECSC, establishing Community Rules For State Aid to the Coal Industry, OJ 1993 L 329/12; the Coal Aid Code is valid from 1994 until 22 July 2002.
5. Art. 1 (1) a) ii) of Council Regulation 994/98/EC on the application of Arts. 92 and 93 of the Treaty establishing the European Community to certain categories of horizontal state aid, OJ 1998 L 142/1.
6. OJ 1996 C 45/5.
7. Commission Communication amending the Community Framework for State Aid for Research and Development, OJ 1998 C 48/2.
8. OJ 1986 C 83/2.
9. Cf. Art. II (2) together with Annex 1 A of the WTO Agreement.
10. Cf. para. 1.9 of the Framework.
11. Cf. paras. 2.2, 2.3 and Annex I of the Framework:
    – fundamental research: "any activity designed to broaden scientific and technical knowledge not linked to industrial or commercial objectives";
    – industrial research: "planned research of critical investigation aimed at the acquisition of new knowledge, the objective being that such knowledge may be useful in developing new products, processes or services, or in bringing about a significant improvement in existing products, processes or services".
    – precompetitive development activities: "the shaping of the results of industrial research into a plan, arrangement of design for new, altered or improved products, processes or services, whether they are intended to be sold or used, including the creation of an initial prototype which could not be used commercially. This may also include the conceptual formulation and design of other products, etc. provided that these cannot be converted or used for industrial applications or commercial exploitation. However, this does not include the routine or periodic changes made to products, production lines, manufacturing processes, existing services and other operations in progress, even if such changes may represent improvements".
12. Para. 5.14 of the Framework, as amended 1998.
13. Ibid. Art. 6
14. Ibid. Art. 2.
15. Confirmed by the Court of First Instance of the EC CFI in Case T-243/94 *British*

Steel, [1997] ECR II-1887, at para. 47.

16. See para. 3.3 of the "Community Framework for State Aid to the Motor Vehicle Industry", OJ 1997 C 279/1; and para. 4.2.6 of the "Community Guidelines on State Aid for Small and Medium Enterprises", OJ 1996 C 213/4.

17. Cf. para. 2.4 of the Framework.

18. Cf. para. 2.5 of the Framework.

19. Cf. paras. 3.2-3.4 of the Framework.

20. For these eligible costs see Annex II of the Framework.

21. As above.

22. Cf. paras. 5.7-5.9 and 5.12 of the Framework.

23. Cf. para. 5.10 of the Framework.

24. Cf. 5.14 of the Framework, as amended in 1998.

25. Cf. paras. 6.1-6.5 of the Framework.

26. Cf. the Commission Communication on *"de minimis"* aid, OJ 1996 C 68/9; para. 4.5 of the Framework.

27. Art. 93(3) of the EC Treaty; cf. para. 4.6 of the Framework.

28. Cf. para. 4.7 of the Framework

29. See hereinafter Chapter 4 c.

30. Cf. the Commission's "Yellow Book" (Competition Law in the EC), Vol. IIA (Rules applicable to state aid [as per 31 December 1994]), at pp. 73 *et seq.*

31. Cf. Annex III to the Framework.

32. See e.g. para. 2.5. of the "Community Guidelines on State Aid for Rescuing and Restructuring Firms in Difficulty", OJ 1997 C 283/2.

33. Cf. para. 4.7 of the Framework.

34. Cf. para. 9 of the Framework.

35. Adv.-Gen. Lenz in Case C-135/93, *Spain v Commission re Car Framework I*, [1995] ECR I-1653, at p. 1661, para. 33.

36. See Case C-313/90, *CIRFS*, [1993] ECR I-1125 (1186-1189).

37. Case T-243/94 *British Steel*, [1997] ECR II-1887; Case T-150/95 *UK Steel*, [1997] ECR II-1433; however, R&D aid is the main issue in the pending case T-59/98 *Honeywell*, in which a competitor seeks nullification of an authorisation, by the Commission, of R&D aid to be granted to the French company Sextant Avionique for developing an aircraft piloting system.

38. For references, see the Annex to this note.

39. See Commission Decision 91/500/EEC, *Friuli region*, OJ 1991 L 262/29 at p. 34; Commission Decision 96/615/EC, *IFP*, OJ 1996 L 272/53, pp. 59 *et seq.*

40. See Commission Decision 96/615/EC, *IFP*, OJ 1996 L 272/53, p. 60.

41. Case 47/69 *France vs. Commission*, [1970] ECR 487.

42. See Commission Decision 90/188/EEC *Dutch parafiscal charges I*, OJ 1990 L 101/35; Commission Decision 90/189/EEC, *Dutch parafiscal charges II*, OJ 1990 L 101/38; and Commission Decision 95/456/EC, *Greek pharma*, OJ 1995 L 265/30.

43. Art. 1 (1), Art. 2 of Commission Decision 96/615/EC, *IFP*, OJ 1996 L 272/53.

44. Ibid. at pp. 58-60.

45. Commission Decision 92/327/EEC, *Belgian programme contracts*, OJ 1992 L

182/89.
46. Commission Decision 96/573/ECSC, *Halyvourgia*, OJ 1996 L 252/19.
47. Commission Decision 95/519/EC, *French coal industry*, OJ 1995 L 299/18.
48. Commission Decision 95/519/EC, *French coal industry*, OJ 1995 L 299/18.
49. Commission Decision 95/437/ECSC, *Georgsmarienhütte*, OJ 1995 L 257/37.
50. Ibid. at p. 41.
51. OJ 1996 C 306/9; cf. also EC Bulletin 4/1996 at para. 1.3.37.
52. See OJ 1996 C 358/3, 6/7.
53. OJ 1996 C 358/3.
54. Commission Decision No. 94/172/EEC *Valtellina*, OJ 1994 L 79/24.
55. See OJ 1996 C 168/2.

CHAPTER 6

HORIZONTAL GUIDELINES: DO THEY FACILITATE JOB CREATION? THE EXAMPLE OF EMPLOYMENT SUBSIDIES

Guy Cox

This Chapter addresses two questions. First, which horizontal "subsidies" related to employment are permitted in Europe? Second, what is the link between employment and job creation?

Section 1 gives a brief survey of the conditions invoked by the Commission under which measures reducing labour costs are not to be considered as subsidies or where such measures are compatible with the principles of the common market. Section 2, then, briefly describes the link between labour costs and employment by making use of some theoretical and practical schemes.

1. Conditions under which labour cost reduction is not considered to be a subsidy or is considered to be compatible with the common market

In this period, in which the majority of the Member States are suffering from unprecedented high unemployment rates, job creation is the first concern of the Commission. As long as there is no effective solution to structural unemployment in Europe, it will be difficult to convince the European population to subscribe to the goals of the European Union.

The employment subsidies used by some Member States in order to improve the situation in their labour markets often appear to be inappropriate instruments. Moreover, there is a risk that problems are not solved by subsidies but only moved to other Member States: unemployment, then, is exported. As employment subsidies might distort competition among European companies, which would consequently be reflected in their employment rates, the Commission's supervision of subsidies is meant to prevent this situation by making sure that employment subsidies are not

S. Bilal and P. Nicolaides (eds.), Understanding State Aid Policy in the European Community, 119–128.
© 1999 *Kluwer Law International. Printed in the Netherlands.*

incompatible with the goals of the Community.

Following the extraordinary European Council meeting on employment, held in Luxembourg on 20 and 21 November 1997, the 15 Member States have adopted "employment guidelines" for the first time.[1] This new process was introduced within the framework of the anticipated implementation of the Amsterdam Treaty: such guidelines will be annually approved and have to be converted into national action plans. Employment throughout the Union will thus benefit from a conversion strain that provides support for the promotion of employment.

Concerning the rules of competition in the field of government subsidies, the first series of employment guidelines recommends that this government aid promotes economic efficiency and employment without disturbing competition.

One of the instruments used by the Member States in their battle against unemployment is *labour cost reduction*. This is not so astonishing in itself. Ever since the White Paper on "Growth, Competitiveness and Employment" in 1993, the European Commission has emphasised the necessity of taking measures to improve employment on a European scale.[2] Based upon this publication, the European Council at a meeting in Essen, in December 1994 defined five priorities in matters of employment. One of the priorities is the reduction of indirect labour costs.

In the section on "Developing entrepreneurship", the 1998 employment guidelines, as adopted in Luxembourg, also contain a guideline advocating the reduction of fiscal pressure on labour and non-wage labour costs. This guideline obliges the Member States in their national action plans to try and make their taxation systems more friendly to employment and in doing so reverse the trend of the ever increasing taxation of labour. The taxation of labour has risen in Europe from an average of 35% in 1980 to over 42% in 1995. In particular, the 1998 employment guidelines state that each Member State shall:

> "set a target, if necessary and taking account of its present level, for gradually reducing the overall tax burden and, where appropriate, a target for gradually reducing the fiscal pressure on labour and non-wage labour costs, in particular on relatively unskilled and low-paid labour, without jeopardising the recovery of public finances or the financial equilibrium of social security schemes. It will examine, if appropriate, the desirability of introducing a tax on energy or on pollutant emissions of any other tax measure."[3]

It is obvious that the Commission is convinced that labour cost reduction is one of the substantial means to stimulate job creation.

In order to clarify the circumstances under which the measures to reduce labour costs are subject to the rules of ballot, the Commission published some guidelines on employment subsidies in December 1995.[4] Furthermore, a communication from the Commission, published in January 1997, deals with government subsidies monitoring and labour cost reduction.[5] I will try to schematise, as well as to occasionally illustrate, the framework as set out by the Commission in both documents.

Roughly speaking, the Commission distinguishes between measures authorised because they do not contain any subsidies and measures which are in principle unauthorised because they do contain subsidies. However, within this second category the Commission can consider certain measures as being compatible with the common market.

1.1 AUTHORISED MEASURES

Authorised measures are those:
(i) tailored to the economy of a member state as a whole; and
(ii) which apply in an automatic and non-discretionary way.

These are the recommended measures as far as the Commission is concerned, for they do not favour any specific companies or industries and following Art. 92 (1) of the Treaty are not to be considered government subsidies.

Examples of such authorised measures:

a) A general reduction of social security contributions. In 1995, Denmark decided to levy new taxes on certain industrial pollutant emissions by means of an energy bill. The profits from the new taxes have been returned to industry through a general reduction of the employers' social security contributions. On the basis of objective criteria and given the fact that every company has benefited automatically from this system, the Commission has decided not to consider these subsidies as government subsidies following Art. 92 (1) of the Treaty.

b) Measures relating to certain categories of workers (low-paid labour, the relatively unskilled, youngsters in work experience programmes, the long-term unemployed, part-time workers, etc.) provided these measures are applied automatically and without any distinction.

In evaluating subsidies, the Commission checks whether the company has, in addition to hiring those previously unemployed for instance, provided other services in return, such as training.

Within this context, we can also refer to the proposal the Commission made to the authorities in, for example, Sweden in order to guarantee the compatibility of the Swedish recruitment and employment systems with the open market. These cases are typical examples of the policy the Commission intends to introduce in this field. It is made up of a number of precautionary measures in order to render the objective of stable, net job creation fully effective. As far as the first measure is concerned, the Commission held the opinion that the support had to be aimed more specifically at the deprived categories of unemployed and that as far as the mere purveyance of labour for the relinquished jobs was concerned, support was only possible provided the jobs were relinquished out of free will. Concerning the second measure it is considered that support can only be granted for the creation of new jobs. In both cases, the Swedish authorities were requested to reduce the excessively large scope of the initially proposed field of implementation. They were also asked, amongst other things, to guarantee the stability of the jobs created, be it by using contracts of unspecified duration, including training, or by maintaining the newly created jobs for a minimum period.

c) Measures concerning career guidance, counselling and vocational training for the unemployed. The Commission considers the training of workers to be a crucial element in maintaining employment and in developing the Union's competitiveness. Therefore, it encourages companies to invest in training. Whenever this is done by making use of government subsidies, the Commission must ensure that these subsidies do not disrupt competition.

In order to clarify under which circumstances government subsidies for training can be considered as compatible with the common market, the Commission has formulated a draft framework regulation on subsidies for training. It hopes to be able to adopt this framework regulation in the course of 1998.

d) Measures meant to improve the general labour legislation or to adapt the educational system.

e) A final category of measures are those authorised not primarily due to their nature, but rather due to the *limited effect* they have on the cross-border trade. The *de minimis* rule states that Art. 92 (1) does not apply to subsidies amounting to a maximum ECU 100,000 over a three-year period. Therefore, contrary to the other examples, we are dealing here with genuine "subsidies" that are "tolerated".

The preceding measures (and examples) are not considered to be government subsidies following Art. 92 (1) of the Treaty.

In order to make the distinction between government subsidies and general measures, one should refer to the four criteria mentioned in Art. 92 (1) as a means of establishing what determines a government subsidy, bearing in mind that those four elements must all be present for a measure to fall under Art. 92 (1).

Those four elements are:

–   the subsidies are financed out of state resources;

–   the subsidies distort competition or threaten to do so;
–   the subsidies favour certain companies or productions;
–   the subsidies adversely influence commercial exchanges between Member States.

1.2   MEASURES TAILORED TO CERTAIN COMPANIES OR PRODUCTIONS ARE UNAUTHORISED

Examples of unauthorised measures

a)   Sectoral measures. In this context, the Commission has already given a negative evaluation of the Italian subsidies to its shoe industry; the French plans for its textile industry; and the Belgian Maribel 2 and 3 regulations granting a tax cut to employers whose activities belong to a sector that is exposed to stiff international competition.

In contrast, the modification to the Maribel regulation in 1997 (Maribel-quarter) was accepted by the Commission as a general measure since it was aimed at the modification of the social security contributions of all branches, depending on the percentage of "blue collar" workers amongst the personnel employed. This is an objective and transparent parameter that does not discriminate against companies or entire branches. At present, Belgium is working at further generalisation of its Maribel measure, giving it an even more horizontal nature.

b)   Measures favouring certain regions

c)   Measures applying to companies of a certain size. The Commission decided that the Swedish support scheme had to be considered as government support for certain enterprises since it applied solely to enterprises employing up to 500 workers, thus advantaging those enterprises in comparison to the enterprises employing over 500 workers.

These measures which are not allowed are considered to be support in the sense of Art. 92 (1), but can nonetheless be declared compatible with common market principles by the Commission.

1.3   MEASURES COMPATIBLE WITH THE COMMON MARKET

The measures that can be compatible with the common market are those which:
–   create employment opportunities (cf. below);
–   maintain employment opportunities subject to certain conditions;
–   are applicable to certain sectors that are exposed to international competition but to a lesser extent.

1.3.1 Measures that create employment opportunities. This is taken to mean a net increase in the number of places at work. The Commission is always looking to see whether the jobs are stable and whether the companies are offering something in return, such as training.

For example:

– support for the creation of new jobs in small and medium-sized enterprises and in areas eligible for regional support;

– support that encourages categories of employees that have particular difficulties in the job market joining or rejoining that market;

– support for measures for the division of work, such as stimulating part-time work.

1.3.2 Measures that aim at maintaining employment opportunities provided that they fulfil certain conditions.

– the support must serve to repair the damage done by natural disasters or other unusual occurrences;

– the support is awarded to regions that are eligible for supportive measures that encourage economic development in areas where the standard of living is extremely low or where there is a serious lack of employment opportunities;

– the support is applicable to a lesser extent to some of the sectors that are exposed to international competition (e.g. the communication of the Commission of the Council and the European Parliament concerning a European strategy for the stimulation of local initiatives for development and employment opportunities).[6]

2. What is the connection between support for employment opportunities and job creation?

Neither the European Commission, nor the OECD, nor internal institutes have any doubts that the cost of labour has an influence on job creation and on employment opportunities in general.

The cost of labour is naturally influenced by the level of the net salary and the total of all the deductions by the government via personal taxation as well as employers' and employees' contributions to social security. The government can raise or lower its deductions, generally or selectively and so influence the cost of labour.

There is unanimity over the proposition that a lowering of labour costs has a positive impact on employment opportunities. The effects can, however, differ according to the ways that are chosen by which to lower these labour costs.

In order to bring about an output of goods and services, companies introduce various production factors which they can purchase on the market for a certain price. These production factors can be grouped under: (i) labour, (ii) capital, and (iii) energy and non-energy intermediate inputs. The sum of the costs of all the production factors is the total production cost.

The proportion of the total production costs that each of these production factors amounts to varies considerably from sector to sector. So the recovery of the cost of the labour production factor makes up a good 55% of the total costs in the services sector, while only amounting to scarcely a quarter of the total costs in the industrial sector. The intermediary inputs by contrast make up a good two thirds of the total costs in industry, against scarcely a quarter in the service sector.

A certain production volume can normally be achieved in different ways, characterised by a certain combination of production factors. Changes in the relationship between the prices of production factors can give rise to substitution effects in the production process, whereby relatively expensive production factors are replaced by relatively cheaper ones, in so far as the production processes allow substitutions between labour, capital and intermediary inputs. If, for example, the cost of labour increases more sharply than that of capital, then it is more rewarding to introduce capital, than labour. On the other hand, if even a moderate increase in wages is in prospect, that reduces the advantage that can be expected from rationalising investment. The choice made by companies in terms of methods of production is influenced by the anticipated relative level of cost changes in the different factors of production.

The determinants of the relative cost changes are:
– the cost of labour, which is made up of the gross pay plus social contributions;
– the cost price of the intermediary inputs (energy and non-energy material costs); and
– the cost of capital (that is to say the annual real cost of financing and the annual depreciation of capital goods).

The impact of labour costs on employment opportunities is expressed in terms of elasticity, indicates by how many percent employment opportunities grow or diminish when the relative cost of the labour production factor goes up or down by 1%.

Many studies have already questioned the elasticity of labour with respect to labour costs, and their results differ sharply. Hamermersch demonstrates in a review of the American literature that the long-term elasticity, according to the economic method or subdivision by sector, can swing from between -0.15 and -0.75. As regards to France, Dormont thinks that this elasticity can lie between -0.5 and -0.8. For Belgium there are numerous estimates that give a fairly broad spread of results. The Hermes-Belgium macro-sectoral model provides us with a possible model (separated by sector), according to which the long-term elasticity should amount to approximately -0.4.

The econometric estimates on the basis of the National Bank of Belgium model provide similar results. Hence, it appears that if the relative price of labour (labour costs in comparison with the measured average of the costs of other production factors) increases by 1%, and all other circumstances remaining constant, the intensity of employment falls by approximately 0.5%. Put another way: the long-term elasticity of employment in relation to the relative cost of labour (with growth remaining the same and productivity increasing independently) amounts to around -0.5.

A moderation in labour costs has a favourable effect on employment opportunities via three channels:

–   an improvement in competitive power whereby the companies can drive up their market share, both within the European market and abroad;

–   an increase in the profitability of investments, by means of which potential growth is increased;

–   a slowing of the substitution of the labour production factor by the capital production factor.

Without going into details, I would like to indicate that the methods by which labour costs are lowered can be very different. One of the techniques that is often used, including in Belgium, is the lowering of the employers' social security contributions. Within this choice there are various options that differ from a general lowering of contributions, which is often disadvantageous for employees and employers, to the other extreme, namely a selective reduction in contributions that are subject to conditions (for example for taking on someone who has been a member of the long-term unemployed).

These different methods each have different results. In Belgium we take the view that a mix of different formulas is preferable so as to allow the economy and employment opportunities to be stimulated to maximum effect. In fact, it appears that by following this policy, economic growth has become more labour intensive in recent years.

3. Conclusion

In order to translate economic growth into employment opportunities to the maximum extent, the relative cost of the labour production factor must be sufficiently low. At the same time, for social reasons, but also for economic reasons (consumption), the available incomes must stay sufficiently high. This obliges Member States to lower the burden on labour by means of general and/or selective measures.

These measures must as a general rule not extend as far as artificially stimulating particular sectors in a country, because that would result in moving unemployment problems to another country, rather than solving them. In this context, the European Commission has formulated guidelines which allow the evaluation of admissible government measures to influence labour costs. The lack of transparency of and simplicity in the rules does not make the application of this easy, as illustrated by the many disputes between Member States and the Commission.

One example of the lack of transparency is the vagueness of the thin borderline between general measures in the field of cost reduction (permitted) and social measures (not permitted). As things are now this borderline is hard to determine before the measures in question have been decided on by the Commission. It is even harder to do so since both the Court and Commission accept general measures which are gradually introduced (e.g. for budgetary reasons).[7]

Bearing this in mind, the harshness with which the Commission implements its vague rules is, if not astonishing, at least out of proportion. One can also wonder whether this harshness (which could well turn into an obligatory recovery under the menace of penalties) could not end up undermining employment within the Community.

This would have a negative effect as far as the European unification is concerned. And such cannot be the intention, can it?

The economic logic on which the Commission has forged its position holds.

The vagueness in its implementation in reality and in time however does a lot less. This calls for a transition period in order to create more clarity within the rules followed by gradually more harshness in their implementation as time passes by.

This is a normal chronology.

NOTES

1. Council Resolution of 15 December 1997 on the 1998 Employment Guidelines, O.J. No C 30/01 of 28.1.1998.
2. Commission of the European Communities, *Growth, Competitiveness, Employment: The Challenges and Ways Forward into the 21st Century*, White Paper, 1993, COM(93) 700 final.
3. Cf. supra, Guideline 11.
4. O.J. No C 334/04 of 12.12.1995.
5. O.J. No C 1/05 of 3.1.1997.
6. O.J. No. C 265/03 of 12.10.1995.
7. See decision 80/932 of 15.09.1980, O.J. No L 264 of 8.10.64. Indeed, what other qualification is there for the controversial Maribel bis/ter than an intermediary phase in the implementation of a general measure since almost half the blue collar workers were already concerned.

CHAPTER 7

DO STATE AID GUIDELINES FACILITATE
IMPROVEMENTS IN COMPETITIVENESS?
THE EXAMPLE OF MARITIME TRANSPORT

Alfons Guinier

1. Introduction

The establishment and maintenance of a system of free and fair competition is one of the basic principles of the European Community (Art. 3 of the EC Treaty). Consequently, state aid is incompatible with the common market unless it falls within one of the derogations under Art. 92 of the Treaty. Further, the Commission, in cooperation with Member States, is obliged to keep under constant review all systems of aid existing in those States and to take decisions on the compatibility of new or altered aid with the common market (Art. 93 of the EC Treaty).

In monitoring state aid, the Commission relies on Art. 92 of the EC Treaty, which in principle bans all aid, although it allows the Commission to make exceptions to this general ban. Such exceptions can in particular be granted in the case of aid that promotes the development of certain economic activities and certain economic areas, if this does not conflict with the Community's interest in having fair trading conditions that are free of distortions of competition.

Under the EC Treaty provisions, competition is consequently not an absolute principle and the control of competition must not therefore be an end in itself: Member States are in principle free to develop their national economies through state aid even if competition is affected as a result. This is incidentally an instance where the principle of subsidiarity has been applicable from the start.

But it is also evident that the granting of national aid is limited where the Community has an overriding interest in ensuring undistorted competition. Determining such limits, i.e. weighing up the common interest, is the Commission's central task in the monitoring of state aid. The following

S. Bilal and P. Nicolaides (eds.), Understanding State Aid Policy in the European Community, 129–142.

principles governing positive assessment may be deduced from Art. 92.

–   The aid must be economically necessary in order to bring about the desired development, i.e. the assisted measure would not be carried out without the aid.

–   The amount and duration of the aid – which also means the extent and duration of the distortion of competition – must be in proportion to the objective pursued through the aid.

–   Assistance should always be confined to pump priming. Aid that is unlimited in time and intended to cover the day-to-day operation of a firm – known as operating aid – cannot be authorised, any more than export aid within the Community.

–   National interest, or the interest of particular firms alone, does not justify the authorisation of aid, which must be of benefit to the Community as a whole.

–   Lastly aid which fits coherently into Community policies or into measures on which there is a Community-wide consensus can more easily be deemed compatible with the common market. Conversely, aid in sectors in which there is over capacity and particularly fierce competition throughout the Community can be authorised only subject to strict conditions. For example, the Commission is more willing to authorise aid for basic research, or for small and medium-sized businesses, than aid to the textile or motor vehicle industries. In addition, in the steel and shipbuilding area the subsidies will only be allowed under strict conditions.[1]

The decision of the Commission and Member States to allow and to recommend state aid for the shipping industry is based on EU maritime policy, in particular on the Commission communication "Towards a New Maritime Strategy" presented by Transport Commissioner Neil Kinnock in March 1996.[2]

The rationale of the Commission and Member States for this decision originates from their conviction that the EU, as a main trading entity on a global basis cannot do without maritime know-how. This know-how finds its basis in a strong and competitive shipping sector and extends to the whole maritime area. The EU shipping industry's competition is international and not so much intra-EU competition. State aid for shipping should consequently reflect the "international-competition" environment.

The very nature of EU international shipping activities, not only between Europe as a whole and the rest of the world but also through the provision of direct services between third countries outside the EU (cross trade), makes the shipping sector distinct from the shipbuilding sector, which competes on the world market but is regionally based. This physical difference becomes even more evident when one considers the nationality of a ship i.e. the Flag or the Register (including its tax base), which can easily be changed at any moment without too many difficulties, offering attractive financial operating conditions – whilst the control of capital remains in Europe. The so-called EU controlled fleet. Such an easy and often applied transfer is physically impossible for a land-based industry such as shipbuilding. Aid to the shipping sector should consequently not be confused with aid to shipbuilding, which is dealt with on the basis of completely different criteria.

This special international character and operating base of shipping is an important subject which is unavoidably repeated when considering state aid in the shipping sector.

Following this introduction we will give some background on developments in EU shipping and explain the rationale and contents of state aid guidelines for shipping.

2. Historical background

The discussions on support measures in the European shipping sector started back in the 1980s. The reason was clear. Since the beginning of the 1980s the EEC registered fleet as a percentage of the world fleet decreased from 29.6% in 1979 to about 14-15% in the 1990s. This also had obvious consequences on employment, with a reduction of about 45-50% of EC seafarers on EC vessels.

This evolution was in sharp contrast to the importance of trade and shipping to the EC in that period:
– With about 25% of world trade the EC was one of the key players in the world economy;
– 90% of the Community's external trade was carried by sea;
– 33% of intra-Community trade carried by sea.[3]

Whereas some Member States had taken individual measures to remedy the above anomaly, safeguard their national shipping and maritime know-how and improve the competitive position of the sector versus global competition structurally, it took about 15 years for the EC to develop a concrete policy in this respect.

We learnt from inner circles that is was Commissioner Narjes – then in charge of Industry (DG III) – who in the mid-1980s launched the idea of support measures for European shipping during intra-Commission discussions. The idea was not carried forward. Commissioners Contegeorgis and Lord Clinton-Davis also worked out some ideas on positive measures for European shipowners but in the event nothing was agreed.

In 1986, the so-called first phase of the EU shipping policy was established by the Council of EU Transport Ministers through the adoption of the interim well-known Four Shipping Regulations, which was mainly aimed at a free market in shipping within Europe and worldwide.[4]

When agreeing this policy package, the Council – aware of the decline in the number of vessels on EU registers and of the fall in employment of EU seafarers – invited the European Commission to work on a second phase of EU shipping policy and particularly on measures to improve the competitive (operational) position of EU shipowners under EU national registers versus world competition.

Following this Council statement, discussions between all involved went on, some Member States enhanced their own measures in support of their own fleets, but at Community level nothing concrete happened until 1989 when the then Transport Commissioner Karel Van Miert presented a new policy document on the future of Community shipping and on measures to improve the operating conditions of the EU merchant fleets.[5]

This policy paper also gave birth to "EUROS", a parallel register – to run simultaneously with the national register of the relevant Member States – under which positive measures would be allowed.

Since this was the first document launching the so-called second phase of the EU shipping policy, it was in the first instance welcomed by most of the parties involved. Indeed, at last something happened.

The Van Miert document gave a description of the alarming position of the EU merchant fleets since 1980:

–   There had been a decline in the EU registered fleet from 117 million Gross Registered Tonnes (GRT) to 59 million GRT in 1988, i.e. a decline in tonnage of 50%;

–   There had been a reduction in the number of vessels from 11,218 to 6,512;

–   the European share of the world fleet had declined from 29.7% to 15.4%;

–   The number of EU seafarers employed had been reduced from 307,000 to 169,000 (a reduction of 45%).

In the paper the Commission suggested the need for an EU merchant fleet for the European economy and the necessity of having positive measures to improve the competitive position of EU shipowners on EU registers.

According to the Commission, these positive measures should concentrate on the cost of seafarers, notably in terms of fiscal and social security contributions, company taxation, assistance with investment costs, repatriation of seafarers, training, etc.

As already mentioned, the first reactions were positive because at long last something happened. However, after a more detailed study, reactions were no longer that positive. The package was often described as an empty box because it did not contain any concrete action, or as a pure state aid package without concrete contents. Therefore, the Commission was invited to work on something better.

After further studies and analysis of the different regimes under European and worldwide registers, between five and 10 different proposals were brought forward by the European Commission, either formally or informally.

Although it would be interesting to go into the details of each of them to get a clearer picture of the decision-making machinery of the European institutions, this is not appropriate in the context of this contribution.

The main elements of the positive measures contained in the different proposals can be summarised into:

 — reimbursement of seafarers' income tax
 — reduced income tax
 — reimbursement of social security contributions
 — reduced social security contributions
 — payments/reimbursement of the cost of repatriation of seafarers
 — aid to assist the training cost of seafarers
 — exemption from company tax for modernisation schemes on profits from the sale of merchant ships reinvested in the purchase, modernisation or transformation of another merchant vessel
 — support to ensure high quality ships and equipment by upgrading existing ships to higher international safety standards
 — tax-free provisions for reinvestment in vessels
 — tonnage tax
 — flexible depreciation rules
 — the carrying forward/carrying back of losses.

National measures could continue to exist if this was the wish of the Member States involved. Also, manning schemes changed from a requirement for 100% of officers and 50% of ratings to be EU nationals to more flexible and more ad hoc schemes.

The first proposals were mandatory in character, but when confronted with the negative reactions of Member States they was later changed into a mandatory minimum level of positive measures with a voluntary maximum level, leaving it to Member States to apply measures of their choice on basis of these limits.

However, since Member States could still not accept this mandatory approach, the proposals were further refined into a suggestion for a Council Resolution encouraging Member States to take positive measures and leaving them free to choose a non-mandatory scheme within minimum/maximum limits. Even so, apart from underlining the importance of a healthy EU shipping industry, no commitment on Community policy could be obtained from Member States.

The Kinnock strategy paper of March 1996, "Towards a New Maritime Strategy", eventually offered a breakthrough with clear suggestions on aid measures and workable state aid guidelines, taking into account the international trading and operating environment of EU shipping. We shall elaborate in more detail on the new approach in section 4.

3. The need for an effective EU shipping policy

LOOKING BACK: THE EU SHIPOWNER'S VIEW

Looking back into the history of the positive measures, one is tempted to compare it with the procession of "Echternach".

For those not familiar with continental culture, Echternach is a place in Luxembourg, where they organise a Catholic procession around Whitsun. The characteristic feature of this procession is that the participants proceed hand in hand taking three steps forward, two steps back and alternating from the right to the left. All this accompanied by polka music. However, they eventually arrive at their destination. We leave it to the reader to judge whether, apart from the polka music, our story on positive measures is the same...

Having given a brief historic review on support measures for EU shipping, a logical question might be what did the, European shipowners, think about it? Or, why did it take such a long time to come up with something concrete?

These positive measures (EUROS) – although dealt with on a political level – are, in our opinion, in the first instance purely economic. We are afraid this is often forgotten.

First of all, EU shipping (ECSA[6]) fully supports the philosophy that Europe, as one of the main trading entities in the world, needs a strong EU shipping sector.

It should be realised that, whereas shipping remains the core activity, it has an automatic effect on all the surrounding sectors such as shipbuilding, ship repair and marine equipment manufacturing, marine insurance, broking, banking, law, ports surveying, education, etc. All these sectors are underpinned with essential skills and know-how provided by Community shipping.

In a study made by Dutch and Belgian academics in 1994 for the Dutch Government on the future of the Dutch shipping sector, the catalyst effect of shipping on all maritime sectors was abundantly clear.[7] It resulted in the Dutch Government's decision to produce a "pro-active maritime policy", the main policy objective being the creation of sustainable added value and employment.

From what we have seen to date, most, if not all, of EU Member States accepted the need for a strong shipping sector. To play the role of a catalyst, EU shipping must be strong and competitive. Therefore, positive measures, as advocated by EU shipowners since 1986, are essential. The consideration of positive measures and state aid for shipping should be seen against the background of the growing globalisation of shipping industry itself and its customers. In this international playing field, one cannot ignore:

- the dependence on international financial and capital markets;
- the increasingly integrated labour market;
- the uniquely mobile tax base of shipping, enabling companies to take advantage of fiscal and labour cost benefits on a world-wide basis;
- the realities of the information revolution which make the shipping world even more international.

This scenario offers both opportunities and problems for EU shipping in the fight to remain competitive in the world market. The core aim of positive measures must therefore be to create a sympathetic economic and political climate for investment in the shipping industry with the aim to:

- enable EU shipping to compete on at least level terms with world competition;
- repatriate capital and attract new capital to EU shipping and encourage the setting up of new activities in the EU;
- encourage employment opportunities for EU nationals within the first two goals.

The aim of positive measures should therefore not be to harmonise within Europe but rather to meet the needs of the flexible international shipping environment. One imagines that the philosophy the Commission originally adopted to harmonise the support measures of Member States, or to impose measures on the States, was the main reason for the delay in arriving at something concrete at the European level. This method quite simply could not work since the approach, tax, social security systems, etc. are different in all Member States. It has also been a mistake to take the intra-EU competitive position of EU shipping as a yardstick. We stressed earlier as a kind of *"leitmotiv"* that shipping is *de facto* international. The yardstick of competitiveness should therefore clearly be world competition.

The measures needed to fulfil these objectives have been mentioned in the previous sections; nevertheless, to sum up they are:

- a flexible and stable tax environment for EU shipping;
- a reduction in the overall costs of employing seafarers, e.g. through appropriate income tax and social security relief in order to strengthen the competitiveness of the EU shipping industry, including making it attractive to employ European seafarers;
- flexible manning possibilities in terms of nationality;
- increased emphasis on the recruitment and training of seafarers.

It is also of key importance that existing national regimes or measures, which have been set up to meet the above objectives, including fiscal regimes, should be allowed to continue if the individual Member States so wish it.

This brings us back to state aid guidelines. We do realise it is not an easy subject but, nevertheless, such guidelines should be transparent and should contain provisions to address the risk of international distortions of competition and, consequently, not be solely inward looking with respect to the EU. They should offer EU shipping a stable fiscal and operating cost framework within which EU shipowners can build up their operations within a long-term view.

Although it is perhaps superfluous to say it, there should be a distinction between aid to shipping and general schemes and state aid falling outside the scope of aid to the shipping industry, such as aid to shipbuilding.

4. The Kinnock strategy paper – Community guidelines on state aid to maritime transport

As mentioned above, the Commission Communication of March 1996 offered a new approach to support measures for EU shipping by abandoning the previous ideas on harmonisation and by recognising that the competitive market for shipping was not European but global. The strategy paper also advocated support measures for EU shipping but left it to Member States to apply them within their means and national systems while controlled by state aid guidelines to avoid distortion of competition, as well as to avoid a subsidy race on a European or global basis. It is also a clear policy that the guidelines should act as an incentive for Member States to implement support measures, rather than as a policing instrument.

A brief analysis of the key points and rationale of this policy on state aid as expressed by the Commission in the strategy paper and the state aid guidelines themselves provides clarity on the principles contained in the guidelines. In this summary we often refer to the Commission's position to stress the underlying policy.

4.1 GENERAL

In its Communication "Towards a New Maritime Strategy" of March 1996 and in the introduction to the Community guidelines on state aid to maritime transport published on 5 July 1997, the Commission stressed the necessity of support measures for EU shipping to remedy the disadvantages EU shipping faces such as:

–   the strict manning conditions to be respected;
–   Member States fiscal and social arrangements for companies and their employees, which make it expensive to operate EC registered ships with EC seafarers on board;

– few costs for third country operators entering the open trades;

– direct competition with these third country operators – who benefit from more competitive operational conditions – in both international and Community trades.

It was also stressed that the shipping industry is extremely mobile and that an onerous regime can easily be avoided through registering vessels in other countries (giving absolute freedom in manning) and, if necessary, establishing a nominal level of administration or management outside the EU (to avoid Member States' fiscal systems). The Commission also acknowledged that, in recent years, there had been a large supply of seafarers available from low-wage third countries, giving shipowners a low-cost option when selecting crews.

The above circumstances led to a decrease of the percentage of EU registered vessels from 32% in 1970 to 14% in 1995. The share of the major open registry countries increased over the same period from 19% to 28%. It is evident that there has also been a correspondingly steady decrease in the number of EU seafarers over the same period.

The Commission also recognised that the flagging out of vessels (i.e. changing the registration of a vessel to a non-EU country) is, however, not the end of the problem. Where flag States outside the EU offer an attractive international service infrastructure, flagging out has tended in recent years to be followed by relocation of ancillary activities (such as ship management) to countries outside the EU, leading to an even greater loss of employment, both on board ship and on shore. An evident consequence has been a loss of maritime know-how, which has obvious negative consequences for the whole maritime field.

4.2 STATE AID GUIDELINES

Recognising that some Member states had taken measures on a national level to safeguard the economic viability of their national shipping industry, taking into account their specific national structures, the European Commission adopted revised state aid guidelines on maritime transport on 6 May 1997.[8] The guidelines, which are very much based on the philosophy expressed in the "Strategy Paper on Maritime Transport" issued by Commissioner Neil Kinnock in March 1996, have as general objectives of:

– safeguarding EC employment, (both on board and on shore);

– preserving maritime know-how in the Community and developing maritime skills; and

– improving safety.

In the context of the above objectives they allow for state aid to be granted generally only in respect of ships entered in Member States registers. In certain exceptional circumstances measures which do not require an EU flag may be approved where a benefit to the Community is clearly demonstrated.

Key measures which can be approved can be summarised as follows:

– *Fiscal treatment of shipowning companies:* fiscal schemes with alleviation to improve the fiscal climate of shipowning companies including the tonnage tax regime. These alleviation schemes require as a rule a link with a Community flag. However, they may exceptionally be based on an economic link (i.e. flag neutrality) subject to the necessary safeguards and monitoring by the Commission.

– *Labour-related costs:* reduced rates of income tax and social security contributions for EC seafarers on board ships registered in Member States.

– *Crew relief:* reimbursement of costs of repatriation of EC seafarers on board ships entered in Member States registers.

– *Training:* whereas vocational and academic training is exempted from state aid regimes, aid may be granted for on board training of EC seafarers on board of EC registered vessels. Exceptionally, training of EC seafarers on board other vessels may be supported where justified by exceptional criteria, such as the lack of available places on vessels in a Member State's register.

Investment aid for new ships must respect the relevant EU directives or any other Community legislation as relevant in this respect. In certain restricted circumstances aid may be permitted to improve equipment on board of EC registered vessels or to promote the use of safe and clean ships.

For regional aid and restructuring aid the EU's general rules apply.
Public service obligations and contracts have received particular attention taking into account their specific nature and the importance of services to peripheral regions. This will be dealt with on the basis of the usual public service commitment rules/arrangements.

The Commission has abandoned the previous complex and hypothetical calculation of ceilings to aid and introduced *a straightforward and transparent ceiling of zero taxation and social charges for seafarers and corporate taxation of shipping activities as the maximum level of aid which is permitted.*

The state aid guidelines became effective as from 5 July 1997, the date of their publication in the Official Journal of the European Community.

ECSA (representing the shipowners of the EU and Norway) welcomed the new guidelines as a generally clear, balanced and acceptable approach to a complicated issue. The new guidelines are flexible in that they take into account the very different structures and characteristics to be found in Member States. They also recognise the global character of shipping, have effective safeguards against excesses and are in compliance with international obligations and internationally agreed yardsticks.

ECSA expressed the hope that they will act as an incentive for EU Member

States to take action as appropriate to maintain a healthy European shipping industry and the essential maritime know-how.

5. Positive measures as taken to date and expectations for the future[9]

Since the date of the introduction of state aid guidelines, in spring 1997, the position in the EU Member States and Norway in respect of the introduction and the application of measures to improve the competitiveness of their national shipping industry has developed substantially.

Substantial support measures or progress can be reported in the following countries:

– *Netherlands*: The Commission formally approved the Dutch shipping aid programme in July 1997, and no changes were requested. The Dutch Parliament has recently adopted a new crewing act incorporating more flexible crewing possibilities. As mentioned in the guidelines, the system is subject to monitoring.

– *Norway*: A package of positive measures for the shipping sector – largely based on the Dutch programme – has been approved by the EFTA Surveillance Authority.

– *Germany*: In June 1998 the Government agreed a package of measures supporting German shipping. The package was approved by the Commission.

– *Italy*: An Italian second register allowing a package of measures in line with the EU state aid guidelines has recently been approved by the Italian Government and is now being gradually enacted.

– *France*: In April 1998 the French Transport minister announced a new set of support measures replacing the "Quirat" system.

– *Denmark*: In addition to the conditions under the DIS (Danish International Shipping Register) changes to support training have been introduced and were notified to and agreed by the Commission. The Danish Shipowners have also requested that their government consider the introduction of a tonnage tax system.

– *Spain*: In addition to the conditions allowed under the Canary Island Special Ship Register further fiscal measures are under consideration.

In other EU Countries less progress can be reported but discussions are taking place:

– *Belgium*: Following an agreement between the shipowners' association and the seafarers union, the government agreed to reduce social contributions. Further *démarches* on fiscal alleviation, possibly a tonnage tax, are being considered to improve competitiveness. Most of the vessels previously registered under the Belgian flag have been transferred to the Luxembourg register to benefit from more attractive fiscal schemes.

– *The United Kingdom*: A working group has been established comprising owners, unions, and Ministries to investigate a package of measures. The group is reporting to the Vice-Prime Minister, who supports the drive for action. Clear proposals are expected in the near future.

– *Sweden*: The Swedish shipowners are involved in intensive discussions with the government on positive measures based on the Dutch and Norwegian aid programmes. Shipowners and seafarers' unions reached an agreement on a joint position strengthening the pressure on the government.

– *Finland*: A similar position to Sweden.

– *Portugal*: Discussions with the government are ongoing. However, results are not forthcoming mainly due to a lack of success in convincing the Finance Minister.

– *Greece*: Having the benefit of a tonnage tax system, Greek shipowners do not have a specific project for the introduction of new measures increasing the competitiveness of the flag. On the contrary the increase in the seafarers' taxation, introduced in 1997, has raised negative reactions by the industry. Discussions are going on to avoid "negative" measures. The EU state aid guidelines and the new positive measures taken by other EU Member States contribute positively to these discussions.

– *Ireland*: An independent survey has revealed that Irish tax laws hinder the competitiveness of the Irish shipping industry. Working under the Irish flag and being resident in Ireland are the worst options for an Irish seafarer. The Irish Chamber of Shipping is putting pressure on the government for urgent measures to rectify this position. Concrete results are expected soon.

6. First results of the application of state aid guidelines for shipping

The EU state aid guidelines for shipping as well as the positive measures introduced by Member States – with the guidelines as an incentive – are still rather new. Therefore the results for most of the Member States are difficult to assess at this moment.

Nevertheless, we can report encouraging results in the Netherlands where the national fleet has increased by 100 vessels over the last two years. With 3.3 million GRT the fleet has again reached the 1986 level. Moreover, a substantial number of shipowners have established themselves in the Netherlands or have extended their activities there. Other shipowners are considering starting up new shipping activities from the Netherlands. The effects on employment are positive. A recent prognosis indicates, however, that there will be a substantial shortage of qualified seagoing and shore based staff with shipping knowledge by 2004. Even today shipowners have difficulties in finding qualified Dutch or European officers.

In Norway the national fleet is also growing and employment has steadily increased (with more than 1,000 employees at the time of writing). Furthermore, increased confidence in the sector contributed to boosting new shipbuilding orders from Norwegian companies, a big percentage of which was placed with national shipyards.

As mentioned above, the application of new measures is so recent that in many Member States substantial results cannot yet be seen. It is however clear that the positive measures have avoided and stopped the flight of national shipping companies to more economically attractive regimes.

The conclusion to be made on the results of the state aid guidelines is therefore very positive. The state aid guidelines have also clearly acted as an incentive for the different Member States to consider and take action to maintain a viable shipping sector and the maritime know-how which is essential for their economies.

The only negative point is that the positive measures and the guidelines which are steering them have in many instances been introduced much too late. The European shipping industry has been stressing for many years that such measures were overdue. The present situation regretfully confirms this statement. Not only in the Netherlands but also in other EU countries there is a clear shortage of qualified national seafarers and qualified shore staff. Europe is therefore still running the risk of loosing its know-how in the whole maritime field.

The European social partners in the shipping sector – ECSA and FST – are jointly involved in a study to find ways and means to attract young people to maritime education, and to set up systems for the training and retraining of seafarers.

We do hope that our efforts will give concrete results which together with the introduction of attractive investment and operating regimes for the shipping sector Europe will succeed in maintaining a highly qualified shipping industry which it clearly needs as a main trading entity in the world.

NOTES

1. Commissioner Karel Van Miert – Bonn 5.7.98.
2. COM (96) 81, final Communication from the Commission to the Council, the European Parliament, the Economic and Social Committee and the Committee of Regions of 13 March 1996. (Kinnock Strategy Paper).
3. Information source: ECSA (various annual reports).
4. OJ 1986 L 378/1, Council regulations 4055, 4056, 4057, 4058.
5. COM (89) 266 – A future for the Community Shipping Industry: Measures to improve the operating conditions of community shipping.
6. ECSA –The European Community Shipowners' Association – formed in 1965 under the name of the Comité des Associations d'Armateurs des Communautés Européenes (CAACE) and taking its present name in 1990, comprises the national shipowner associations of the Community and Norway. ECSA works through a permanent Secretariat in Brussels and a Board of Directors, as well as a number of specialised Committees. Its aim is to promote the interest of European shipping so that the industry can best serve European and international trade and commerce in a competitive, free enterprise environment to the benefit of shippers and consumers.
7. Prof. C. Peeters and Prof. N. Wijnholst, De *toekomst van de Nederlandse Zeevaar sector,* 1994.
8. OJ 1997 C 205/05, Community guidelines on state aid to maritime transport.
9. ECSA Annual Report 1997-1998.

CHAPTER 8

STATE AID IN THE ENERGY SECTOR IN THE EC: THE APPLICATION OF THE MARKET ECONOMY INVESTOR PRINCIPLE

Piet Jan Slot

1. Introduction

The EC Treaty has several provisions which could be applied to the regulation of prices. The general rules of the EC Treaty in particular Arts. 30 and 36, as well as Arts. 85 and 86 may of course be relevant. Nevertheless, as this article will demonstrate, it is the application of the EC rules on state aid which is the main mechanism for supervising prices in the energy sector and therefore this article will be limited to an analysis of the application of these rules.

At first sight it may be somewhat surprising that the application of the EC rules on state aid has given rise to the supervision of prices. One might have thought that the rules on competition would lend themselves more readily to such supervision. However, as is well known among competition lawyers, the rules of Art. 85 EC and even more so of Art. 86 EC have hardly been developed and applied in the control of price levels. While it is, of course, true to say that Art. 85 EC prohibits price-fixing it does not allow the competition authorities to affect the level of prices of individual undertakings (in this case utilities) although Art. 86 EC does allow some control of prices in situations where the utilities occupy dominant positions. Nevertheless, ever since the judgement of the Court of Justice of the European Union (ECJ) in the *United Brands* case, it has been clear that attempts to challenge prices, which are unreasonably high and therefore constitute an abuse, is a task beyond the capabilities of the competition authorities.[1]

The judgement of the ECJ in the *SACEM* case raised hopes that Art. 86 EC could be applied to control prices. In this judgement the Court ruled that when a company with a dominant position charges considerably higher prices for its services than similar enterprises in other Member States this may be taken as refutable proof of an abuse under Art. 86 EC.[2] Expectations have not

S. Bilal and P. Nicolaides (eds.), Understanding State Aid Policy in the European Community, 143–157.
© 1999 *Kluwer Law International. Printed in the Netherlands.*

materialised. Apparently even the *SACEM* case petered out in the course of proceedings before French courts. The EC Commission has also been very reticent about challenging prices on the grounds that they are excessive in relation to the economic value of the product supplied.[3] Price discrimination is easier to challenge under Art. 86, as the judgement of the ECJ in the *United Brands* case demonstrated,[4] although actions on this basis are nevertheless rare.[5]

The next section will be devoted to the specific questions related to the supervision of energy prices. In the final section we will offer some conclusions.

2. Energy prices and the EC state aid rules

2.1. INTRODUCTION

In order to explain why the EC state aid rules are important for the energy sector we must look at the relevant rules for the application of the provisions on state aid in the EC Treaty as they are found in three judgements of the ECJ: joint cases 67, 68 and 70/84, *Kwekerij Gebroeders van der Kooy*[6], case 169/84, *COFAZ II*[7] and case C-56/93, *Belgium v. Commission*.[8] It will in fact be sufficient to discuss here the judgements in cases *Gebroeders van der Kooy* and *Belgium v. Commission* because the last judgement also summarises the facts and the judgement in the *COFAZ II* case. Since the issues in these cases are rather complicated, an extensive summary of the background and the facts of these cases will be given.

2.2. *KWEKERIJ GEBROEDERS VAN DER KOOY*

2.2.1. Background and facts. The facts of this case were rather complicated.[9] In the northern countries of the Community, significant quantities of vegetables and flowers are grown in heated glasshouses. This form of cultivation is particularly widespread in the Netherlands where a substantial proportion of the production is exported.

In the 1970s Dutch horticultural producers heated their glasshouses with heavy fuel oil. However, because of the resultant air pollution the Dutch Government encouraged conversion to natural gas, which now accounts for 95% of the energy consumption of Dutch horticultural producers.

The transport, importation and exportation of natural gas in the Netherlands are carried out by N.V. Nederlandse Gasunie, Groningen, a company governed by private law, and of which 40% of the shares are owned by the Staatsmijnen (the Dutch State mines which in turn are wholly owned by the Dutch State), 10% by the Dutch State and the remainder by two private oil companies.

Gasunie is administered by a board consisting of eight members, one of whom is appointed by the Minister for Economic Affairs, three by the Staatsmijnen and two by each of the private oil companies. Gas prices are set by the Board of Directors, acting according to a 75% majority. Since 1963, prices and delivery conditions for the supply of gas to public distributors and to other parties have been subject to the approval of the Minister of Economic Affairs.

Gasunie enters into individual standard contracts with gas purchasers whose consumption exceeds 170,000 cubic metres per year, whether they are direct users or distributors. In 1981 Gasunie entered into a contract with Vegin and the *Landbouwschap* (agricultural board) for the sale of gas to horticultural producers (represented by the *Landbouwschap*).

According to the Commission, the contract tariff amounted to a preferential tariff and provided for conditions which were particularly advantageous for horticultural producers. The Commission took the view that the advantage should be regarded as an aid incompatible with Art. 92 of the EC Treaty, and on 15 December 1981 it therefore adopted Decision 82/73,[10] in which it required the Dutch Government to take the necessary measures to discontinue the aid in question.

Actions for the annulment of that Decision were brought before the Court by the Dutch Government, the *Landbouwschap* and by certain horticultural producers. In the meantime, negotiations took place between the Commission and the Dutch Government and a new agreement was concluded on the following conditions:

– The market gardening tariff was aligned with the industrial tariff, taking into account the caloric parity between gas and heavy fuel oil;

– The price determined by the average of CBS prices was to be increased for horticultural producers by a *premium* of 0.5 cents (NL) per cubic metre.

As a result of that agreement, the Commission, by Decision 82/518 of 22 July 1982,[11] repealed its earlier decision. The proceedings brought before the Court against the decision were also withdrawn.

On 28 September 1984 a further contract was entered into between Gasunie and the *Landbouwschap* for the period from 1 October 1984 to 1 October 1985.

The Dutch Government informed the Commission of the new contract between Gasunie, Vegin and the *Landbouwschap*. The Commission considered that the contract entailed aid incompatible with Art. 92 (1) of the EC Treaty, and it opened the procedure of Art. 93 (2) of the Treaty. However, the Dutch Government denied that the new gas tariff for horticultural producers constituted state aid. It argued *inter alia* that:

"...there is an increasing danger that a large number of horticultural producers will convert to coal, because of the increase in the price of gas and the simultaneous fall in the price of coal; for some horticultural producers conversion would be attractive if the price of coal rose beyond about 37 to 38 cents/cubic metre; in order to avoid losing customers Gasunie is obliged to lower the price of gas."

Several Member States and a number of other persons submitted observations to the Commission in which they stated that the preferential tariff for the gas at issue constituted state aid incompatible with the common market. Only the *Landbouwschap* took the contrary view.

On 13 February 1985 the Commission adopted Decision 85/215.[12] According to the Commission the tariff fell within the prohibition of Art. 92 (1) EC. The Commission took the view that the tariff had been imposed by the Dutch State. It concluded that even if the Dutch State held only a 50% share of Gasunie, it may nevertheless have influenced its pricing decisions by means of the ministerial approval to which Gasunie's tariffs are subject.

The Commission accepted that a company such as Gasunie may decide to vary its tariffs depending on the use of the goods which it sells, but considered that such variations "must have sound and comprehensible economic reasons, *e.g.* to ensure the competitiveness of gas on the various user markets, and must not discriminate between horticulture and other consumers in a comparable situation".

The Commission accepted that the price of gas may be fixed on the basis of the price of a fuel other than heavy fuel oil, in particular coal. However, it doubted whether a tariff with a application limited to one year would have a significant impact on the decisions of growers concerning whether or not to convert to coal.

It observed that the arguments based on the need to avoid competition from coal and on the need to provide against existing instability in the price of fuel oil were valid not only with regard to horticultural producers but also with regard to other sectors using gas, such as industry. In that sector too there is a risk of conversion to coal and it too needs stable energy prices. According to the Commission, the Dutch Government had not shown why horticultural producers need a more advantageous gas tariff than the industrial sector.

The Commission argued that the equilibrium price, the price at which horticultural producers have no incentive to convert to coal, is between 43 and 44.3 cents (NL) per cubic metres. However, at a price between 46.5 and 47.5 cents per cubic metres Commission estimated that 30% of the natural gas used in horticulture would be replaced by coal in less than three years. According to the Commission the gas tariff applied to horticultural producers was too low and was discriminatory.

Moreover, by imposing such a tariff the Dutch State was giving up revenue which it could have received from its interest in Gasunie, and the resulting advantage for horticultural producers thus came from state resources.

The Commission further concluded that "Dutch horticultural production ...enjoys an advantage which necessarily affects intra-Community trade, especially as the major part of Dutch produce is exported to other Member States".

It therefore considered that the aid does not fulfil the conditions set out in Art. 92(3) of the EC Treaty.

2.2.2. The judgement of the Court. Was the tariff the result of action taken by the Government of the Netherlands? The first issue involved in these cases was the question of whether the fixing of the contested tariff was the result of action by the State of the Netherlands. On this point the Court found, in paras. 35-38 of its judgement in *Kwekerij Gebroeders van der Kooy,* that the documents before the Court provided considerable evidence to support the view that the fixing of the disputed tariff was the result of action by the Dutch State.

First of all, the shares in Gasunie are distributed so that the Netherlands State directly or indirectly holds 50% of the shares and appoints half the members of the supervisory board – a body whose powers include that of determining the tariffs to be applied. Secondly, the Minister of Economic Affairs is empowered to approve the tariffs applied by Gasunie, with the result that, regardless of how that power may be exercised, the Dutch Government can block any tariff which does not suit it. Lastly, Gasunie and the *Landbouwschap* have on two occasions given effect to the Commission's representations to the Dutch Government seeking an amendment of the horticultural tariff, first following Commission Decision 82/73, which was later repealed, and then again following Decision 85/215, which *was* challenged in these proceedings.

Considered as a whole, these factors demonstrate that Gasunie in no way enjoys full autonomy in the fixing of gas tariffs but acts under the control and on the instructions of the public authorities. It is thus clear that Gasunie could not fix the tariff without taking account of the requirements of the public authorities.

It may therefore be concluded that the fixing of the contested tariff is the result of action by the Dutch State and thus falls within the meaning of the phrase "aid granted by a Member State" under Art. 92 of the Treaty.

Pricing policies: The ECJ noted first of all that the Commission had not challenged the risk of conversion to coal, the price of which had recently fallen considerably. It then went on to assess the Commission's contention that the contract price level was below the level needed in order to guard against the risk of conversion. The ECJ found that there was no need for Gasunie to align its general horticultural tariff with the equilibrium price for the least efficient type of undertaking. At least in the medium term, the position of these enterprises would inevitably become marginal, so that it would not be commercially justifiable of Gasunie to fix its horticultural tariff by reference to such undertakings. The Court therefore concluded that the Commission had correctly found that the contested tariff was lower than necessary in order to take account of the risk of conversion to coal.

2.3. CASE C-56/93 *BELGIUM V COMMISSION*

2.3.1. Background and facts[13]. This is an action for the annulment of a Commission decision of 29 December 1992 terminating the procedure regarding a preferential tariff system applied in the Netherlands to supplies of natural gas to Dutch nitrate fertiliser producers.

The relationship between the Dutch gas supplier, Gasunie, and the Dutch nitrate fertiliser manufacturing industry has occupied the attention of those whose interests are affected, Member States, the Commission, and the Court, on state aid grounds for over ten years. Natural gas is the chief raw material and represents 90% of the costs of production of ammonia. Ammonia is, in turn, the chief constituent in the manufacture of nitrate fertilisers. As a result, gas, in effect, represents 70% of the cost of production of such fertiliser. Up to the 1980s, Community nitrate fertiliser manufacturers largely produced their own ammonia.

As Gasunie has a *de facto* monopoly of the supply of gas in the Netherlands and of the export of Dutch gas, the Court, in *Van der Kooy & Others v Commission,* concluded that the fixing of a Gasunie tariff (in this case, a preferential horticultural tariff for natural gas supplies) was the result of action by the Dutch State and was to be considered aid under Art. 92 of the Treaty.

The Commission first initiated proceedings under Art. 93(2) of the Treaty against the Netherlands in October 1983. According to the Commission, Gasunie, under an aid scheme which then applied, granted special rebates to Dutch ammonia producers by means of a two-tier tariff structure, which had the effect of reducing the cost of natural gas used by them as a raw material. The ammonia industry was charged the standard industrial price for gas used in respect of production for sale in the European Community and a substantially lower price for gas used in the production of ammonia exported to third countries. In the course of the proceedings, the Commission delivered 84 a reasoned opinion on 13 March 19 in which it found that this tariff structure constituted state aid within the meaning of Art. 92(1) of the Treaty and did not qualify for any of the derogations provided for in Art. 92(3).

The Dutch Government informed the Commission that Gasunie had abolished the contested tariff and had added to its industrial tariff structure a new tariff known as tariff F, with retroactive effect from 1 November 1983. Tariff F was made available to very large industrial users established in the Netherlands, other than those in the energy industry (and essentially, as we shall see, to the ammonia sector), on condition that they:

(a) consumed at least 600 million cubic metres of gas per year;

(b) operated a load factor of at least 90% (i.e. operated for at least 90% of the time, assuring regularity of consumption);

(c) agreed to total or partial interruption of supplies, at the discretion of Gasunie (with 12 hours notice, where possible); and

(d) accepted supplies of gas of varying calorific values.

The new tariff F was invoiced at the price applicable under tariff E, which applied to users with an annual gas consumption of between 50 and 600 million cubic metres (per year), less 5 cents (NL) per cubic metre. It later transpired that the minimum annual consumption required for tariff F use was 500 million per cubic metre, and that the 5 cents rebate was a maximum, but the actual rebate fell to as low as 2 cents per cubic metre on occasion.

The Commission continued its investigation, in the light of the new tariff, which, it concluded, secured economies in the cost of supply for Gasunie which were greater than the value of the 5 cents rebate, principally because of the combined effects of large volume and regularity of demand. It also concluded that tariff F formed part of the general tariff structure for gas users in the Netherlands, which did not discriminate between sectors, and contained no element of state aid. It therefore decided on 17 April 1984 to terminate its proceedings against the Netherlands under Art. 93(2) of the Treaty.

This decision was challenged in annulment proceedings taken by a number of French competitors of the Dutch nitrate fertiliser manufacturing industry, in *CdF Chimie Azf v Commission*. The Court commissioned a report from three expert consultants on the gas industry (hereinafter "the experts' report") upon which it based the findings of fact in its judgement. The experts' report analysed the savings for Gasunie attributed by the Commission both to the individual elements of economies of supply and also to the total effect of such elements. In each case they found that the Commission had committed a manifest error of appraisal:

– It had overstated by a factor of five the savings attributable to the volume of gas consumed and the load factor.

– It had attributed savings both to the possibility of interrupting supplies of gas at short notice and to the possibility of varying the calorific value of the gas supplied, when neither of these elements conferred any economic advantage on Gasunie.

–   Finally, it was difficult to identify total savings in excess of 0.5 cents per cubic metre in respect of elements valued by the Commission at over 5 cents per cubic metre.

The experts reported that the tariff F rebate must be attributable to other considerations. The Court decided that the Commission had committed a manifest error of appraisal and annulled the Commission's decision in its judgement of 12 July 1990.[14]

Although the economies of supply which were originally advanced in justification of tariff F no longer figure in the arguments, and the Commission, in the decision discussed here, has replaced them by quite different grounds, the fact remains that the Court had already considered tariff F in *CdF Chimie*. It is useful to recall two particular aspects of the judgement of the Court. On the one hand, the Court rejected the contention by the French applicants that tariff F was a special and secret arrangement, negotiated only with the Dutch nitrate fertiliser manufacturers on a confidential basis. It held that it was "a public tariff whose conditions of availability are public and perfectly open", and that it was "available to all customers who fulfil the objective conditions prescribed for its application". On the other hand, the Court upheld the argument that tariff F was essentially intended to apply to the ammonia manufacturing industry and that its provision to a single undertaking outside that industry did not undermine its essentially sectoral nature.

The Commission reopened the procedure under Art. 93(2) of the Treaty in January 1992, publishing a notice which pointed out both the apparently neutral objective conditions for tariff F and the fact that the Dutch ammonia producers had been its chief beneficiaries. It also pointed out in this notice that the rebate was variable, with 5 cents per metre representing merely its maximum value.

The Commission adopted a decision (hereinafter called "the decision") on 29 December 1992[15] once more to terminate the procedure. The Commission drew upon the experts' report, which suggested that, while the alleged savings had not materialised, there might be other commercial justifications for tariff F, viz. ensuring that valued customers for natural gas were not charged unaffordable prices which would drive them either out of business or to sourcing their ammonia elsewhere. The Commission stated:

> "[W]ith regard to Gasunie's tariff F, the aim was to resist competition on the nitrate fertiliser market from ammonia produced in other countries, notably non-Community countries. A nitrate fertiliser manufacturer ... can himself produce the ammonia needed to produce nitrate fertilisers or he can buy it from other producers and use it to manufacture his product ... . If the price of the gas which he uses in order to manufacture the ammonia he requires is too high, he will decide to purchase the ammonia,

if possible, elsewhere at a lower cost than he would have to pay if he produced it himself .... This was the situation in the Community ammonia industry in the 1980s, and if Gasunie had not granted the Dutch nitrate fertiliser producers special tariffs, they could perfectly well in the long run have shut down the ammonia producing factories, obtained their ammonia supplies from outside the Community and continued nevertheless to produce nitrate fertilisers."

The main element of the decision was that Gasunie needed to protect very large and vulnerable gas customers:
– which took 30% of its industrial gas at a time when it had lost other markets;
– which could switch to very cheap imported ammonia with ease (there was some evidence that this had occurred);
– which were in turn suffering loss of market share in the Community market for nitrate fertilisers to Eastern European exporters;
– with a price which responded to lower tariffs or differentiated pricing in other Member States;
– with a price at which costs were covered, so that profits could still be made, and greater revenue secured (thus ensuring a more rapid return on investment);[16]
– and at a price which was also made available, indirectly, to ammonia producers in other Member States which imported gas from the Netherlands.

The Commission concluded (i) that tariff F was commercially justified, (ii) that it gave no preference over other Member State producers and (iii) that the absence of any loss of revenue showed that the Dutch State had not acted differently from any ordinary shareholder. Conclusions (i) and (iii) are effectively the same point, stated differently. The question of whether the Commission's conclusions (i) and (ii) (which I regard as the principal bases of the decision) are interdependent is of some significance, and is discussed further below.

Gasunie abandoned tariff F in 1991 in favour of a distinct pricing system for gas when used as a raw material rather than as an energy source. The new system was approved by the Commission on the condition that its terms, and any subsequent modifications thereto, be extended to export markets. The Commission later approved a decrease in this price (in the Dutch as well as the export market) on grounds identical to those expressed in conclusion (i) of the impugned decision in the instant case, viz. the need in a period of heightened competition from non-Community ammonia producers to respond to the potential loss of a very significant market.

2.3.2. The judgement of the Court.

Introduction: Before we start our summary of the most important parts of the Court's judgement, it may be useful to point out that there are two issues involved here, relating to the interpretation of Art. 92(1), i.e. the question of what constitutes aid.[17] The first is whether the tariff constitutes a normal commercial response by Gasunie to the specific difficulties of the Dutch ammonia industry. This question concerns the specific application of the "market economy investor principle" discussed above. The second is the question as to whether the tariff gave the Dutch ammonia producers an advantage over their competitors in the other Member States. This in effect questions whether or not there is a distortion of competition as described by Art. 92(1). The second question only becomes relevant if the first question is answered positively. In other words, if Gasunie's commercial behaviour is justified its effects on competitors in other Member States are not addressed by the EC prohibition on state aid.

At the same time it is relevant to point out that the question of whether a certain tariff is commercially justified cannot, in cases involving exports to other Member States, be answered without looking at the effect on its customers elsewhere in the Community. Customers in other Member States, which are in the same position as the Dutch ammonia producers, cannot be discriminated against. Thus, while these two questions may be raised separately, they can, in situations involving exports, only be answered jointly.[18]

The problem may also be stated differently. In this case the complication arises from the fact that two different action's by Gasunie are being scrutinised: tariff F and the tariff which Gasunie sets for its exports. A further complication arises because the export tariff provides a composite price. Gasunie's export tariff is a weighted average, whereby the average is computed from prices per user sector and the relative volume used. This weighted average tariff is designed to enable distribution companies in the importing Member States to conduct their own pricing policy.

The ECJ did not follow the above distinctions when answering the arguments made by the Belgian Government, but instead followed the latter's less than clearly structured arguments.

The main elements of the judgement: The Court first addressed the Belgian argument that the Commission's finding that the tariff was justified on commercial grounds had been ill founded.

The ECJ first reiterated that a preferential tariff does not constitute aid if, in the context of the market in question, it is objectively justified by economic reasons such as the need to withstand competition in the same market. It went on to note that in the context of a complex economic appraisal, its function must be confined to verifying whether the Commission complied with the relevant rules governing procedure and the statement of reasons, whether the facts on which the contested finding had been based had been accurately stated and whether there had been any manifest error of assessment or a misuse of powers.

There was, according to the ECJ, nothing to support a conclusion that, in supplying natural gas to the Dutch nitrate fertiliser producers in accordance with tariff F, Gasunie behaved differently from any other private undertaking in normal market conditions. Belgium's contestation of the Commission's findings that both Gasunie's variable and fixed costs were well below tariff F, so that the company could increase its net revenue through sales at tariff F rates and yet make sure that it retained important customers, was dismissed by the ECJ. It noted that the fact that the average purchase price was higher than tariff F does not undermine the Commission's argument. This price is calculated from the various final sales prices in the different markets, less its costs and profits.[19] Consequently, the Commission's statement concerning Gasunie's variable and fixed costs could not be shown to be false merely on the basis of information regarding the average purchase price.

The ECJ went on to reject the challenge that the Commission had failed to assess exports as an alternative to the sales for the fertiliser industry in the Netherlands. Belgium contended that exports would have been a more attractive commercial alternative. The Commission maintained that, but for tariff F, Gasunie would immediately have lost an important outlet, which could not have been replaced by export outlets. The ECJ noted that Belgium had failed to establish that the Commission had committed a manifest error.

A related argument by Belgium was that it would have been more attractive for Gasunie and the Netherlands to limit its natural gas production so as to prolong the life of its natural gas fields. The ECJ also rejected this argument. It referred to the opinion of the Advocate General who, in para. 71, pointed out that this would have resulted in a decrease in revenue and, therefore, in a less rapid return on the money invested. The ECJ also rejected a final argument by Belgium, i.e. that tariff F was not necessary in order to withstand the competition from ammonia, a substitute for the use of natural gas as a feedstock.

The ECJ then went on to consider the arguments related to the Commission's conclusion that tariff F did not favour Dutch ammonia producers in relation to their counterparts in other Member States.

The ECJ started to note that it is common ground that the method used to calculate the frontier price agreed between Gasunie and Distrigaz was the "netback" system which is based on the market value of natural gas according to the various uses to which it is put in the importing country. Belgium contested the Commission's conclusion that this system also accommodated the volumes intended for the Belgium fertiliser industry. The Court endorsed the Commission's reasoning. The ECJ also rejected Belgium's argument that the negotiations between Gasunie and Distrigaz did not allow the latter to match Dutch tariffs for the nitrate fertiliser producers.

In a separate argument related to the interpretation of Art. 92 EC Treaty, Belgium maintained that the Commission should have indicated that Gasunie had not foregone any profit in granting tariff F. The implication of Belgium's argument is that any behaviour leading to foregone profits must be considered to be state aid. The ECJ did not share this view. It observed that the Commission has given precise reasons for supporting the finding that Gasunie acted according to market conditions. Furthermore, the ECJ stated that in such a case the fact that a practice also furthers a political aim does not mean that it constitutes state aid.

3. Conclusion

The above discussed case law of the Court of Justice on state aid in the energy sector provides ample guidelines for the conduct of commercial operations of government controlled public utilities. It is by no means a coincidence that it was developed in the context of the commercial operations of Gasunie. Gasunie has, starting in the 1960s, developed a truly Community-wide gas market,[20] indeed it has been a true market leader. At the same time allegations of favourable tariffs constituting state aid have also been levelled in other energy sectors, notable the electricity sector. The Commission has in several instances looked into alleged cases of state aid.[21]

The extensive discussion of the facts and the context of the above cases show that it will be difficult to lay down precise criteria for the pricing of energy sources. However, some tentative conclusions about the determination of energy prices may be offered here.

Prices lower than the regular, listed energy tariffs of enterprises controlled by governments are justified in one or more of the following circumstances:

(1) if such lower tariffs are the result of real cost savings such as volume discounts;

(2) to the extent that they form part of a general tariff which is applicable to the entire industry;

(3) to the extent that there is an objective justification. This is sometimes referred to as the market economy investor principle;

(4) if such lower tariffs serve an objective that is recognised in Community law and to the extent that they are necessary and proportionate.

It is also useful to note that a deliberate foregoing of profits does not automatically result in state aid. The market economy investor principle serves as a shield against rash judgements in this respect.[22] It should also be noted that the initial fears that the application of the rules on state aid would result in a very narrow straightjacket for government controlled utilities seem no longer justified. It is interesting to see that the ECJ in its judgement *Belgium v. Commission* has endorsed the view that commercial behaviour may be guided by a desire to make an appropriate return on money invested.

Together with the application of the market economy investor principle, the principle of non-discrimination is the main standard of reference. Customers in similar markets and conditions must be given similar tariffs.[23]

Even if the above conclusions are rather comforting for those involved in commercial actions in state controlled public utilities there is, nevertheless, concern at the procedural level. As has been explained above, all fresh state aid has to be notified to the EC Commission. Non-notification results in the illegality of such measures.[24] After reviewing commercial action in relation to energy prices, it is clear that it may in practice be difficult to assess whether or not such action amounts to state aid. The easiest way to resolve such questions would be to notify. In practice this may not always be an attractive option as governments may be less than willing to subject themselves to the judgement of the Commission. This may leave the utility in the unenviable position of being caught between a reluctant uncooperative government and the possibilities of challenges against tariffs not being cleared by the Commission under the market economy investor principle, or otherwise under the rules on state aid. On the other hand this position is hardly different from the situation under the competition rules and companies have learnt to cope with that. Contrary to the situation under Art. 85 and 86, however, is the relatively recent awareness that energy tariffs may be subject to supervision by the Commission.

The Court's ruling in the *Van der Kooy judgement* that the actions by Gasunie could be imputed to the Dutch Government has had important implications for the restructuring of public utilities. Half-hearted privatisation in which government control over the utility and the supervision of tariffs is retained means that EC rules on state aid are applicable. On the other hand fully-fledged privatisation necessarily entails releasing government control. Privatisation thus implies that the tariff policy of the utilities is no longer be subject to supervision by the Commission.

NOTES

1. Case 27/76, *United Brands v. Commission*, [1978] ECR 207.
2. Joint Cases 110, 241 & 242/88, *Lucazeau v. SACEM*, [1989] ECR 2811.
3. I do not discuss predatory pricing here as it is not a matter of great concern in the energy sector, but see: Bellamy & Child, *Common Market Law of Competition*, 4th edition, Sweet & Maxwell, London 1993, p. 620.
4. See note 2, the Commission's charge that United Brands practised discriminatory prices was upheld by the ECJ.
5. See Jones, Van der Woude and Lewis, *E.C. Competition Law Handbook*, 1996 edition, Sweet & Maxwell, London 1996, p. 264 citing seven Commission decisions and two ECJ judgements dealing with this issue.
6. [1988] ECR 219.
7. [1990] ECR I-3083. In the first judgement in this case [1986] ECR 391, the ECJ ruled that the French Cofaz company had standing to bring an appeal against the Commission decision approving the Dutch gas tariffs.
8. [1996] ECR I-767. Judgement of 29 February 1996.
9. The full description can be found in the report of the hearing: this section is a summary based on it.
10. OJ 1982 L37/29.
11. OJ 1982 L1229/38.
12. OJ 1985 L97/49.
13. This summary of the background of the case is taken from the opinion of the Advocate General Fennelly, paras. 1-11. The footnotes have been omitted.
14. Case 169/84, *COFAZ II*, [1990] ECR I-3083.
15. OJ 1992 C 344, p.4.
16. What the Commission does not mention here is that this gas would have produced more revenue if it had been sold to other sectors. This point is raised by the Advocate General in para. 59 of his opinion.
17. Cf. para. 15 of the conclusion of the Advocate General.
18. This is a point that in my opinion is overlooked by the Advocate General who proposes a separate assessment of the two questions. The ECJ does not follow its Advocate General in this approach.
19. This system of calculation of gas prices is called the netback system.
20. This process has been described by R.D. Visser; "The European Natural Gas Market", in: P.J. Slot and M.H. van der Woude (eds): *Exploiting the Internal Market; Cooperation and Competition toward 1992*, Deventer 1988, pp. 117-140.
21. Cf. the Report of the Hearing in case C 313/90, *CIRFS v. Commission*, [ECR] 1993 I-1125. In this report, the Commission observes that it has made an enquiry into alleged state aid in the form of lower electricity tariffs given by EDF in France. See also the Report on Competition Policy 1994, p513 on the decision on the Danish electricity company SEAS.
22. Cf. G. Abramonte: *The Market Economy Investor Principle*, ECLR, 1996.
23. It is an interesting question whether Art. 86 EC Treaty requires similar treatment.

It will be recalled that this provision prohibits, *inter alia*, applying dissimilar conditions to equivalent transactions with other trading parties, thereby placing them at a competitive disadvantage. The question is whether the application of the market economy investor principle can lead to dissimilar conditions.

24. N.B. that illegality can be cured afterwards by the Commission's approval of the aid as has been discussed above in para. 2.3 b.

CHAPTER 9

REGIONAL DEVELOPMENT GUIDELINES:
DO THEY REALLY HELP REGIONAL DEVELOPMENT?

Carlos Lambarri and Eduardo Fernández Ezkurdia

1. Introduction

The main issue when dealing with regional aid systems is the need to achieve consistency between two opposing goals of EC policy: on the one hand the efficiency of the economy at the EU level, and on the other hand the need to promote regional development in targeted areas. The absence of aid penalises poor or peripheral regions, as it is the main tool that can be used to reduce their lack of competitiveness. Hence, it can even be argued that doing nothing distorts competition, as in such circumstances poor regions are not allowed to use aid to improve their competitiveness. This chapter examines what can be done to reconcile undistorted competition with the goal of regional development.

Art. 130(a) of the Treaty of Rome provides that "the Community shall aim at reducing disparities between the levels of development of the various regions and the backwardness of the least favoured regions, including rural areas".

On the one hand, Structural and Cohesion Funds make use of European resources to apply those EC policies which aim at promoting the development of regions in need. On the other hand, the Commission provides guidelines for Member States concerning the granting of internal regional aid out of their own financial resources. In fact, an underdeveloped region has the opportunity to enjoy the benefits of both Structural Funds to finance investment and complementary regional aid. Therefore, it is crucial that there is consistency between both kinds of aid to prevent Member States from granting aid contrary to the goals of Structural Fund policy.

This Chapter aims to identify the main issues that we believe should be taken into consideration when analysing the effects of aid on the economic

S. Bilal and P. Nicolaides (eds.), Understanding State Aid Policy in the European Community, 159–171.
© 1999 *Kluwer Law International. Printed in the Netherlands.*

development of the underdeveloped regions of Europe. Our point of departure is considering whether the regulation of regional aid leads to constraints on the economic growth of underdeveloped regions.

Regional aid systems can be considered as just one more of the economic policies of different countries. They can be as important as factors of production such as professional skills. However, we are also concerned about the need to control the application of such systems, and will now try to outline the key points in order to define a new framework for competition that can help regional development.

Firstly, the Community's control of state aid in itself distorts competition at EU level, as it does not give equal treatment to the different competitive tools used by the Member States. Furthermore, the actual applicability of the Community's control of state aid contains weaknesses, as the area covered by this control is not clear enough. For example, does it cover general fiscal policies?

The guidelines for the application of state aid rules are another controversial issue. Regarding this point, we will defend the need to distinguish between defensive aid (aimed at preserving existing industry, and which must be free to compensate other regional disadvantages), and aggressive aid (in order to attract new investment, and which must be controlled).

Finally, technical issues connected to the practical application of the rules should be modified to improve the relationship between EC policy on state aid and the objective of reducing disparities within the EU. Issues such as the classification of the regions, the problems of comparing different regions, the political definition of the criteria, etc. are worth discussing further.

In examining these issues this Chapter is structured as follows. A brief description of the EC rules is presented in Section 2, which also discusses the basic principles of the regulation of state aid: its scope, the mechanism for the distribution of the approved aid, and the different purposes or objects for which aid is granted and its levels. Section 3 outlines the recent evolution of the regulation and its expected future changes. Section 4 includes a critical analysis of the regulation, and the key points discussed are put together under four headings: Competition versus regional development; Applicability of the regulation of state aid; Guidelines for the application of the regulation; and The practical application of the rules. We will conclude with some suggestions and proposals, derived from the analysis, which will be put forward in Section 5.

2. The prevailing rules

2.1 INCOMPATIBILITY AND EXEMPTIONS

The legal basis of the EC competition policy and, therefore, of regional state aid is the general rule of the incompatibility of state aid, as it affects trade between Member States, with the common market under Art. 92(1) of the EC Treaty. However, some exemptions are defined: Art. 92(2) provides for types of aid that "shall be compatible with the common market" and Art. 92(3) types of aid that "may be considered to be compatible with the common market".

Given the above, regional aid is designed to develop the less-favoured regions by supporting investment and job creation in a sustainable context. Member States consider that regional aid can play the role that is assigned to it effectively, and hence the consequent distortions of competition are justified, provided that it adheres to certain principles and obeys certain rules, particularly regarding the *exceptional nature* of the instrument.

2.2 THE SCOPE OF THE RULES

In trying to define the scope of application of the exemptions considered under Arts. 92(2) and 92(3), and the consequent guidelines, we first find that sectors with specific guidelines (such as some agricultural products, fisheries, the coal industry, transport, steel, shipbuilding, synthetic fibres and motor vehicles) are excluded from the application of the general guidelines on regional aid. Furthermore, specific rules apply to investment covered by the multisectoral framework for regional aid to large projects, and ad hoc aid for firms in difficulty is governed by specific rules and not classified as regional aid.

According to Art. 92(2), the following are compatible with the common market: social aid accorded to individual consumers, unless it is discriminatory because of the origin of the products; aid for the repair of damage caused by natural disasters; and aid targeted at certain German regions as a consequence of the former division.

However, the most interesting point about regional aid is the possible exemptions provided in Art. 92(3). And we say "possible" because the Treaty says that these cases "may be considered to be compatible with the common market", which introduces a strong component of discretion in the Commission's decisions.

Under Art. 92(3), the following kinds of aid may be considered compatible with the common market:

a) "Aid to promote the economic development of areas where the standard of living is abnormally low or where there is serious underemployment".

To qualify for this exemption, the region, delineated a NUTS level II geographical unit, must have a per capita Gross Domestic Product/ Purchasing Power Standard (GDP/PPS) of less than 75% of the Community average, which is the same criterion used for the qualification for Objective 1 status in Structural Funds.

b) "Aid to promote the execution of an important project of common European interest or to remedy a serious disturbance in the economy of a Member State".

c) "Aid to facilitate the development of certain economic activities or of certain economic areas, where such aid does not adversely affect trading conditions to an extent contrary to the common interest".

This provision enables a Member State to grant aid intended to further the economic development of areas of that State which are disadvantaged in relation to the national average.

Sections (a) and (c) of Art. 92(3) are the main references when discussing regional aid, as section (b) applies in only occasional cases.

2.3 DISTRIBUTION OF THE APPROVED AID

For the distribution of the approved aid, the Commission sets a global limit for the coverage of regional aid in terms of population to which both derogations of Art. 92(3)(a) and (c) are applicable so that the recipient regions have less than 50% of the total national population.

Aid is automatically allowed for regions which qualify as a result of the derogation in Art. 92(3)(a) on the basis of the criterion of per capita GDP/ PPS. The rest of the total approved regional aid is distributed amongst the different regions put forward by the Member States as candidates for the derogation of Art. 92(3)(c).

The final distribution for the 92(3)(c) regions depends on the results derived from a comparison between indices for the GDP/PPS per capita and the unemployment rates of the regions and "reference indices" of the same factors for each Member State. Hence, the bigger the difference between the indices calculated for a given region and the ones calculated for its Member State is, the larger the amount of aid received by this region will be (remembering that the derogation of Art. 92(3)(c) is based on a comparison of conditions within the Member State, not with the whole EU). This means that the relative position of a 92(3)(c) region, in terms of GDP/PPS per capita and unemployment, within its country, defines the amount of aid that can be provided from the money available (once the 92(3)(a) regions are satisfied).

2.4 OBJECT AND LEVEL OF AID

Regional aid can be given for three different purposes:
   – *Productive investment:* in this case, aid for initial investment is calculated as a percentage of the investment's value, always defined in terms of Net Grant Equivalent (NGE)[1]. Table 1 shows the different ceilings of intensity allowed.
   – *Job creation:* permitted aid concerns jobs linked to the carrying out of an initial investment project. The amount of aid must not exceed a certain percentage of the wage cost of the person hired, calculated over a period of two years. The percentage is equal to the intensity allowed for investment aid in that area.
   – *Operational aid:* regional aid aimed at reducing a firm's current expenses is normally prohibited. However, it might be granted in regions eligible under the derogation in Art. 92(3)(a), as well as in the outermost regions of low population density qualifying for the exemption under Art. 92(3)(a) and (c), where aid intended to offset additional transportation costs may be authorised.

3. Recent developments and future evolution

There is expected to be a reduction in the coverage of allowed state aid for the 2000-2006 period, because of a reduction in population in areas where the derogation of Art. 92(3)(a) is applicable, and because the economic evolution of the EU will increase the unity of the internal market. This will mean that regional aid will have a more significant effect on competition.

In parallel, a trend towards the concentration of regional aid can be observed. This is to avoid the loss of effectiveness caused by its generalisation. However, when considering the prospective new Member States and their relative position within the Community it can be expected that the expansion process (Agenda 2000) will cause new difficulties, since the number of underdeveloped regions will grow very rapidly.

Another main issue will be the need to increase coherence between state aid policy and cohesion policy, avoiding the paradox of a region receiving Structural Funds but being excluded from the state aid map.

Regarding the operational rules for the Commission, more transparency

Table 1

Aid	Ceiling
Art. 92(3)(a)	
General rule	50% NGE
Outermost regions	65% NGE
NUTS II regions with per capita GDP/PPS over 60% of the average	40% NGE
NUTS II outermost regions with per capita GDP/PPS over 60% of the average	50% NGE
Art. 92(3)(c)	
General rule	20% NGE
Low population density (less than 12.5 inhabitants per km^2) or outermost regions	30% NGE
Regions with both a higher per capita GDP/PPS and a higher than the average unemployment rate	10% NGE
Low population density or outermost regions with both a higher per capita GDP/PPS and a lower unemployment rate than the average	20% NGE
Regions adjoining an Art. 92(3)(a) region	20% NGE

is needed, with all the guidelines defined in a single document and with discretion replaced by a standard and automatic criteria for the qualification of regional aid.

4. Critical analysis

4.1 COMPETITION VERSUS REGIONAL DEVELOPMENT

The existing Commission guidelines on regional aid have been defined to prevent distortion of competition. However, competitiveness is not only an economic issue, it also includes geographical, cultural, political and population issues. Hence, rules set out to prevent distortion of competition might end up introducing a distortion themselves. If a poor region can not compete by means of regional aid systems, it will never overcome its other handicaps (lack of infrastructure, remoteness from the market, unskilled workers, etc.).

Therefore, we can identify a possible contradiction between the necessity for a regional development policy and the constraints that these guidelines entail. Must a peripheral region be disadvantaged in relation to the economic centre of a country?

If a ceiling is defined, will it reflect the lack of competitiveness compared to other regions? For instance, if the Azores had a GDP/PPS per capita of 40% of the EU average, would a ceiling of aid up to 60% of the investment value be enough, if one compares its situation to the Ile de France which receives no aid but has a GDP/PPS per capita of 180%?

We can also identify a second contradiction between the possibility of conditions existing in a region which allow regional aid to be applied and the capacity to develop this kind of activity. The idea that regional aid can be a complementary instrument to EU Structural Funds does not take into consideration the fact that the poorest regions suffer from a lack of financial resources to afford these policies, while some rich regions in the Community (which are allowed to obtain regional aid because of their relatively underdeveloped position within the Member State itself) have plenty of financial resources to carry out these activities. The effect can easily be a widening rather than a narrowing of the differences.

Connected to the previous point, a coherence between the Structural Funds and regional aid policies is not guaranteed. A "poor" German region, which may not be poor in EU terms, can enjoy relatively larger amounts of regional aid than a poor region in Portugal, which is. Such a situation is contrary to the goal of the Structural Funds favouring economic convergence among regions.

Another key issue in this area is the criteria used to define which regions need regional aid. Currently it depends only on GDP per capita or unemployment rates. However, many other structural factors (lack of infrastructure, inefficient education system, lack of resources for R&D activities, few leisure activities, etc.) can be the reason why a region lacks competitiveness, which in turn makes it unattractive to new investment.

It is not too ambitious to ask for a revision of the purely economic criteria and their reasoning with new criteria that can help identify the underdeveloped regions better.

Examining in greater depth the need to improve the concentration of aid among the most needy regions, we face the derogation in Art. 92(3)(c), which is aimed at allowing the Member States some flexibility when deciding the regions that can be given national regional aid in order to reduce the significant differences within their national territories. However, this internal comparison amongst regions within a Member State does not make sense if you consider the internationalisation of markets and the globalisation of the economy (particularly in EMU). Hence, the qualification for the regional aid should be based on the relative underdevelopment of an area in comparison to the European average level.

4.2 APPLICABILITY OF THE REGULATION ON STATE AID

Although measures for regional promotion are under Community control, there is no regulation harmonising public policies, either regarding taxation or expenditure (social expenditure, infrastructure, individual or corporate taxation, even indirect taxes, financial markets, etc.) that is decisive for the decision-making process regarding new investments.

In the particular case of taxation, Arts. 92 to 94 only aim to prevent fiscal policies from being applied to particular regions or sectors. Problems can arise when considering the different levels of administrative decentralisation, and if the Community control of state aid discriminates against the political development of the subcentral levels of government. Who decides on regional policies? The central government or the regional government?

For instance, a Member State could decide, as a generally applicable tax measure, to eliminate corporate income tax, or to subsidise the establishment of industrial estates for companies. These measures would not be constrained by the Commission although they could clearly distort competition.

The Basque case is very interesting in this respect. How can the Commission control decisions on public policies made by the Basque Government in a fully autonomous area such as the Basque Country, given that such policies are generally only applicable in its territory? It is not the same as the Spanish Government deciding to apply a special regime in the Basque Country without extending it to the other Spanish regions.

In this second case, if Spain decided to grant the Basque Country a general investment incentive by levying a corporate income tax of 10% for investments over ECU 1 million, it might distort competition inside Spain, but does it distort competition in Europe if you consider that it is possible that the tax rate are much higher in Spain than in some other Member States?

Going even further, what would happen if the 17 Autonomous Communities in Spain decided to have their own personal income tax regulation, each one different from the others? How could we make a comparison in order to define what is state aid in fiscal matters? Should all of them be compared to one creating the highest tax burden? It is not clear at all.

To sum up this point, the Commission should never prejudge on the basis of who defines the policies, the national or the regional government. The generality of the fiscal measures will depend on the degree of political decentralisation within the country.

Another element is the extreme difficulty of making proper comparisons between any two regions in Europe. The Commission would have to compare the same industry in two very different regions, such as Malmö and Palermo, to have a real overview of the intensity of the regional aid granted in both areas. Furthermore, it would also have to be able to take into account the different cultural and social conditions of the regions compared.

4.3 GUIDELINES FOR THE APPLICATION OF THE REGULATION

Following the point presented above, there is a clear contradiction between the restrictions on regional aid and the freedom Member States have in defining public policies. The Member States can, to a great extent, determine their own policies regarding fiscal issues, public expenditure, social programmes, privatisation of public companies, sectoral regulation, etc. However, the Community imposed limitations on the intensity of certain types of regional aid cannot benefit from this autonomy in making policy decisions.

If a Member State sets its corporate tax rate at 20%, can the Commission ban another State from granting a tax allowance of 15% for certain investments if the tax rate in this second country is 40%? Who is offering better investment conditions?

Therefore, the problem is on the definition of what is considered regional aid and what is excluded from this definition. Table 2 provides a brief overview.

Table 2

Measures considered as state aid	Measures not considered as state aid
Direct subsidies for investment and job creation	Public policies on taxation (generally applicable)
Tax allowances	Public policies on infrastructure
Special tax regimes for certain companies	Public policies on environmental issues
Construction of infrastructure for particular companies	Sectoral regulation
Discounted interest rates	Establishment of financial markets
Reduced tax rates for certain companies	Social expenditure programmes
	Privatisation programmes
Construction of infrastructure for particular companies	

There are numerous indirect factors generated by the freedom to set (national and regional) public policies, even without the direct participation of the administration, which can subsidise investment that escapes the

Community's control of national regional aid. There are also grey areas such as public policies which aim to promote the development of new industries, by means of creating favourable economic conditions. For instance, the administration could make a deal involving private banking, agreeing to promote a local financial centre in return for private support to companies that will never be subject to Community control of state aid.

Environmental investment, job creation, R&D activities, the internationalisation of companies, etc. are all areas that can receive indirect aid, for example a general programme for the financing of recycling plants by means of an increase of 1% in personal income tax could be introduced. The Commission cannot ban this policy.

We can identify three main objectives of state aid:

– *To attract investment:* in relation to this, constraints to the freedom of the regions to grant aid mean a distortion of competition in favour of the rich.

– *To improve competitiveness:* if aid for transportation from the outermost regions is prohibited, how can they compete? They can only do so by being much more efficient than the rich centre (i.e: lower production costs).

– *Other goals:* taxation on holding companies, the price of industrial land, etc. If there is no aid related to these issues, who will then choose the peripheral regions?

Besides, aid can also be classified as:

– *Defensive or corrective:* in order to correct competitive disadvantages.

– *Offensive or proactive:* in order to attract industrial activity.

Established industries would be punished if the first type of aid were not allowed, while the second kind must be selectively granted to allow for a reduction of regional disparities. Both kinds of aid need to be distinguished, and different ceilings have to be defined for them. They also need different types of support systems.

We can now turn to a very important question. Is state aid really such a big problem? Is regional aid really significant in influencing the decision-making processes of investors? We must be aware that the decision-making process regarding new investment is a very complex activity where a lot of different criteria are involved. The following criteria, ranked in order of importance, are the determinants of business locations:

(1) The business: In the first place is the business itself, including the structure of prices and costs, the resources and labour skills needed, etc. All these issues are decisive when deciding on the kind of economic activity to start.

(2) The market: Once the business has been chosen, the size, closeness, growth trends, etc. of the targeted market are crucial to the new business, and condition its success in the chosen location.

(3) Basic infrastructure: Together with the specific conditions of the

targeted market, the basic infrastructure of the chosen region regarding transport, telecommunications, services, etc. are also key elements to determining the evolution of the business.

(4) The environment: The economic, social, entrepreneurial and educational aspects should all reinforce strengths observed in the market.

(5) Aid: a) Direct (subsidies)

b) Indirect (taxation)

The aid available to companies willing to start a new business in a new place can only be decisive if all the criteria mentioned above are satisfactorily complied with. In such cases, a firm can make its decision because of the additional support promised by the regional or national authorities. If the criteria are not complied with even the best aid system is destined to failure.

Only 5(a) could ever become a third or fourth level criterion if the intensity is high enough. And only 5(b) could reach higher if it relates to the fiscal strategy of an international corporate group (as it may give particular importance to tax allowances or special regimes of international taxation).

Spain can again offer a clear example of the relative insignificance of regional aid in influencing investment decisions. Cantabria and the Basque Country are neighbouring regions. Although Cantabria is an Objective 1 region with regard to Structural Funds and is eligible under the derogation in Art. 92(3)(a), the Basque Country has always been preferred by international investors because of other factors, such as infrastructure, closeness to the rest of Europe, communications, etc.

4.4 PRACTICAL APPLICATION OF THE RULES

The first problem is the basis of the comparison among the Member States. It is difficult to measure the amount of effective aid. Consider the following examples:

– The corporate tax rate may be higher than other countries, but the tax allowances are higher as well.

– The corporate tax rate is comparatively lower than other States, but other taxes are higher, or there are additional taxes that do not exist anywhere else, or taxation on dividends is higher, etc.

– Direct subsidies are granted, although the corporate tax rate is higher.

Hence, with very different taxation systems, there is a serious problem of comparison amongst the different European regions. Is it possible to quantify them in an absolute amount of NGE? Moreover, how can we compare fiscal systems that are completely different in relation to such items as payment terms, criteria for the application of allowances, and even indirect fiscal burdens (administrative requirements)?

Regarding more technical issues, why are eligible regions defined at

NUTS II level? Why not NUTS III? This second option would avoid the possibility of an underdeveloped NUTS III region being excluded from the aid map because it belongs to an average or rich NUTS II region.

The enlargement of the EU to the Central and Eastern European countries will significantly increase the number of regions qualified to benefit from the derogation in Art. 92(3)(a). This will make the goal of concentrating the permitted aid more difficult, unless many of the regions that currently enjoy regional aid are replaced by the new regions.

5. Suggestions and proposals

To conclude, the new regulation for the granting of regional aid should facilitate the granting of aid to under-developed regions. For this reason I would suggest the following reform of the guidelines on regional state aid.

(1) Corrective aid systems must be defined, including tax measures (excluding allowances for the establishment of new companies), for the promotion of the international competitiveness of the recipient regions.

For this kind of aid, no limits on aid amounts are advisable as such limits discriminate against existing industries. Furthermore, the establishment of a special European programme should be considered.

(2) There should be a relaxation of the control of proactive aid intended to attract new investment (e.g. tax allowances, direct subsidies, etc.).

This type of aid must have ceilings, as it does currently, but they should be significantly higher for the outermost regions or for regions with important structural problems. The ceiling band should be widened, keeping the lowest intensity levels as they are while almost doubling the highest to allow aid for more regions.

(3) The level of concentration must be improved. The aid must be classified in two different programmes addressing the problems of the poorest peripheral regions and other needy regions.

These are just some initial thoughts that should be further developed in order to achieve a new and better system for the regulation of state aid that could at the same time protect competition and promote regional development. Although aid is not the most important point in determining the location of new investments, underdeveloped regions will never have a chance to overcome their backwardness if they are denied the possibility of attracting larger amounts of state aid compared to the direct public support available in the more developed areas of the European Union.

We hope that this chapter has achieved its goal of making the reader think about the several issues connected to the EC state aid policy. Furthermore, that it has started a line of reform destined to define a new system which concentrates aid in the really needy regions where it can really be effective in reducing regional disparities.

NOTE

1. The calculation of Net Grant Equivalent (NGE) consists of reducing all the forms of aid connected with an investment to a common measure irrespective of the country concerned, i.e. the net intensity, for the purposes of comparing them with each other or with a predetermined ceiling. The net intensity represents the final benefit which a firm is deemed to derive from the value of the aid before tax in relation to the assisted investment.

CHAPTER 10

COMPETITION POLICY, COHESION AND COHERENCE? MEMBER STATE REGIONAL POLICIES AND THE NEW REGIONAL AID GUIDELINES

Fiona G. Wishlade

1. Introduction

The last year or so has been an active period in policymaking with respect to the most high profile aspect of Community cohesion policy, the Structural Funds. Following the publication of Agenda 2000, the Commission's forward look at Community policies across a range of areas and the implications of enlargement, preparations for the next round of Structural Funds plans are underway. These developments have attracted considerable media and academic attention as nations and regions consider how the changes will affect their jurisdictions, and gear up for the intensive negotiations over eligible areas and financial allocations due to take place during the Austrian and German (and even the Finnish) Presidencies. At the same time, but attracting little publicity, the competition directorate of the European Commission, DGIV, has issued new guidelines on national regional aid[1] (RAGS), which involve significant changes and are set to apply from the start of the year 2000. In parallel, a new framework will limit the scope for regional aid to assist large investment projects (LIPS).[2] As a regulatory rather than a spending policy, the competition rules lack the glamour of the Structural Funds and their ability to complement national policy efforts with potentially significant contributions from the Community budget. However, there is evidence of policy maker disquiet at the nature of the new rules and their potential implications for national and Community regional policies alike. Moreover, as the prospect of eastern enlargement looms, and Structural Funds contributions to the current membership decline, some have recognised that the rules governing the operation of national regional policy may be of longer-term significance than Community regional policy *per se*.

Against this background, this Chapter is structured as follows. Following

S. Bilal and P. Nicolaides (eds.), Understanding State Aid Policy in the European Community, 173–206.

this introduction, Section 2 reviews the stated objectives and scope of the Guidelines on national regional aid. In Section 3 the Chapter goes on to consider the impact of the Guidelines on assisted area coverage in the Community. Section 4 assesses the implications of the new rules for Member State approaches to area designation and Section 5 discusses Commission proposals with respect to the "coherence" of national and Community assisted areas. A concluding section highlights some issues for debate.

2. The guidelines on national regional aid

Art. 92(1) of the Treaty of Rome provided for a general ban on so-called state aid "which distorts or threatens to distort competition by favouring certain undertakings or the production of certain goods" to the extent that trade between Member States is affected.[3] Art. 92(3) provides for two regional policy related exceptions to this prohibition in subparagraphs (a) and (c). These provisions have been the subject of extensive interpretation over the past 30 years or so;[4] the most recent expression of Commission policy being the 1988 Communication on the method for the application of Art. 92(3)(a) and (c) to regional aid.[5] Following discussions with Member States in the course of multilateral meetings the Commission recently adopted revised guidelines on national regional aid, which it intends should be applicable from 1 January 2000.

In part, the new Guidelines are intended to consolidate the large number of existing texts related to regional aid.[6] In addition, the new Guidelines involve the formalisation of the Commission's current practice, which is itself a significant departure from the approach outlined in its 1988 Communication (supposedly still in place).[7] However, the guidelines also introduce significant new provisions which will impact on the conduct of national regional policies.

In introducing these changes, the Guidelines conform to the policy framework trend of growing tougher with maturity.[8] In addition, the Guidelines need to be seen in the context of the new Art. 94 Regulation.[9] This Regulation enables the Commission to adopt regulations that exempt certain categories of aid from prior notification and approval by the Commission under Art. 93. Among the categories envisaged for this "group exemption" approach is "aid that complies with the map approved by the Commission for each Member State for the grant of regional aid". In other words, the Art. 94 Regulation could be used to give the national assisted area maps an "independent" existence, impacting directly on other policy areas (such as SME policy) and local authority intervention.

According to the Commission, the new Guidelines are founded on four essential principles:[10]

– *concentration* – that assistance should be focused on the poorest regions in order to improve their efficiency, on the grounds that a scattered pattern of assisted areas is inefficient and may give rise to a "cancellation" effect;

– *reduction in the total volume of aid* – partly reflecting Commission concerns at the distribution of regional aid expenditure between the so-called "cohesion countries", on the one hand, and the richer Member States, on the other;

– *a consideration of the real effect on employment* – reflected in the scope to provide a temporary wage-related subsidy in place of investment-related aid;

– *coherence* – that the spatial coverage and timing of changes to national and Community regional policies should be coordinated.

In addition, the Commission draws attention to the need to counter the negative implications of "delocalisations". Finally, the Commission notes that one of the new elements of the guidelines is that the areas assisted by regional policy will be determined within the context of a Community ceiling on population coverage, which will in turn give rise to population ceilings within each Member State.

This presentation of the Guidelines is striking for a number of reasons. First, it makes no mention of the perceived need to control regional aid in the context of distortions of competition or trade between the Member States; this is, after all, the key function of the competition rules. Second, it is very much concerned with the *substance* of regional policy, focusing on issues of efficiency or problems of relocation; these are the proper concerns of *national* regional policy makers, but surely not of *Community* competition authorities. Third, although the reduction in the volume of aid appears as a principle, there is nothing in the guidelines to impose a reduction in overall spending. Last, and most important of all, the Commission's presentation of the Guidelines conceals some fundamental changes in its approach to controlling regional aid and ones that have far-reaching practical implications. These are essentially four-fold.

First, in respect of spatial coverage, the Commission proposes to reduce overall assisted area coverage to 42.7% of the Community population, compared with the current 46.9%; an absolute reduction of around 15.7 million persons.[11] The definition of Art. 92(3)(a) areas is aligned with that of Objective 1 for Structural Fund purposes, this in turn determines the coverage of Art. 92(3)(c) areas across the Community as a whole (in that the Art. 92(3)(c) areas are 42.7% of the EC population, less the population of those areas eligible for Art. 92(3)(a)). National "quotas" of Art. 92(3)(c) aid is determined by internal (national) disparities in GDP per head and unemployment rates at NUTS III.[12]

Second, Member States are "free" to designate areas up to the population ceiling, subject to a range of stringent parameters to which their area designation methodologies must conform.

Third, the provisions of the Guidelines and the broader commitment to "coherence" between the national and the Structural Fund assisted areas favour a situation in which only areas that are designated for national regional policy can qualify for the Structural Funds.

Last, maximum rates of award are reduced for all eligible regions; combined with the Multisectoral Framework for Large Investment Projects,[13] this could reduce aid intensities for some large projects to levels that may undermine the incentive aspects of regional aid altogether. This fourth element of the Guidelines is not discussed further in this Chapter which focuses primarily on the spatial implications of the new rules.

3. Population coverage

The Commission's approach to controlling the spatial coverage of national regional aid represents the most fundamental change introduced by the Guidelines. The Commission has long considered EC wide and national spatial coverage of regional aids (as a percentage of the relevant population) as a measure of the discipline to which regional aid is subjected; in particular, there is a view that in the more prosperous countries, the assisted areas should include a lower proportion of the national population.

Under the new guidelines, population coverage takes on a pre-eminent role in regional aid discipline. The starting point is the Commission's view that, across the Community, spatial coverage should amount to less than 50% of the population; in practice, the Commission has established a ceiling of 42.7% for EU-15. This is not specified in the published Guidelines, but is mentioned in the letter to Member States, press releases and other announcements. The figure has, according to the Commission, been calculated to accommodate the entire populations of the five CEE countries expected to join during the 2000-6 period (all of which would be expected to fall within the Art. 92(3)(a) derogation) whilst remaining within a ceiling of 50% of an enlarged Community (i.e. EU-21). This is broadly reflected in Table 1, although the outcome differs somewhat from that given by the Commission.

The distinction between Art. 92(3)(a) and Art. 92(3)(c), which has become entrenched through Community case law, is maintained for the purposes of determining spatial coverage. This section briefly reviews the provisions relating to each of these categories, before considering the overall impact of the changes.

Table 1: Population Coverage in the Context of Enlargement

	Pop	Art. 92(3)(a) (% of pop)	Art. 92(3)(a) (millions)	Art. 92(3)(a) (% of EU-21 pop)	Art. 92(3)(a) and (c) (% EU-21 pop)
Hungary	10.2	100	10.2	2.3	2.3
Poland	38.6	100	38.6	8.8	8.8
Estonia	1.5	100	1.5	0.3	0.3
Czech Republic	10.3	100	10.3	2.4	2.4
Slovenia	2.0	100	2.0	0.5	0.5
Cyprus	0.7	0	0	0	0
EU-15	373.0	19.8	73.9	16.9	35.7
EU-21	436.3		136.5	31.3	50.0

Allowable coverage (Art. 92(3)(a) and (c) as % of EU-15 population (a+c))	41.7

Source: Author's own calculations based on Eurostat data.

3.1 ARTICLE 92(3)(a).

Art. 92(3)(a) provides that "aid to promote the economic development of areas where the standard of living is abnormally low or where there is serious underemployment" may be considered compatible with the common market.

This article is clearly aimed at areas that are particularly disadvantaged. More specifically, the ECJ has emphasised that:

"the use of the words 'abnormally' and 'serious' in the exemption contained in Article 92(3)(a) shows that it concerns only areas where the economic situation is extremely unfavourable *in relation to the Community as a whole*."[14] [emphasis added]

The new approach to designating areas under Art. 92(3)(a) is substantially the same as that under the 1988 Communication; however, there are differences in approach which will impact on some areas that currently qualify under this derogation. Under the new guidelines, Art. 92(3)(a) areas are defined as:
– NUTS II regions
– with GDP per head measured in purchasing power standards (PPS) of

less than 75.0% of the Community average;
– where the regional and the Community averages relate to the last three years for which data are available.

Previously, the basic unit for designation was the NUTS III level, although account was taken of the situation of the NUTS II level for determining eligibility; the new guidelines focus exclusively on NUTS II. In addition, the 1988 Communication extended eligibility to Northern Ireland "because of its particularly difficult situation" and to Teruel (Spain), even although neither met the stated criteria;[15] this discretionary approach is absent from the new Guidelines which take account only of quantitative criteria. Table 2 sets out the coverage based on calculations undertaken by the European Commission.

At present, coverage of Art. 92(3)(a) areas amounts to 23.6% of the Community population. According to the Commission's current calculations, after 1 January 2000, coverage would fall to 19.8% of the EC population (subject to probable revision by 1 January 1999). The difference partly reflects changes in the situation of the regions since the Commission last considered coverage in the various countries. In addition, a strict application of the criteria is implied by the guidelines, with the consequence that Northern Ireland, which was an *explicit* exception, is excluded.

Arguably the most significant changes which can be determined from the Commission's figures are that the Republic of Ireland would cease to qualify under Art. 92(3)(a), whereas the country is entirely covered by this derogation at present; and that the Lisbon region of Portugal, which contains around a third of the national population, would also cease to be eligible under the Art. 92(3)(a) derogation.

The underlying implication of the Guidelines is that areas which meet the Art. 92(3)(a) criteria would be included in the national assisted areas map; in other words, there would be no capacity to exchange areas which qualify under the Art. 92(3)(a) derogation for those that do not.

3.2 ARTICLE 92(3)(c)

Coverage of Art. 92(3)(a) effectively determines coverage of Art. 92(3)(c) – assuming that the overall ceiling is maintained. The classification of 19.8% of the Community population under Art. 92(3)(a) leaves 22.9% of the population as a "quota" for Art. 92(3)(c), to be distributed among the regions *not* covered by Art. 92(3)(a).

It is in applying Art. 92(3)(c) that the key difference between the new guidelines and the 1988 Communication emerges. Under the 1988 Communication the measurement of internal regional disparities in GDP per head and unemployment rates constituted the first stage in determining *which*

Table 2: Population Coverage under the New Guidelines –
Commission Calculations[16]

	Total Pop (millions)	Art. 92(3)(a) (% pop)	Art. 92(3)(c) (% pop)	Total (Art. 92(3)(a) and (c)) (% pop)	Current coverage (% pop)
Belgium	10.137	0	35.2	35.2	35.0
Denmark	5.228	0	19.2	19.2	20.0
Germany	81.662	17.4	18.3	35.7	38.1
Greece	10.454	100	0	100	100
Spain	39.210	54.3	22.9	77.2	76.0
France	59.704	2.6	35.2	37.8	42.4
Ireland	3.582	0	100	100	100
Italy	56.640	30.7	10.4	41.1	48.9
Luxembourg	0.398	0	32.0	32.0	42.7
Netherlands	15.457	0	15.0	15.0	17.3
Austria	8.047	3.4	27.1	30.5	35.1
Portugal	9.916	66.6	33.4	100	100
Finland	5.108	13.8	34.4	48.2	41.6
Sweden	8.627	0	15.6	15.6	18.5
UK	58.613	2.2	26.3	28.5	38.2
EU-15	372.983	19.8	22.9	42.7	46.7

Note: Figures are based on data available at 15 October 1997.
Source: Unpublished memorandum of the European Commission.

regions could qualify for regional aid under Art. 92(3)(c). In contrast, under
the new Guidelines, a broadly similar mechanism is used to determine *what*
share of the overall total of Art. 92(3)(c) regions a given Member State will
be allocated. Under this new approach, the Member States determine the
actual areas to be designated, subject to Commission approval both of the
area designation methodology and of the regions proposed by the Member
States.

　　In practice, however, the quotas allocated by this process are subjected to
a series of adjustments which mitigate the impact of the exercise by taking
account of: minimum and maximum Art. 92(3)(c) coverage for each country;
a ceiling on the reduction imposed; and special provision for former Art.
92(3)(a) areas.[17]

3.3 IMPACT OF THE GUIDELINES ON NATIONAL ASSISTED AREA
     COVERAGE[18]

The impact on assisted area coverage implied by the Guidelines varies widely
between Member States. This is illustrated in Figure 1, which considers two
dimensions of the impact of the changes: the change in coverage as a
percentage of the current coverage; and the change in coverage in percentage
point terms.

In terms of the *direction* of change (i.e. whether coverage is expanded or
reduced), clearly, both measures tell the same story: three countries would
actually be able to *increase* assisted area coverage under the new guidelines
(Finland, Spain and Belgium); three of the cohesion countries (Greece,
Ireland and Portugal) would experience no change; and the remaining
Member States would be obliged to cut back on coverage. However, the
relative magnitude of the change differs according to whether the percentage
point change in coverage or the change as a proportion of the previous
coverage are considered.

In terms of percentage point change, i.e. the change in actual coverage, the
countries most affected are Italy, the UK and Luxembourg, all of which
would have to cut coverage by more than 7% of the national population.
These reductions are even more significant when viewed in *relative* terms.
Luxembourg and the UK, for example, would lose more than 25% of their
assisted areas on this basis.

For the remaining six countries obliged to reduce coverage, the impact is
not so dramatic (although it may be no easier to accommodate domestically).
Denmark and Germany are less affected than the Community as a whole, both
in percentage point terms and relatively speaking. For Sweden and the
Netherlands, the percentage point cutback is less than the Community
average, but amounts to more than 15% of current coverage; France and
Austria bear slightly more of the cutbacks than the EC average on both
measures.

At the other end of the spectrum, based on current Commission calculations,
three countries would be expected to enjoy an increase in authorised assisted
areas coverage. In Spain and Belgium, the increase is arguably not significant
(although will certainly ease policy choices). However, in Finland, the
increase is substantial both in relative terms (an expansion in coverage
amounting to more than 15% of current coverage) and in population terms –
a further 6.6% of the Finnish population could be included in the assisted
areas map, on the basis of the figures in the Commission's memorandum.

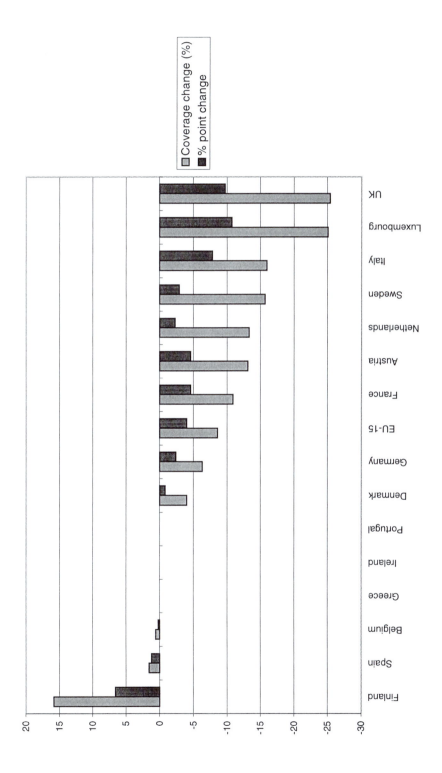

Figure 1: Changes in Assisted Area Coverage under the Guidelines

4. Area designation and the Member States

The population coverage established by the Commission sets the broad framework within which area designation under the Art. 92(3)(c) derogation is undertaken by the Member States. In addition, however, the guidelines set out a further series of constraints with respect to territorial units, indicators and area designation methodologies. Further, the options facing the Member States are complicated by the Commission's emphasis on coherence between the national assisted areas and those designated for the purposes of the Structural Funds. This section begins by setting out the requirements of the Guidelines before going on to discuss each of these aspects in turn, with particular reference to the current and past policy practices of the Member States.

4.1 AREA DESIGNATION REQUIREMENTS UNDER THE GUIDELINES

A key change introduced under the Guidelines is that Member States are required to notify to the Commission under Art. 93(3) of the methodology and quantitative indicators which they wish to use to determine the eligible areas for Art. 92(3)(c), as well as the list of regions they propose for the Art. 92(3)(c) derogation. More specifically:

– The *methodology* must be objective, enable socio-economic disparities to be measured, highlighting significant differences, and it must be presented in a clear and detailed manner to enable the Commission to "assess its merits".

– Up to five *indicators*, including both simple indicators and combinations of indicators, may be used. They must be:

• objective and relevant to the examination of the socio-economic circumstances of the regions;

• based on time series including "at least the three years prior to the moment of notification" or derived from the latest survey, in the case of non-annual surveys;

• drawn up by reliable statistical sources.

– The *regions* must fulfil the following conditions:

• They must be NUTS III, or, where justified, a different homogeneous unit – importantly, however, only one type of unit may be used by each Member State;

• Individual regions or groups of contiguous regions must generally have a minimum population of 100,000; a fictitious population of 100,000 will be imputed to calculate the population coverage if the population is less. Exceptions to this are:

* NUTS III regions with a population of less than 100,000;

       *   islands and "other regions characterised by similar geographical isolation";

       *   Luxembourg.

- The list of regions "must be arranged on the basis" of the chosen indicators; the selected regions must show "significant disparities" – half the standard deviation) compared with the average of the potential 92(3)(c) regions of the Member State concerned.

- Subject to the population ceiling, regions with a population density of less than 12.5 km^2 may also qualify for the Art. 92(3)(c) derogation.

- Regions eligible under the Structural Funds may also qualify, subject to the population ceiling *and* to the conditions set out in the second indent of the condition relating to eligible regions, i.e. that designated areas must generally involve a minimum 100,000 population.

4.2 TERRITORIAL UNITS

There are two major constraints imposed on the Member States in relation to territorial units. First, the regions must conform to NUTS III or another territorial unit; the same territorial unit must be used in relation to all the indicators used. Second, designated areas must form "compact zones" and, in general, must contain a population of at least 100,000.

As far as the use of NUTS III is concerned, few Member States are likely to view this as a viable option for area designation purposes. Commission policy is centred around the notion of so-called NUTS regions, but while the use of NUTS is common for Community policy purposes, any notion of comparability is really quite illusory, both within countries and between them. This is clearly illustrated in Table 3, which shows the vastly differing physical scales of regions that are intended to be comparable.

In terms of surface area, the average Finnish NUTS III region is 25 times the size of the average German or Belgian unit. Across the Community as a whole, the largest NUTS III unit is almost 10,000 times the size of the smallest one.

As significant, perhaps more, are the differences in regional populations of the areas under comparison. These are illustrated in Table 4. At NUTS III, the population varies from 892,000 (UK) to just 148,000 (Germany) and even within Germany the population of the largest NUTS III unit is over 200 times that of the smallest. At the Community level, the most populous NUTS III region has over 400 times the population of the least populous.

The scale of these differences cannot but cast doubt on the value of comparing data at these levels across regions and countries. This is all the more so since some indicators are highly sensitive to the spatial unit of analysis. (This is particularly true of GDP per head;[19] it is therefore a matter

Table 3: Surface Area of the EU Regions (1,000 km²)

	NUTS I			NUTS II			NUTS III		
	Average	Min	Max	Average	Min	Max	Average	Min	Max
B	10.2	0.2	16.8	3.4	2.40	4.4	0.7	0.10	2.0
DK	43.1	43.1	43.1	43.1	43.10	43.1	2.9	0.10	6.2
D	22.3	0.4	70.6	8.9	0.40	29.5	0.7	0.03	2.9
GR	33.0	3.8	56.8	10.2	2.31	19.1	2.6	0.33	5.4
E	72.1	7.2	215	28	0.03	94.2	9.7	0.01	21.7
F	70.4	12.0	145.6	24.4	1.10	83.9	6.3	0.11	83.9
IRL	68.9	68.9	68.9	68.9	68.90	68.9	7.7	3.32	12.2
I	27.4	13.6	44.4	15.1	3.30	25.7	3.2	0.21	7.5
L	2.6	2.6	2.6	2.6	2.60	2.6	2.6	2.60	2.6
NL	10.3	7.3	11.9	3.4	1.40	5.7	1.0	0.13	3.4
A	28	23.6	34.4	9.3	0.41	19.2	2.4	0.41	4.6
P	30.7	0.8	88.9	13.1	0.80	27	3.1	0.80	8.6
FIN	169.1	1.6	336.6	56.4	1.55	136.1	17.8	1.55	98.9
S	410.9	410.9	410.9	51.4	6.5	154.3	17.1	2.90	98.9
UK	22	7.3	77.1	6.9	0.70	30.6	3.7	0.38	25.3
EU-15	68.1	0.2	410.9	23.0	0.03	154.3	5.4	0.01	98.9

Note: These figures do not include the revised boundaries for the UK which were announced in Summer 1998.
Source: Eurostat, 1995.

Table 4: Population of the EU Regions – 1992 (1,000)

	NUTS I			NUTS II			NUTS III		
	Average	Min	Max	Average	Min	Max	Average	Min	Max
B	3,348	951	5,810	1,116	236	2,258	234	38	951
DK	5,171	5,171	5,171	5,171	5,171	5,171	335	45	608
D	5,039	684	17,595	2,015	492	5,273	148	17	3,456
GR	2,578	1,004	3,540	793	195	3,540	202	21	3,540
E	5,584	1,502	10,502	2,171	127	6,984	752	56	4,910
F	6,546	1,539	10,862	2,266	134	10,862	589	73	2,540
IRL	3,549	3,549	3,549	3,549	3,549	3,549	444	195	1,371
I	5,169	1,584	8,868	2,843	117	8,868	599	92	3,923
L	393	393	393	393	393	393	393	393	393
NL	3,796	1,605	7,117	1,265	238	3,284	380	55	1,292
A	2,638	1,750	3,336	879	273	1,570	226	21	1,570
P	3,286	238	9,366	1,408	238	3,479	329	50	1,832
FIN	2,527	25	5,030	842	25	1,787	266	25	1,278
S	8,668	8,668	8,668	1,084	397	1,728	361	57	1,662
UK	5,273	2,089	17,703	1,657	278	6,905	892	72	6,905
EU-15	4,238	25	17,703	1,830	25	10,862	410	17	6,905

Source: Eurostat, 1995.

of grave concern that this indicator should be the determinant factor in establishing eligibility for the Art. 92(3)(a) derogation as well as playing a major role in setting the Art. 92(3)(c) quotas).

A wider issue is the nature of the regions defined by NUTS levels and their appropriateness for the measurement of economic and social disparities. For the most part, NUTS areas do not correspond to any functional unit (such as labour market or Travel-to-Work Areas (TTWA)). In other words, they are largely areas of statistical convenience and often lack internal homogeneity or coherence. Reflecting this, many Member States have, in past area designation exercises, used specially defined areas that are viewed as more meaningful from an economic and social perspective. For example, German policy makers have traditionally used labour-market areas, whilst Dutch area designation has tended to be based on the COROP regions, functional divisions of the country based on labour market criteria. Similarly, in Britain, policy has been based around TTWAs, which are viewed as approximations to self-contained labour market areas.

Other Member States have opted for smaller administrative units as "building blocks" for area designation – communes in Portugal; cantons in Luxembourg and municipalities in Sweden, for example.

This divergence of practice between countries is indicative of the "trade off" between the relevance of the units and availability of the statistics. Quite simply, statistics are often gathered in relation to administrative boundaries in order for subnational authorities to provide appropriate services within their jurisdictions, and there tends to be a wider range of data available in relation to administrative units than for functional units; the latter, on the other hand, are better at reflecting accurately the socio-economic circumstances of the areas covered.

These factors make the choice of unit difficult for policy makers in many countries. The decision is complicated further by the constraints contained in the Guidelines which impose the use of one type of unit only. It is unclear quite what this means. For example, some data, particularly those related to employment, may be most appropriately measured in the context of labour-market areas, but for other characteristics, indicators may only be available (or relevant) at a higher level of spatial aggregation. Does this constraint preclude the imputation of data relating to the larger unit on the smaller one? If it does, then this is a severe constraint on national area designation systems: the number of indicators actually available at any given level is likely to be very limited. A further consideration is that, in practice, there may be sound justification for splitting geographically large areas and focusing policy on only part of the unit, however, this would appear to be excluded under the Guidelines.

The second principal constraint in relation to designated units is the condition that areas must, in general, form compact zones comprising a population of at least 100,000. The exceptions to this are NUTS III regions with a population of less than 100,000, islands, other regions characterised by geographical isolation (this is not defined) and Luxembourg. Over 15% of NUTS III regions have fewer than 100,000 inhabitants, but reflecting the lack of comparability of NUTS units across the Community, these are heavily concentrated in Germany, and to a lesser extent in Belgium and Greece. In short, the prevalence of low population NUTS III regions in a given Member State could quite arbitrarily facilitate pinpointing in area designation, which is precisely what the Commission is seeking to discourage. On the other hand, Member States which choose to designate on the basis of units other than NUTS III (e.g. communes or labour market areas) or which have larger NUTS III areas, will be obliged to aggregate up the units concerned in order to meet the minimum threshold.

4.3 STATISTICAL INDICATORS

The guidelines impose significant constraints on the indicators which can be used for area designation purposes. The most obvious of these is the limitation of five indicators. As Table 5 shows, this will be an important restriction on some countries which, in the past, have used a far greater number of indicators. In Portugal, for example, the last area designation exercise involved an analysis of 23 indicators, unusually, as will be seen, within a wholly quantitative system. Elsewhere, however, it is commonplace for more than five indicators, either singly or in combination to be used. In this context, it is unclear what is meant in guidelines by the reference to "combinations of indicators" or why a limit is imposed on the number that can be used.

It seems likely that the cap on the number of indicators will prove to be an important constraint on countries, particularly those that contain only limited (or no) Art. 92(3)(a) areas, but nevertheless have problem regions of considerable diversity. This is the case in the UK and France, for example, which both contain thinly populated and isolated regions, areas of urban deprivation and industrial closure areas. In both countries it will be a challenge to identify five "objective and relevant" indicators that reflect this diversity.

A further concern about the conditions attached to the selection of indicators is the extent to which they are backward looking and problem-centred. In Germany and the UK, attempts have been made to take account of *future* employment trends in assessing regional problems. The guidelines do not appear to allow for such an approach, focusing instead on data relating to "at least the last three years" or, where annual data are not available, to the

Table 5: Problem Region Indicators at the National Level

	B	DK	D	E	F	I	NL	P	FIN	S	UK
Climate									✓	✓	
Distance to market/peripherality/accessibility			✓		✓			✓			✓
Population density		✓	✓		✓			✓		✓	✓
Population change		✓			✓			✓		✓	
GDP per head	✓					✓				✓	
Tax income											
Industrial/activity structure	✓		✓	✓	✓	✓		✓		✓	✓
Infrastructure/amenity			✓				✓	✓			
Economic prospects	✓		✓	✓	✓						✓
Demographic trends	✓		✓		✓						✓
Unemployment		✓	✓	✓	✓	✓	✓		✓		✓
Structure of unemployment											✓
Employment trends			✓							✓	✓
Future employment		✓	✓							✓	✓
Active population			✓					✓		✓	✓
Qualifications/occupational structure			✓								
Income								✓			
Living conditions								✓			

Source: Wishlade F. and Yuill, D. (1997) *Measuring Disparities for Area Designation Purposes: Issues for the European Union*, Regional and Industrial Research Paper Series, 24, European Policies Research Centre, University of Strathclyde.

latest survey. The wholly retrospective nature of the approach is an important issue in the context of assisted areas maps which, in principle, appear to be intended to apply to the year 2006.

The problem-centred nature of the guidelines may also constrain policy makers. In recent years, a number of countries have considered issues of regional *potential*, in particular the notion that it may be more effective to apply policy to an area adjacent to that shown up on the basis of the indicators, rather than directly on the area concerned. In France, for example, in the last area designation exercise, which was a highly discretionary, even covert process, account was taken not only of measures of prosperity or unemployment, but also of the extent to which areas could be expected to benefit from the types of investment promoted through the regional policy grant. Similarly, in the UK, small areas of London with good sites and infrastructure and accessible from areas of high unemployment were designated in the 1993 exercise.

4.4 AREA DESIGNATION METHODOLOGIES

It is arguably in the context of area designation methodologies that Member States will find most difficulty in conforming to the demands of the new Guidelines. Before going on to discuss this in detail, it is important to note that there are two "derogations" from the methodology.

The first concerns areas that are sparsely populated. According to Annex II to the Guidelines, these are "made up essentially of NUTS III level geographic regions with a population density of less that 12.5 inhabitants per square kilometre." In addition, the Annex allows for "a certain flexibility" in the selection of areas. This special provision for sparsely populated areas was absent from at least one draft of the guidelines. On the face of it, its inclusion in the final version should ease significantly the area designation process in the Nordic countries. It essentially separates out issues of population density from other types of regional problem in the countries concerned enabling a simpler measure to be used in the northern territories and more pertinent indicators to be applied elsewhere.

The second derogation from the area designation methodology concerns the inclusion of areas eligible for Structural Funds assistance. This issue is discussed in further detail below (see Section 5), but the essence of the provision is that regions eligible for the Structural Funds may be included in the list of areas eligible for national regional policy, subject to the population ceiling and the rules relating to minimum population "blocks", described above.

Under the guidelines, Member States are required notify to the Commission under Art. 93(3) of the methodology and quantitative indicators which they wish to use to determine eligible areas for the Art. 92(3)(c) derogation, together with the list of eligible areas and the relative intensities. The list of regions must be "arranged on the basis of the indicators" and must show "significant disparities (half the standard deviation) compared with the average of the potential 92(3)(c) regions of the Member State concerned, in respect of one or other indicator used in the method."

The key questions here are what degree of flexibility is allowed, if any, and how far, if at all, can the current policy practice of the Member States conform to these requirements? In considering these questions, it is useful briefly to review the range of experiences in the Member States.[20]

At one extreme, in *Portugal*, the exercise is purely statistical. There is no adjustment made to the ranking produced from the analysis of 23 indicators; communes that fall below the national average on the ranking are designated: those that are above average are excluded. However, designation in the Portuguese context has less *absolute* importance than in many other countries. All of Portugal is currently treated as an Art. 92(3)(a) region by the Commission, allowing investment support *throughout* the country even though the regional incentive system (SIR) is restricted to designated problem regions. Although Lisbon loses Art. 92(3)(a) status at the end of 1999, the whole of the region will qualify as an Art. 92(3)(c) until 2006: it is only really at that time that the impact of the new rules might be felt in Portugal.

The *German* system is also based very much on quantitative indicators. Importantly, and in line with the Art. 92(3)(a)/(c) division in the Commission process, the latest area designation exercise involved separate assessments of the old and new *Länder*. As in past re-designations, a two-stage process for reviewing the GA areas in West Germany was undertaken. The first stage involved an assessment of the 167 West German labour market areas according to a set of weighted regional indicators: the average unemployment rate between 1992 and 1995 (40%); per capita gross average annual salaries and wages of those eligible for social security (40%); an infrastructure indicator measuring the attractiveness of the area to the private sector (10%); a forecast of future employment development (5%); and developments in the unemployment rate (5%). These data were normalised and a ranking produced; the first 46 areas, accounting for 22% of the West German population, were deemed GA areas. However, in a second stage, the *Länder* were able to modify the map to include their own preferred areas (with clearly definable regional problems) through a process of "exchange" of areas, whilst remaining within the 22% population ceiling. This flexibility is provided to allow account to be taken of regional problems not given due weight by the designation procedures (with their essentially historical view of the situation).

In some respects, the German system appears close to the method proposed by the Commission. However, there are important differences. Mention has already been made of the use of forecasting data rather than purely retrospective or historical data. Perhaps more significant, however, is the lack of flexibility implied by the Commission's approach to the rankings. In the German context, this scope for a *qualitative* appraisal of *quantitative* outcomes is important both from the perspective of the rationale and integrity of policy, and for political reasons. The second stage of analysis is in part recognition of the fact that purely statistical processes may not accurately reflect the real nature of the regional problem, and indeed can produce anomalous results. In part it also reflects the shared responsibility for regional policy between the Federal and the *Land* levels. There appears to be no provision for such flexibility or discretion in the model proposed by the Commission.

Further along the scale, in the 1993 *British* area designation exercise there was an extensive analysis of quantitative indicators. This exercise was of particular interest for the approach adopted to obtaining a common overview of the regional problem. Instead of utilising a "combined indicator", as in Germany, the government drew up indices of nine separate factors each of which was given a variety of weights. This is illustrated in Table 6.

Table 6:
British Area Designation Criteria

Factor	Range of Weights (%)
Current unemployment	0-100
Structural unemployment	0-100
Long-term unemployment	0-5
Future jobs gap	0-10
Occupational structure	0-5
Activity rate	0-10
Peripherality	0-10
VAT growth	0-5
Population density	0-5

By varying the weights a broad picture was obtained of the basic problems facing different areas. Through an iterative process, it was possible to focus particularly on the appropriate status of areas on the margin or between tiers;

and to take account of the wider regional policy needs of broader areas of the country. In addition, special account was taken of the needs of areas facing major significant known unemployment problems as a result of large-scale closures or rundowns. As already mentioned, a particular issue concerned the position of London which, at the Travel-to-Work Area (TTWA) level, had been suffering from above-average unemployment and had very high rates of unemployment in some inner city areas. In recognition of these problems, it was decided to designate specific (small) parts of London containing good sites and infrastructure either in, or in close proximity to, major areas of unemployment which could be attractive to new investment. In a number of other parts of the country – centred mostly on city areas – the decision was exceptionally taken also to split some TTWAs with a view to focusing assistance on areas in most need.

In the UK context too, there would be obvious difficulties in replicating the 1993 system in the context of the new Guidelines. The special account taken of the unemployment situation in London, and the splitting of TTWAs, the chosen unit, in particular circumstances is out of line with the requirements in respect of units described above. As in Germany, the use of forward-looking measures would also be problematic. As already noted, the number of indicators exceeds that permitted under the guidelines. On a more technical level, it is unclear whether the absence of a single ranking would conform to the Commission's demands or whether this requirement could be accommodated by combining the rankings on the different indicators. In any case, there would appear to be no scope for qualitative inputs following the initial ranking and weighting process.

Until its accession to the EU, the process of area designation in *Austria* was relatively informal, with an emphasis on regional *problems* rather than problem *regions*. As a consequence of EU membership, the system has become much more formalised, with a clear demarcation of those areas eligible for regional support. In preparing for the negotiations with the EFTA Surveillance Authority (ESA) – in the context of EEA membership – the Federal authorities used the Commission's 1988 Communication as the basis for the area designation methodology. The Austrian analysis showed that Burgenland qualified under Art. 92(3)(a) as an underdeveloped region. The remaining regions were then reviewed (at NUTS III) in terms of their structural unemployment over the previous five years and gross regional product per inhabitant. Having established which areas would qualify on the basis of the Commission's published thresholds, the outcome was passed to ÖROK (the *Österreichische Raumordnungskonferenz* which acts as a forum for cooperation between the different actors in the regional policy field) for revision and was then submitted to ESA for approval.

In Austria, EEA membership provided a new context for regional policy and area designation clearly followed closely the methodology outlined in the 1988 Communication. This approach would not appear to conform to the new guidelines. In particular, as noted earlier, the new guidelines offer no scope for qualitative adjustments to the list of regions meeting the quantitative criteria. It is worth recalling here the differences between the 1988 Communication and the new guidelines: the 1988 methodology provided for GDP per head and unemployment thresholds which constituted a "first stage" eligibility test for assisted area status; in the 1998 rules, this same test is used to determine the population coverage of the assisted areas, not the actual areas.

In *Italy* and *Spain*, area designation for national regional policy has been closely associated with the areas eligible for the Structural Funds. Both countries contain significant Art. 92(3)(a) (and Objective 1) areas and are likely to continue to do so post-2000. However, for the purposes of the Art. 92(3)(c) derogation, a new approach would be required in the context of the new guidelines. On the other hand, in the Spanish context especially, area designation for the Structural Funds can be expected to play a key role, and may even indirectly increase flexibility.

In *Sweden*, designation of the standard aid areas was based on statistical analyses at the municipal level of factors such as unemployment, labour force participation rates and migration – measures which focus mainly on the problems facing the remote northern parts of the country. In contrast, designation as a temporary area generally reflects the unemployment situation in the region concerned. A review of the Swedish Aid Areas is imminent – in line with the agreement reached with the Commission in 1995 to reconsider area designation within three years of accession. The main criteria to be used for designation purposes will be: population trends, population density, proportion of elderly, employment trends, share of public sector employment, division of employment by sex, education levels, tax powers and state transfers. Under the terms of the guidelines, this exercise may be conducted in line with the 1988 Communication, provided that the map expires at the end of 1999. In practice, the area designation process in Sweden may be eased by the derogation in favour of sparsely populated areas. On this basis, the methodology and ranking would need to be devised only in order to accommodate other types of problem region.

In *France*, the most recent review took place in 1993/94 and followed longstanding disagreement with DGIV over the total coverage of the assisted areas, and considerable pressure for coverage to be significantly reduced. The approach adopted by the French authorities to the review is interesting. In the light of the problems which were associated with the designation of Structural Fund areas in 1993 – and, in particular, the political pressures which they generated – it was decided to give no active publicity to the fact that a new map was being prepared. The designation process was largely empirical – based on sound and detailed knowledge of the country rather than on an explicit system. The old map was taken as a starting point and was reviewed in the light of a set of Commission-driven parameters. The outcome was a map which had broad similarity to its predecessor (holding 40.9% of the national population as against 41.9% previously), but which incorporated significant differences in detail. In particular, the map focused on areas of genuine industrial development potential – omitting tourist-oriented coastal areas and town centres with no industrial sites and, in some areas, taking explicit and detailed account of the location of industrial estates and major infrastructure routes. From the discussion above it will be clear that a repeat of this process would be quite unacceptable under the new rules.

In the *Netherlands* too, the approach to area designation has been based more on a strategic perception of appropriate areas of intervention rather than detailed statistical analysis. Designated areas have tended to be associated with high unemployment, a poor socio-economic structure and a weak economic structure. Over time, the coverage of the problem regions has been reduced as regional disparities have diminished. By 1990, the general view was that the policy focus should be only on the north of the country; however, Parliament remained concerned at the competitive position of South Limburg (particularly) and Twente in the context of the incentives available in neighbouring regions in Belgium and Germany. As a result, it was agreed that these areas should retain their access to Investment Premium (IPR) support, albeit on a "transitional" basis and only in respect of large projects. In the context of the new Guidelines, this approach would need to be supported by an appropriate methodology and ranking of regions which is not overtly undertaken at present.

5. The Coherence of National and Community Assisted Areas

5.1 THE ISSUES

As noted earlier, the eligibility of a given region for the Structural Funds might be viewed as a "privileged criterion" for inclusion in the national assisted areas map. The aim of this is, quite explicitly, to encourage Member States to aim at coterminosity in the coverage of the assisted areas under national and Community regional policy. The question of the so-called "coherence" of national assisted areas with those aided under the Structural Funds has been on the Commission's policy agenda since the 1989-93 Structural Funds planning period and has been the source of considerable controversy.[21] As Table 7 shows, over 9% of the Community population is in areas which qualify for either national or EC regional policy, *but not both.* This lack of coincidence became of practical importance for two interrelated reasons. First, the Structural Funds involve placing special emphasis on the encouragement of productive investment, for which the main instrument is financial incentives to firms. Second, under the Structural Funds the Commission can part-finance aid schemes, but these must be notified and approved in accordance with Arts. 92 and 93 of the Treaty. In other words, *Commission competition policy makers could control where Commission regional policy makers could intervene.* Once the implications of the discrepancies in spatial coverage came to light, this gave rise to heated debate between the Commission and the Member States, and, indeed, within the Commission. The central issue was whether the two sets of areas should coincide: that is, should the national assisted area maps be the same as the EC regional policy map?

Table 7: Spatial Coherence of National and Community
Regional Policy (% of EC population)

	Structural Funds Areas	Areas *not* Eligible for Structural Funds	**TOTALS**
Areas where national regional aid is authorised	44.0	2.7	46.7
Areas where national regional aid is *not* authorised	6.6	46.7	53.3
TOTALS	50.6	49.4	100

Source: CEC (1998) *Communication from the Commission to the Member States on the links between regional and competition policy: Reinforcing Concentration and Mutual Consistency,* OJ C90 26 March 1998.

The First Report on Economic and Social Cohesion the Commission concluded that:

"the Member States and the Commission need to address, in partnership, inconsistencies between the regions which are supported under national regional polices and those which are supported under Union regional polices. Eligibility for union regional aid should in the future become one of the criteria for allowing assistance under Member States' own regional policies".[22]

Subsequently, Agenda 2000 took up the theme. It noted that:

> "The percentage of the population of the Union covered by Objective 1 and 2 should be reduced from 51% to 35-40%. This figure will be smaller than the population covered by Arts. 92(3)(a) and (c), which should also be reduced from 1 January."[23]

In relation to Objective 1 it stated that:

> "the threshold of a *per capita* GDP of 75% of the Community average should be applied strictly. Care should also be taken that there is complete congruence with the regions assisted by the Member States under Art. 92(3)(a) of the Treaty".

With respect to the new Objective 2, coverage should be "as consistent as possible with the areas assisted by the Member States".

This emphasis is reiterated in the preamble to the proposed new Structural Funds Regulation submitted in March 1998:[24]

> "the regions whose development is lagging behind where per capita GDP is less than 75% of the Community average should be the same as the areas assisted by the Member State under Art. 92(3)(a) ...similarly, in accordance with the communication of the Commission on regional policy and competition policy the areas undergoing economic and social change should correspond as closely as possible to the areas assisted by the Member State under Art. 92(3)(c) of the Treaty, and the areas that Member States accordingly propose as eligible for assistance towards economic and social conversion should essentially only be those areas notified to the Commission under Art. 92(3)(c) of the Treaty."

5.2 THE COMMISSION PROPOSALS FOR COHERENCE

In a Communication dated 17 March 1998,[25] the Commission sets out the issues with respect to "coherence" of national and EC assisted areas and makes the following proposals.

First, the "classic" Objective 1 eligibility criteria (GDP per head in PPS of less than 75.0% of the Community average) should be applied strictly so that the areas coincide exactly with Art. 92(3)(a) and consequent inconsistencies between Objective 2 and Art. 92(3)(c) are avoided.

Second, the Commission "calls on" Member States to notify under Art. 92(3)(c) those regions assimilated with Objective 1 or benefiting from special arrangements. In this context, it is assumed that these provisions apply to the Canary Islands, which are currently above the GDP per head threshold for Objective 1 and Art. 92(3)(a),[26] and to sparsely populated regions formerly covered under Objective 6.

Structural Funds	National Regional Policy
Objective 1 "classic"	Art. 92(3)(a)
Objective 1 "other" (Canaries; Objective 6)	Art. 92(3)(c) (Depending on whether proposed by Member State)

Third, in principle, the Commission will not consider for inclusion in the new Objective 2 any region which the Member State has not included in its list of proposed assisted areas under Art. 92(3)(c). However, in justified cases, regions outside Art. 92(3)(c) can be included, subject to a national ceiling of 2% of the population and the overall aim of concentration (i.e. that Objectives 1 and 2 together should cover 35-40% of the EC population).

Fourth, the Communication draws attention to the fact that eligibility for the Structural Funds is a "privileged" selection criterion with respect to Art. 92(3)(c), provided that the population ceiling for national regional aid is respected *and that the regions eligible for the Structural Funds are not chosen later than the national assisted areas.*

Fifth, it envisages that the two area designation exercises be undertaken such that the two new maps enter into force on 1 January 2000. It proposes that the Member States submit their proposed Objective 2 areas by 31 March 1999. As far as *national* assisted areas are concerned, these should be submitted to the Commission as soon as possible, but in any event not later than 31 March.

In the present context, it is the relationship between Objective 2 and Art. 92(3)(c) which is relevant. Accordingly, the section which follows reviews the proposals for Objective 2 coverage for the period 2000-2006.

5.3 OBJECTIVE 2 COVERAGE AND CRITERIA

As already mentioned, Agenda 2000 and the proposed Structural Funds Regulation provide for a new Objective 2 to cover areas undergoing socio-economic change in the industrial and service sectors, declining rural areas, urban areas in difficulty and depressed areas dependent on fisheries.

Reflecting the emphasis on concentration, the draft Structural Funds regulation proposes a ceiling of 18% of the Community population for Objective 2 coverage.[27] Within this limit, the Commission plans to propose

a population ceiling for Objective 2 for each Member State on the basis of a number of factors:
— the population in NUTS III areas which meet the eligibility criteria for designation as industrial or rural areas;
— the seriousness of the structural problems at the national level, as compared with other Member States, assessed on the basis of total and long-term unemployment outside the Objective 1 regions;
— the maximum reduction in population covered by Objective 2 (including the areas that were formerly Objective 1 but which now meet the Objective 2 criteria) is set as one-third of the population covered by Objective 2 and 5b in the 1994-99 period.

Of these three factors, only the third, the minimum coverage of the new Objective 2, can readily be calculated; this is illustrated in Table 8.

It is worth noting that the sum of the national minima amounts to 16.9% of the Community population, just 4 million persons fewer than the Commission's suggested maximum of 18% of the Community population for Objective 2 coverage. The lack of room for manoeuvre suggests either that the 18% limit will be breached or that the coverage of the new Objective 2 areas will not be significantly above the minimum for most Member States. Moreover, these constraints must, in principle, be combined with two further parameters governing assisted area coverage, namely, the distinction between different types of assisted area within Objective 2 and the emphasis on coherence between the national and the Community assisted areas maps.

Within the proposed overall ceiling for Objective 2 of 18% of the Community population, the Commission has indicated that two further criteria should apply.

First, the preamble to the draft regulation,[28] suggests the following indicative breakdown between assisted areas types across the Community:

•	industrial areas:	10%
•	rural areas:	5%
•	urban areas:	2%
•	fisheries areas:	1%

Second, unless objectively justified, Objective 2 coverage in each Member State shall be at least 50% comprised of industrial and rural areas.

Published Europe-wide data are only available in respect of the criteria relating to industrial and rural areas. In consequence, this discussion is limited to these two categories of assisted area: as already noted, these account for the bulk of areas expected to be designated as Objective 2. However, in practice there are significant difficulties and data lacunae even where EC-wide data are, in principle, available.

Table 8: Current Objective 2 and 5b Coverage and Future Objective 2 Minima

	Objective 2		Objective 5b		O2 and 5b	New O2
	Pop (millions)	% pop	Pop (millions)	% pop	total (%)	min (%)
Belgium	1.4	14.0	0.448	4.5	18.5	12.3
Denmark	0.44	8.8	0.361	7.0	15.8	10.5
Germany	7	8.8	7.823	9.6	18.4	12.3
Greece	0	0	0	0	0	0
Spain	7.9	20.3	1.731	4.4	24.7	16.5
France	14.6	25.9	9.759	17.3	43.2	28.8
Ireland	0	0	0	0	0	0
Italy	6.3	10.8	4.828	8.4	19.2	12.8
Luxembourg	0.13	34.2	0.03	7.4	41.6	27.7
Netherlands	2.6	17.3	0.8	5.4	22.7	15.1
Austria	0.637	8.2	2.276	28.9	37.1	24.7
Portugal	0	0	0	0	0	0
Finland	0.787	15.5	1.094	21.5	37.0	24.7
Sweden	0.965	11.0	0.757	8.6	19.6	13.1
UK	17.7	31.0	2.841	4.9	35.9	23.9
EU-15	60.459	16.4	32.748	8.8		16.9

Source: EPRC calculations from Commission data reproduced in CEC (1996) *Structural Funds and Cohesion Fund – Regulations and commentary*, OOPEC, Luxembourg.

In Table 9, EPRC calculations of population coverage for Objective 2 are set alongside the Art. 92(3)(c) ceilings given to Member States. Clearly, much of what is being discussed here is subject to revision. This has already been mentioned in the context of the scope for revised population ceiling under the guidelines on National Regional Aid, but is also true of Structural Fund area designation, which will use more up-to-date figures than those that are currently available.

Nevertheless, it is evident that the Commission faces serious problems in achieving coherence, and ones which are not likely to be eased by more recent data. Part of the problem is the fact that, for some Member States, the proportion of the population meeting the hard criteria for Objective 2 is higher, sometimes considerably higher, than the Objective 2 "safety net". This is the case for France and Finland where the areas apparently eligible for Objective 2 have been impacted by high levels of employment. More basically, in Sweden and the Netherlands, the two-thirds safety net for Objective 2 is simply higher than the Art. 92(3)(c) population ceiling.

Table 9: Article 92(3)(c) and Objective 2 Coverage Compared

	Revised O2 (% population)	Art. 92(3)(c) (% population)
Belgium	12.30	35.2
Denmark	10.50	19.2
Germany	12.30	18.3
Greece	0.00	0.0
Spain	30.20	22.9
France	40.60	35.2
Ireland	46.08	100.0
Italy	12.80	10.4
Luxembourg	27.70	32.0
Netherlands	15.10	15.0
Austria	24.70	27.1
Portugal	4.60	33.4
Finland	59.88	34.4
Sweden	17.03	15.6
UK	23.90	26.3
EC-15	21.49	22.9

Source: Table 2, above, and own calculations based on Eurostat data and the draft Structural Fund Regulation.

6. Conclusions

This Chapter has outlined the context for the area designation exercises which all of the Member States face over the coming year or so. The framework for this review of regional policy targeting is radically different from the past and presents a significant challenge to Member States, not only with respect to the schedule for change, but also in terms of the substantive reforms to area designation practices implied by the guidelines. Against this background, a number of issues of concern arise.

(i) Population coverage has become the principal measure of regional aid discipline but it is employed in a largely arbitrary fashion. Ultimately, this may constrain national regional policies in ways not justified by competition concerns. Population coverage as a measure of regional aid discipline has become so embedded in the Commission's psyche that the underlying logic of its approach has ceased to be questioned: at best, it can be viewed as an arbitrary and indirect proxy for seeking to prevent distortions of competition through regional aid. The key problem with the emphasis on a Community-wide population ceiling is that it presupposes some relationship between the regional problems and policies of different countries. This is quite misguided because a deterioration in the economic conditions of a region in one Member State has, in general, no material impact on the economic conditions of regions in another Member State: it merely affects their relative prosperity. The relative prosperity of regions across Europe is only relevant if policy intervention is at the Community level, necessitating a prioritisation of areas for the targeting of funds. For competition policy purposes, it is the targeting of *national* resources which is at issue.

From a practical point of view, there are considerable short-term uncertainties about the final population coverage figure within which Member States must designate assisted areas. This is due to be notified to Member States by 1 January 1999, at the latest. In some cases these ceilings may change quite radically on the strength of one year's new data – Spain, for example, could lose a significant proportion of the national population from Art. 92(3)(a) – and yet the ceilings notified at the start of 1999 are set to apply until the end of the year 2006, some eight years later. Moreover, in the case of GDP data, that information will be a decade old by the time the assisted areas maps expire. Furthermore, population coverage will be determined for a period of seven years (timed to coincide with the Structural Funds planning period), which takes no account of the practical realities of the emergence of new regional problems. In practice, these are unlikely to be compensated for by an unexpected improvement in the fortunes of other regions, thereby justifying the exchange of assisted areas within the approved population ceiling.

Aside from concerns at the over-emphasis on population coverage, it is also curious that substantial reductions in assisted area coverage are being sought from the *current* membership in order to accommodate an enlargement that seems increasingly unlikely to take place on schedule.

(ii) The area designation methodology stipulated in the guidelines is at odds with past area designation traditions in every Member State and arguably contrary to the principle of subsidiarity. No Member State currently operates an area designation methodology which is readily accommodated within the terms of the new guidelines: most Member States are likely to find the task of producing *sensible* assisted area maps within the constraints of the guidelines to be a considerable challenge.

Some of the conditions imposed by the Commission have no stated justification – Portugal and the UK, for example, use more than the specified maximum of five indicators; no reasons are given as to why area designation on the basis of nine or 23 indicators should threaten to distort competition any more than designation on the basis of five.

Other elements are unclear: no definition of "combined indicators" is provided; the stipulations with respect to territorial units make no reference to aggregating up or to imputing data relating to a larger unit onto a smaller one – in most countries this is likely to prove necessary in order to generate a sufficient range of appropriate indicators; it is not apparent how the conditions related to minimum level of disparity are to be incorporated into the ranking.

Of particular importance in the context of past national policy practices, the Commission's methodology appears to allow no place for a *qualitative* appraisal of the outcomes of statistical analyses. Of the countries which use a detailed assessment of quantitative criteria to develop rankings, most notably Portugal, Germany and the UK, only in Portugal is that ranking used as the basis for area designation without further adjustment. Moreover, as already noted, Portugal can be regarded as a special case in this context: the resulting map does not dictate eligibility for regional aid and in any case the results produce a clear split within the country. In other countries with marked internal divides (notably Italy and Germany) statistical data alone would certainly reflect those disparities. However, in the context of finer distinctions or more complex regional problems, statistical analysis alone is inadequate to the task of assessing regional problems and targeting regional development. In this context it is odd that the methodology *does* allow scope for regions to be "exchanged" during the lifetime of the approved maps, while not allowing this flexibility at the outset.

Related, the methodology proposed by the Commission is essentially problem-centred and backward looking. There is no scope for policy maker analysis of whether instruments are best targeted at areas adjacent to those which show on the problem region analysis nor is there apparently any possibility of taking account of likely future developments.

Of key concern, the Commission's methodology presupposes that regional policy is essentially a national level responsibility. As already discussed, the *Land* level input which currently takes place after the initial ranking of regions is an explicit recognition of the fact that regional policy in Germany is a *shared* responsibility. In Belgium, however, the situation is quite different. The legal basis for regional policy lies in framework legislation passed prior to decentralisation, but this is very much of an outline nature and responsibility for all practical aspects of policy design, implementation and funding lies at the regional level. Moreover, since the mid-1980s, regional development policies in Flanders and Wallonia have diverged considerably. In this context, the imposition of a *national* population ceiling and a single methodology and ranking of regions would appear to undermine any plausible interpretation of the principle of subsidiarity.

(iii) The difficulties of achieving coherence between national and Community assisted areas are not solely arithmetical, rather they reflect a failure to define policy objectives and policy responsibilities at the different institutional levels. The Commission's proposals with respect to the coherence of assisted areas are the product of history, institutional rivalry and a flawed notion of policy coherence. The starting points and internal rationale for national and Community regional policies are quite distinct, and yet DGXVI has consistently sought so-called policy coherence through coterminosity of maps.

The dispute between DGIV and DGXVI over the coverage and coincidence of the national and EC maps has been documented elsewhere. On balance, DGIV came off worst in what was essentially a triangular dispute. The hasty compromise early in the 1989-93 Community Support Frameworks effectively suspended DGIV reviews of national assisted area maps until the end of 1993. By this time, the new Structural Fund maps had been devised with a significant role accorded to *national* priorities, policies and indicators. Moreover, the political commitment to achieving coherence made it difficult for DGIV to question the eligibility of areas under national regional policy if they had already been designated for the Structural Funds. This arguably led to a weakening of DGIV's position during the current Structural Funds planning period.

The provisions in the new guidelines suggest that DGIV may be regaining the upper hand. Certainly in terms of timing, the adoption of the guidelines *in advance* of the proposed Structural Funds Regulation suggests that DGIV has stolen a march on DGXVI, and to some extent tied the hands of Community regional policy makers with respect to the conditions attached to coherence. It may be that, through judicious use of the Structural Funds derogation contained in the aid guidelines, Member States can gain increased flexibility in national area designation. However, the prospects for "coherence", in DGXVI's terms, are not bright.

The discussion above suggests that the achievement of so-called "coherent" maps across the Community is an arithmetical impossibility. The impact of precedent, reflected in the application of floors and ceilings to coverage and of eligibility being determined on the basis of widely varying criteria mitigate against likelihood of coterminosity. At the same time, it is surely no accident that the provisions with respect to coherence are contained in a Commission Communication, which does not bind the Member States, and in the preamble to the Structural Funds Regulation, rather than in the body of the text. In any case, it is part of the curious symmetry of European cohesion policies that while the Commission authorises *national* assisted areas in the name of competition policy, the Council of Ministers holds greater sway in determining the coverage of *Community* regional policy.

In reality, it is highly questionable whether coterminous maps have much to do with *policy* coherence. A notable feature of recent developments in Community and competition and regional policy alike is the failure to address the appropriate articulation of regional policies at the different institutional levels. Agreement on the *objectives* of Community regional policy, and the relative responsibilities of the national and Community levels, would resolve coterminosity debate.

NOTES

1. OJ 1998 C 74, 10 March; see Wishlade, F. (1998) *Competition Policy or Cohesion Policy by the Back Door? The Commission Guidelines on National Regional Aid*, European Competition Law Review, 6, Sweet & Maxwell, for an initial analysis of the new Guidelines.
2. OJ 1998 C 107, 7 April.
3. See Evans, A. (1997) *European Community Law of State Aid*, Clarendon Press, Oxford for a full discussion.
4. See Yuill *et al* (1997) *European Regional Incentives 1997-8*, 17th edition, Bowker-Saur, London and Wishlade, F. (1998) "EC Competition Policy: the Poor Relation of EC Regional Policy?" *European Planning Studies* Vol 6, No. 5.
5. OJ 1988 C212, 12 August.
6. See European Commission (1995) Competition law in the European Communities, Volume IIA: Rules applicable to state aid, OOPEC, Luxembourg.
7. In practice, as can be seen with respect to regional aid values, the Commission often does not actually follow the terms of the Communication – see Wishlade, F. and Yuill, D. (1997) "Regional Incentive Policies in the European Union: Rates of Award and Award Values", *Regional and Industrial Research Paper Series*, 23, European Policies Research Centre, University of Strathclyde, Glasgow.
8. Rawlinson, F. (1993) "The Role of Policy Frameworks, Codes and Guidelines in the Control of State Aid" in Harden, I. (ed.) *State Aid: Community Law and Policy*, Trier Academy of European Law, Bundesanziger Verlasges MbH, Köln, Germany.
9. Council Regulation (EC) No 994/98 of 7 May 1998 on the application of Arts. 92 and 93 of the Treaty establishing the European Community to certain categories of horizontal state aid,OJ 1998 L 142, 15 May.
10. DGIV (1998) *Competition Policy Newsletter*, No. 1, February.
11. This ceiling of 42.7% is given in the Commission press release and in the draft Structural Fund Regulation, as well as in the letter to the Member States, but not in the Guidelines themselves.
12. NUTS refers to the Nomenclature of Territorial Units for Statistics established by Eurostat. Examples of NUTS III regions are the French *départements* and the Italian provinces; NUTS II regions are typically larger, for example, Autonomous Communities in Spain.
13. See Wishlade, F. (1998) "EC Competition Policy and Regional Aid for Large Investment Projects: the Other Half of the Pincer Movement", *Regions: the Newsletter of the Regional Studies Association*, No. 217, October.
14. Case 248/84 *Federal Republic of Germany* v *Commission of the European Communities* [1987] ECR 4013 at 4042.
15. Art. 92(3)(a) does not appear to afford the Commission the discretion to do this.
16. The Commission is due to notify the Member States of revised ceilings before the end of 1998, based on 1994-6 GDP data.

17. See Wishlade (1998) *op cit* at Footnote 2 for full details.
18. As noted earlier, it should be stressed that these figures are subject to change following the publication of GDP data for the period 1994-6; new assisted area coverage ceilings are due to be notified to the Member States by the end of 1998.
19. See Wishlade, F. Yuill, D., Davezies, L. and Prud'homme, R. (forthcoming) "Agenda 2000 and the Targeting of EU Cohesion Policy" in *Regional Information Serving Regional Policy in Europe,* Eurostat, OOPEC, Luxembourg for an extended discussion of the drawbacks of using GDP per head at the regional level as a regional development indicator.
20. See Yuill, D. Bachtler, J. and Wishlade, F. (1997) *European Regional Incentives 1997-98,* 17th edition, Bowker-Saur, London and Wishlade, F. and Yuill, D. (1997) "Measuring Disparities for Area Designation Purposes: Issues for the European Union", *Regional and Industrial Research Paper Series,* 24, European Policies Research Centre, University of Strathclyde, Glasgow.
21. See Wishlade, F (1993) "Competition Policy, Cohesion and the Coordination of Regional Aids in the European Community", *European Competition Law Review,* Vol 14, no. 4.
22. CEC (1996), *First Report on Economic and Social Cohesion 1996,* OOPEC, Luxembourg at page 127.
23. CEC (1997) Agenda 2000: For a Stronger and Wider Union COM (97) 2000 final, 15 July 1997, Brussels.
24. *Commission Proposal for a Council Regulation (EC) laying down general provisions on the Structural Funds,* OJ 1998 C 176, 9 June.
25. CEC (1998) *Communication from the Commission to the Member States on the links between regional and competition policy: Reinforcing Concentration and Mutual Consistency,* OJ 1998 C 90, 26 March.
26. In practice, it is possible that GDP per head for the Canaries will fall below the threshold when the 1996 data is issued.
27. Art. 4(2) of the draft Structural Funds Regulation
28. Paragraph 14.

PART III:

FUTURE DEVELOPMENTS

CHAPTER 11

STATE AID PROCEDURES: THE REFORM PROJECT

Adinda Sinnaeve *

1. The Commission's objectives for the future

The growing importance of state aid control, the increasing number of cases dealt with every year, and the prospects of another enlargement led in the middle of the 1990s to a reflection within the Commission on the future of state aid control. After almost 40 years of state aid policy, the question arose whether the procedures, as they had developed over the years on the basis of Art. 93, were still satisfactory within the considerably changed context. On the whole, the Commission's position was that the current system had proved its worth and had functioned in a satisfactory way. However, it left room for improvement in several areas. No revolution was thus needed, but an adaptation to the modified circumstances in which state aid control operates was.

A first objective of the modernisation exercise – which was launched in 1996 and is still ongoing – has consequently been to increase the efficiency of state aid control. Efficiency is to be understood in two senses. On the one hand, the control system should guarantee the effective application and enforcement of the rules on state aid. Where aspects of the existing system could be considered as hampering its proper functioning, reform proposals have had to be made. This is the case, for instance, with regard to the problem of non-notified aid, recovery of aid and the monitoring of Commission decisions. On the other hand, efficiency is also linked to the way resources are used. Therefore, in a situation of scarce resources and an increasing workload, the optimal allocation of resources may require a review of the existing procedures in certain cases, and a clearer focusing on priorities. In practice, the Commission examined whether there was room for a simplification of procedures within an effective control system and for which

S. Bilal and P. Nicolaides (eds.), Understanding State Aid Policy in the European Community, 209–230.
© 1999 *Kluwer Law International. Printed in the Netherlands.*

cases this would be appropriate.

Improving transparency and legal certainty is the other main goal of the reform process. During the last 10-15 years, considerable efforts have already been made to clarify state aid policy. The results of this continuing process are the frameworks and guidelines which have made the assessment criteria of the Commission more transparent and its decisions thereby predictable. Meanwhile, a growing need has also arisen for more transparency with regard to the procedural aspects of state aid control. Various interest groups have sought a codification of procedures which would provide legal certainty.

The importance of those two objectives has been reinforced by the prospects of enlargement. Given the particular situation of the enlargement candidates, the impact of the enlargement process on state aid policy is obvious. It will considerably increase the workload of the Commission's state aid services while, at the same time, no significant additional resources can be expected. It therefore seemed appropriate to streamline and simplify the procedures ahead of the next enlargement. In addition, a codification of the procedural rules would facilitate the Central and Eastern European countries' task of aligning their legislation with Community law.

2. Article 94: the appropriate instrument to realise the objectives

It appears from an examination of the Commission's objectives that only Art. 94 provides the means to achieve them. The current practice of notices and communications[1] is useful to clarify the Commission's interpretation of important procedural issues, but it cannot provide the required legal certainty. Moreover, the envisaged simplification of the procedural rules in the form of exemptions would have automatically conflicted with Art. 93(3) and could therefore only be introduced by a regulation pursuant to Art. 94.

Art. 94 states that "The Council, acting by a qualified majority on a proposal from the Commission and after consulting the European Parliament, may make any appropriate regulations for the application of Articles 92 and 93 and may in particular determine the conditions in which Article 93(3) shall apply and the categories of aid exempted from this procedure".[2]

Although this article seemed to be the perfect legal basis to implement the Commission's objectives, it was not obvious that the Commission would use it. Attempts at using it in the past had not been successful[3] and had left the Commission with a profound scepticism about the expediency of making proposals on the basis of Art. 94.[4] There was indeed a risk that once a proposal was submitted to the Council it would be out of the Commission's control, and the very wide powers which the Treaty conferred upon the Commission would be reduced.

However, the circumstances and the general environment had changed since the first proposals were made at the end of the 1960s. The Commission, supported by the Court, had meanwhile fully established its state aid policy and felt more confident about the general acceptance of its powers by Member States. If the reform projects were to be carried out, there had to be recourse to Art. 94. However, the decisive factor finally came from an unexpected side. It was the Court of First Instance with the *Sytraval* judgement[5] which removed any remaining reticence within the Commission. The Court held in this case that the obligation for the Commission to motivate its decisions could require an exchange of views and arguments with complainants. It also considered that a letter sent from the Commission to a complainant should be taken as a decision: the Commission had always maintained that state aid decisions were addressed to the Member State concerned. The far-reaching consequences which this judgement could have are obvious. The obligation to enter into a an exchange of views and arguments with a complainant during the preliminary examination would not only transform this phase into a formal investigation, but also put an end to the bilateral character of state aid procedures. It would fall not far short of granting rights, such as hearings and access to the file, to third parties. The threat of such a fundamental change in state aid procedures gave a direct impulse to the Commission's plans for Art. 94. Rather than waiting until the Courts changed the procedural framework, the Commission decided to take the initiative itself.

At the Industry Council of 14 November 1996, under the Irish Presidency, the Commission presented its plans to use Art. 94 for the reform of state aid control. The Council welcomed the initiative and encouraged the Commission to submit proposals. The Commission responded with two proposals: one made in 1997 concerning the possibility of group exemptions for certain types of aid (see Section 3), and one for a procedural regulation (see Section 4) made in 1998. The former proposal has been adopted in May 1998, the latter is expected to be adopted by the Council in the beginning of 1999, after the European Parliament has given its opinion.

3. The "Enabling" Regulation

3.1 BACKGROUND AND PURPOSE OF THE REGULATION

On 15 July 1997, the Commission adopted a proposal for a so-called "enabling" regulation[6] and adopted the Regulation itself on 7 May 1998.[7] This empowers the Commission to exempt, by means of group exemption regulations, certain categories of aid from the obligation to notify. For the exempted aid, a system of *ex post* monitoring replaces the existing requirement for prior approval by the Commission. The Enabling Regulation thus provides the legal basis for the different group exemption regulations which are now in preparation to be adopted by the Commission.[8]

The background of the proposal was the realisation that a considerable part of the Commission's work consists of "routine" cases. From the time the Commission started to develop frameworks and guidelines laying down concrete criteria for the assessment of the compatibility of aid, it has received a large number of notifications that are obviously compatible with the common market because they strictly respect the criteria established by the Commission. In a situation where the criteria are known in advance, it is logical that Member States should draft aid schemes which are in line with the rules. Therefore, for such schemes, the Commission needs only to confirm that the criteria set out in the relevant framework are fulfilled: consequently the added value of a Commission decision is very limited. However, in terms of workload, these less significant cases have a substantial impact on the Commission's resources and hinder it from concentrating on the larger, most complex and most distortive cases.

This is why a simplification of procedures is appropriate for those areas where the Commission has reached a level of experience which allows it to define precise, compatible criteria, and where it can be observed that Member States generally respect the published criteria, as is the case for most of the frameworks and guidelines dealing with horizontal aid.

A further important advantage of this procedural simplification lies in the increased transparency. When group exemptions come into existence they will define clear conditions of compatibility in directly applicable regulations and thus improve the possibility of state aid control at national level.

The Enabling Regulation was adopted in a surprisingly short time.[9] This can be explained on the one hand by the fact that it did not change the substance of state aid control, but only the procedure. The definition by the Commission of the material criteria of compatibility will basically not be different from now, whether they are laid down in guidelines or in future group exemption regulations. On the other hand, the procedural change has a clear advantage for both parties. The Commission will be liberated from a number of routine cases, while retaining all its powers to decide on the conditions of compatibility and to control aid. For the Member States, such group exemptions will simplify the administrative burden of notification and allow the immediate award of the aid concerned without a standstill period. The only fear among certain Member States during the discussion on the Enabling Regulation was that the Commission might loosen or weaken the control of state aid. For this reason, it was necessary to provide an effective system of monitoring.

3.2 THE MECHANISM OF GROUP EXEMPTIONS

The categories of aid for which group exemptions are envisaged concern: aid for SMEs, R&D, environmental protection, employment and training, and regional aid.[10] Each group exemption regulation must be defined by means of different parameters. The mandatory conditions that must be attached to a group exemption relate to:
- the admissible purposes of the aid;
- the categories of beneficiaries;
- the admissible thresholds expressed either in terms of aid intensities in relation to a set of eligible costs or in terms of maximum amounts;
- the conditions concerning the cumulation of aid;
- the conditions of monitoring.

In addition, the Commission is allowed to define other conditions in order to ensure the compatibility of aid exempted under a group exemption, in particular to set thresholds for the notification of individual awards of aid or to exclude certain sectors from the scope of the application of a regulation. It appears from the parameters listed above that the approach and contents of the group exemptions will follow the lines of existing practice and mainly translate the criteria of the guidelines and frameworks into another legal form. However, it should be noted that after the adoption of a group exemption, the corresponding guidelines and frameworks will not disappear. Aid which is not covered by the group exemption[11] will not automatically be forbidden but will still have to be notified, as under the current system.[12] The frameworks and guidelines which set out the Commission's position and general approach towards such aid therefore need to be maintained.

The Regulation also enables the Commission to fix a *de minimis* threshold below which aid does not fall under the notification obligation (Art. 2). The reason why this article is included in the Enabling Regulation is mainly to provide a clear legal basis for the *de minimis* rule, because although it already exists[13] uncertainty has risen about its legal basis.[14] Art. 2 makes it clear that the Commission is allowed to decide *ex ante* the threshold below which it considers that the conditions of Art. 92(1) are not fulfilled.

In fact, as the *de minimis* rule is formulated, it does not constitute a real exemption but only clarifies the scope of Art. 92(1). *De minimis* aid is described as aid which does not fulfil all the conditions of Art. 92(1). In practice this means that the aid does not affect intra-Community trade and/ or does not distort or threaten to distort competition. Therefore, it does not have to be notified. As the wording of Art. 2 (therefore) suggests, it is based on the idea that only aid within the meaning of Art. 92(1) is notifiable pursuant to Art. 93(3). This is a change in the position of the Commission, which had always previously considered the scope of Art. 93(3) to be wider than the scope of Art. 92(1). In any case, if notifiable aid is identical to aid fulfilling the conditions of Art. 92(1), and if *de minimis* aid by definition does not fulfil all those conditions, the outcome of this syllogistical argument can only be that the *de minimis* rule does not constitute an exemption to the notification obligation. As to its contents, it may be expected that a future regulation on *de minimis* will not differ very much from the existing rule.

3.3 TRANSPARENCY AND MONITORING MECHANISMS

The main difficulty with a system of group exemptions in the field of state aid is ensuring adequate monitoring. The right balance has to be found between the objective of simplification and the need to make sure that the control of state aid is not watered down. Having regard to the different control safeguards built into the system, it seems that this balance will be achieved.

Firstly, the provisions on transparency and monitoring ensure that the Commission will have full knowledge of the way Member States apply the group exemptions. When implementing exempted aid schemes or exempted individual aid outside any scheme, Member States will forward a summary (like the so-called *cartouches*) to the Commission, with a view to publication in the Official Journal of the EC.[15] In addition, they will be required to record and compile all information on the exempted aid. If the Commission has doubts about the correct application of a group exemption, for instance following a complaint, it will be able to ask the Member State concerned to provide all the information necessary to verify compliance with the exemption. Finally, Member States have to supply the Commission with annual reports on the application of the group exemptions. Those reports will also be made accessible to other Member States and be the subject of a debate in the advisory committee set up under the Regulation.[16]

Secondly, the possibilities of control at national level are significantly improved by the Regulation. Group exemptions will lay down precise and transparent criteria, and will have direct effect. As a consequence, enterprises and third parties will be able to check more easily whether the rules are being complied with. If they suspect that aid granted without notification does not fulfil the conditions for exemption,[17] they may complain to the Commission or to national Courts.

As far as the increase in transparency is concerned, it should finally be mentioned that the Commission will hear all the interested parties at the drafting stage of a group exemption. Art. 6 states that where the Commission intends to adopt such a regulation, it shall publish a draft to enable interested parties to submit their comments. Compared with the procedure to adopt frameworks and guidelines, the possibilities for third parties to express their views on legislation being envisaged are thus considerably improved.

4. The Procedural Regulation[18]

4.1 PURPOSE OF THE PROPOSAL FOR A PROCEDURAL REGULATION

The proposal for a procedural regulation (adopted by the Commission on 18 February 1998,)[19] was the second step in the Commission's initiative under Art. 94. It aimed to improve transparency and legal certainty in state aid procedures by bringing the procedural rules together in one coherent and binding legal text. At present, Art. 93 of the Treaty is the only legal provision on procedures. However, on the basis of this article, a set of rules has been developed through the Commission's practice and the case law of the Court of Justice. Where important procedural issues have arisen or been clarified, the Commission has issued notices and communications, which are normally published in the Official Journal. Legally speaking, these notices have contained no more than an interpretation of certain procedural questions by the Commission and have not provided any legal certainty.[20] Moreover, the piecemeal fashion in which procedures have developed has resulted in a fragmentation of rules, which has reduced the clarity of the system provided for in the Treaty. While aiming to make the rules transparent, the multiplication of texts has actually created less transparency (paradox of less transparency by more transparency). The integration of the procedural rules into one coherent text was thus required.[21]

The second and equally important objective of the proposal for a procedural regulation was to reinforce the efficiency of state aid control. The Commission's long-standing experience had revealed some weak points in the system, in particular with regard to unlawful aid and its recovery. In order to provide the Commission with all the necessary means to ensure effective control, the proposal seeks to enlarge the control system with some new instruments and to tighten the rules on those points where the current system is unsatisfactory.

4.2 CURRENT STATUS OF THE REGULATION

The Commission's proposal was forwarded to the Council on 27 February 1998 and discussed in the Council under the British and Austrian presidencies. The Industry Council first debated it on 7 May 1998, and on 16 November 1998 reached a political agreement on the Regulation. Its formal adoption will be able to take place as soon as the European Parliament gives its opinion, which is expected to be at the beginning of 1999.[22] The Regulation will then enter into force on the 20th day following its publication in the Official Journal.[23]

4.3   CONTENTS OF THE REGULATION[24]

4.3.1   Definitions. The Regulation starts with a chapter on definitions. The most important notions used in the state aid field are defined, as far as they have consequences on the applicable procedures, e.g. existing aid vis-à-vis new aid, and aid schemes vis-à-vis individual aid, unlawful aid, misuse of aid, etc. Those notions have been used for a long time, but except for some interpretative clarifications by the Court, they had never been properly defined.

A material definition of "aid", however, has not been included: the proposal refers only to the criteria of Art. 92(1). This can partly be explained by the difficulty of defining this wide notion in an exhaustive way and the risk that every definition would soon prove to be incomplete. State aid is an evolving concept, gradually developing with the evolution of the common market, and it therefore needs certain flexibility. The concrete filling in of the criteria of Art. 92(1) will continue to be an on-going task of the Commission under the supervision of the Court.

4.3.2   Four different procedures: notified aid, unlawful aid, misuse of aid and existing aid. Chapters II to V lay down the procedural rules for examining state aid and build the main part of the Regulation. Depending on the procedural qualification of the aid (notified, unlawful, misused, existing), a different chapter applies. To a large extent the procedures set out in the Regulation are codifying the *acquis* as it has been developed by the Commission and the Court. The following part will concentrate on the modifications to the present system.

Notified aid: First of all, Arts. 2 and 3 confirm the cornerstones of the system provided for in Art. 93: the notification requirement and the standstill clause. It is important to note that the obligation to notify is explicitly limited to "plans to grant new aid" instead of covering all measures which could possibly constitute aid, as the Commission has insisted in the past.[25] This change in the Commission's position was already indicated by the Enabling Regulation,[26] but is now confirmed. Only aid fulfilling all the criteria of Art. 92(1) will have to be notified pursuant to Art. 93(3), both articles having the same scope. Of course, in case of doubts with regard to the aid character of a measure, it is advisable to notify for reasons of legal certainty, especially in view of risk to the beneficiary of aid being recovered. But it is up to the Member State to decide whether to take this risk or not.

The theory, currently followed, that aid under Art. 93(3) is identical to aid under Art. 92(1) seems indeed more logical from a practical point of view. If the Regulation extended the scope of the notification obligation to all potential aid, this would have disproportionate consequences, in particular with regard to the jurisprudence of the Court. According to the Court,[27] national Courts have to draw all the consequences of an infringement of Art. 93(3). If necessary, they may have to order the suspension and recovery of the aid or take other interim measures. This can be an efficient system as far as unlawful aid is concerned, but it would not be justifiable with regard to measures which could merely *possibly* constitute state aid. Besides, an obligation to notify all measures where state aid cannot be excluded would hardly have been compatible with the Commission's objectives of greater efficiency and concentration of the resources in the most important cases.

With regard to the procedure for notified aid, only a few modifications compared to the present system need mentioning. The Regulation confirms that the preliminary examination must be concluded within two months (*Lorenz*), but it adds that the Member State may only put the aid into effect after giving prior notice to the Commission. Having given notice the Member State can implement the measures concerned unless the Commission reacts within 15 days from the receipt of the notice. From the wording of the *Lorenz* judgement, it had not been clear whether the Commission still had such an additional period at its disposal, when receiving notice that the Member State intended to implement the proposed measure. The Commission had always understood the word "prior" to imply that it may still take a decision to open the procedure within a reasonably short period,[28] but this interpretation was not generally accepted.[29] The proposed 15 days may be needed to avoid distortive aid inadvertently becoming authorised simply because of a breakdown in communication between the Commission and the Member State concerned (e.g. where a request for additional information is not received). For such exceptional cases, it seems justified that the Commission is provided with an opportunity to rectify the situation, since the consequences of a "*Lorenz*" decision are very serious (implicit approval to put into effect possibly incompatible aid and the possible liability of the Commission vis-à-vis competitors, etc.).

In order to speed up decisions, the proposal provides that a notification will be considered to be withdrawn if, after a reminder, the Member State concerned still does not reply to a request for further information. Although it is in the interest of the Member State concerned to complete its notification as soon as possible, quite frequently no reaction to the Commission's supplementary questions is received. The Commission could in such circumstances just wait until the Member State replies, since the standstill clause applies anyhow, but for the purpose of good administration a disincentive to prevent Member States from dragging out the procedure is useful. The consequence of withdrawal is mitigated by the possibility of the Commission extending the period within which Member States should provide the requested information, and by the right of the Member State to ask for a decision if this information is not available or has already been provided, so that the notification should be considered to be complete. The latter possibility for Member States constitutes an important procedural innovation and may become one of the most efficient instruments at their disposal to reduce the duration of the preliminary stage. In future, the Commission will no longer be able to restart the two-month deadline by successive requests for additional information. Member States will stop these – sometimes frivolous – supplementary questions and ask for a decision. Although this may avoid abuses of the system by the Commission, it seems to open the door for more abuses from the other side, since the risk exists that Member States will make incomplete notifications and then say that the additional information requested by the Commission is not available. Moreover, the present wording of the text suggests that in practice it will now often be the Member State which decides when a notification is complete.[30] If the Commission disagrees (e.g. because the Member State has not sufficiently explained why the information is unavailable), it seems that the procedure is deadlocked[31] and that the Court of Justice will finally have to decide.

The Commission's proposal did not contain a time-limit for the formal examination procedure. This could not only be explained by the practical problems such a deadline would bring for the Commission's already understaffed services, but also by the difficulty in establishing an appropriate time-limit, taking account of factors such as differences in the complexity of cases, new questions which may arise following comments from third parties, possible modifications of the original notification in the course of negotiations, etc. Moreover, a question had arisen as to what the legal consequence of the expiry of a time-limit would be. A tacit approval would be more difficult to justify than at the preliminary stage, because the opening of the procedure and the expiry of the time-limit indicate that serious doubts about the compatibility of the aid exist. However, since the acceleration of procedures was one of the main demands of Member States, a compromise had to be found. Negotiations in the Council led to an agreement on a time-limit of 18 months from the opening of the procedure. Once this time-limit has expired, and should the Member State so request, the Commission will have to take a decision within two months. It follows that the total time available for the Commission will still be almost two years at least.[32] In terms of efficiency, this time-limit will thus not be an important improvement, since it will hardly accelerate the decision-making process. On the contrary, two years risks becoming the rule instead of an absolute maximum. Moreover, not respecting the time-limit for the formal investigation procedure does not result in an implicit approval of the aid, as in the preliminary stage, so its effects are limited. Its main function will probably be to prevent the

Commission from leaving certain complex or sensitive cases undecided for several years.

Unlawful aid: Where Member States have infringed the rules of prior notification and standstill, the procedure basically follows the same pattern as for notified aid but it is completed with several additional instruments, which are mainly based on the case law of the Court.

The Regulation codifies the different kinds of injunctions which the Commission has at its disposal during the examination of the compatibility of unlawful aid, including the recovery injunction. This will put an end to the legal debate on the legal competence of the Commission to order such an interim recovery.[33] The recovery injunction as it was foreseen by the Commission's proposal could have become a useful deterrent against unlawful aid. It was also meant to be an important tool for the protection of competitors, because it would have allowed the Commission to act immediately against illegally granted aid, in particular in cases where its complementary part, the suspension injunction, cannot be used.[34] However, the Council, though accepting the principle of a recovery injunction, has made its use by the Commission much more difficult by adding three conditions. According to the final text of the Regulation, a provisional recovery injunction requires that (1) there are no doubts that the measure concerned constitutes state aid; (2) there is urgency; and (3) there is a serious risk of substantial and irreparable damage to a competitor. These conditions come close to the classical criteria for interim relief[35] and could in practice considerably limit the scope of application of the recovery injunction. Besides, it also remains doubtful whether a Member State which does not respect Art. 93(3) will immediately comply with a recovery injunction and whether this instrument, under these conditions, will have any deterrent effect at all.

Since final recovery is the only way to restore an unjustified distortion of competition, the article on recovery has a central place in the Regulation. Art. 14 reinforces the Commission's present practice of systematically asking for the recovery of incompatible unlawful aid by placing an *obligation* on the Commission to do so. This transformation of a possibility into an obligation follows logically from the objective of the Commission's control to ensure undistorted competition. In fact, one could ask if the Commission is not already obliged under the present system to order recovery. By failing to do so in a particular case and not in others, the Commission would not only create an unjustified inequality of treatment between beneficiaries but also fall short of its own task of safeguarding fair competition. An obligation is thus necessary.

What is even more important, however, is the effective execution of recovery decisions. Experience has shown that the present situation regarding compliance with recovery decisions is far from satisfactory. Nearly 10% of the recovery decisions are not executed 10 years after they were taken, in the majority of cases because of pending procedures before national courts. It is clear that such delays make the restoration of competition practically impossible and diminish the effectiveness and credibility of competition policy. If the Regulation is to attain a more effective control of state aid it has to remedy this situation.

The solution to the recovery problems was not evident, however. Following established Court case law, recovery has to take place in accordance with the relevant procedural provisions of the national law in the Member State concerned. Apart from the fact that Art. 94 would not be a proper legal basis for a harmonisation of these procedures, such a harmonisation would be practically impossible because of the different fields of law involved in granting and recovering state aid.[36] Those differences in the applicable procedures should not necessarily be incompatible with effective recovery, especially since the Court has consistently ruled that national provisions are only applicable as long as they do not render recovery practically impossible. With the strict interpretation of the Court, which put aside all the elements of national law that prevented recovery,[37] the present system should normally already ensure that recovery always takes place except in cases of bankruptcy, which can be considered to have the same effect on the market as a reimbursement with regard to the competitive situation. Therefore, to ensure the final result of recovery, the Regulation has only to confirm the jurisprudence of the Court.

However, the actual question is not so much whether the aid will be reimbursed or not, but when it will be reimbursed. Delays in the execution of recovery decisions can be such as to make recovery impossible, because the distortion of competition gradually becomes more irreparable. Such delays are mainly due to the suspensive effect of proceedings which the beneficiary can start under national law against the recovery order of the Member State. There appear to be significant differences between Member States in this regard, so that there is an inequality of treatment between beneficiaries. This is why the proposal of the Commission stated that national procedures should only apply "provided that they allow the *immediate* and effective execution of the Commission's decision" and that "remedies under national law shall not have suspensive effect". This last sentence has disappeared from the final text agreed upon by the Council, mainly because it was considered as a harmonisation provision, for which Art. 94 is not a sufficient legal basis.[38] Surprisingly, the much more important previous sentence, stating that national law should not prevent the immediate execution of the Commission's decision, has remained. The real innovation is to be found there, since on the basis of that clause the Commission can act against delaying procedures in

Member States, including the suspensive effect of certain remedies used by beneficiaries. There is a good chance that the Court of Justice, when confronted with the matter in future, will decide that provisions granting suspensive effect should be disregarded by national judges, as they do not allow for the immediate execution of the Commission's decision and thus infringe the Regulation. In this way, the Commission is likely in the end to achieve the result envisaged by its proposal, so that the consequences of the deletion of the sentence on the absence of suspensive effect are limited.[39] Besides, a new sentence has been included in the Regulation, which reinforces the obligation of Member States to do everything possible in order to obtain immediate reimbursement.

Finally it is worth mentioning that the Council introduced a limitation period for the recovery of aid. After a period of 10 years from the award of the aid, the Commission can no longer ask for recovery. Although at first sight, this provision could be seen to be reducing the Commission's powers, its practical effect should not be overestimated. Cases of unlawful aid of which the Commission has no knowledge (through complaints, press, etc.) for more than 10 years, are not only rare, but can hardly be very distortive. In addition, any action of the Commission with regard to the measure (e.g. a request for information) makes the 10-year period start running afresh. It should also be noticed that the limitation period constitutes a kind of complement to the rule that the Commission is obliged to order the recovery of all unlawful aid which is incompatible with the common market. A limitation period avoids disproportionate consequences of this strict rule introduced by the Regulation.[40] On the whole, it seems that for the few cases where the limitation period may apply this seems justified.

Misuse of aid: Although the misuse of aid may have similar effects on competition as unlawful aid, the procedures are only partly the same for legal reasons. The main difference is that in cases of possible misuse, the aid concerned has been previously approved by the Commission, while unlawful aid does not come under any decision. It follows from Art. 93(2) that aid which has possibly been misused has to be treated as lawful until the Commission concludes the formal investigation procedure with a final decision on the misuse. During the examination the standstill clause does not apply and no provisional recovery should be ordered.

In practice the difference between unlawful aid and misuse is not always easy to make and no consistent practice of the Commission exists in this regard. In order to make a clearer distinction, the Council refined the definition of misuse, limiting it to an infringement by the beneficiary of the aid, while in cases of unlawful aid, the Member State is responsible.

4.3.3 Monitoring. An efficient state aid control system would not be complete without the necessary means to monitor compliance with Commission decisions. The Commission's proposal contained three instruments to reinforce the Commission's ability to do this, two of which were accepted by the Council.

Firstly, a general reporting obligation on all existing aid schemes should allow the Commission to obtain all the information necessary to monitor existing aid schemes according to Art. 93(1).[41] The annual reports required are also an important source of information on pre-accession aid schemes which would otherwise perhaps remain unknown to the Commission.

Secondly, the proposal foresees the possibility of on-site monitoring visits to the beneficiary in cases where serious doubts about compliance with certain decisions exist. On-site monitoring has already been practised in the shipbuilding sector and in certain cases in the car sector on a voluntary basis. It is mainly useful in cases where the Commission has no other way of checking whether imposed conditions (e.g. capacity reductions) have been respected. Whereas the original Commission proposal only foresaw on-the-spot visits for checking the respect of conditional decisions, the scope of the article was widened during the Council negotiations to all decisions authorising aid. The Commission's power to make on-site inspections is certainly one of the main new instruments provided by the Regulation to strengthen state aid control.

The third instrument, a cooperation procedure with national independent supervisory bodies, would have been completely new in state aid control. The Commission proposed that Member States designate an independent body, such as the competition authority or the Court of Auditors, which the Commission could ask to provide a report when it had doubts about compliance with certain decisions. Such national bodies may be better placed than the Commission to obtain certain information and could get a role in the monitoring of state aid through this procedure. However, the Council did not approve this innovative cooperation system and it was deleted from the Regulation.

4.3.4 Third party rights. With regard to the issue of third party rights, the Regulation may not have come up to the legal profession's expectations.[42] It chose not to create specific new rights and in particular not to give complainants a status similar to the one they enjoy in Art. 85 and 86 cases (access to the file, etc.).

In the Commission's view the absence of additional rights for third parties is not a gap but is a logical consequence of the system laid down in Art. 93. The main feature of state aid procedures is their bilateral character as they are based upon a dialogue between the Commission and the Member State concerned. The aid projects which Member States present are not aimed at third parties and do not have intended and targeted effects on other market participants in the way that restrictive practices or dominant positions often do. It follows that the role of third parties in the state aid field is also different. They are mainly a source of information for the Commission where the latter is not in a position to establish the compatibility of aid. In such cases the Commission is obliged to open a formal investigation. This is where third parties can first be involved by submitting comments in order to help the Commission obtain all the information necessary for the assessment of compatibility. Recent judgements[43] of the Courts confirmed that the role of third parties in state aid procedures is limited to the formal examination phase of the procedure. This – important – role of third parties, foreseen by the Treaty, has been codified in the Regulation.

Nevertheless, the question has been raised whether the Regulation should not have gone further. Even if the Treaty does not foresee it, it does not exclude a more active role for third parties. Generally one could say that an extension of third part rights would have been advisable if there was a real need for it – the present protection of third parties being insufficient – or if it led to a more efficient system of state aid control. Neither of those conditions seems to be fulfilled.

Firstly, the present system already gives third parties the possibility of defending their interests at all stages of the procedure:

– Third parties may inform the Commission of any alleged unlawful aid or misuse of aid. According to the rules of good administrative practice the Commission should examine such information and reply to the party concerned.

– Where the Commission concludes its examination of the aid after only the preliminary phase with a decision not to raise objections, third parties can bring an action for the annulment of this decision in order to force the Commission to open a formal investigation in order to preserve their rights.

– In formal investigation procedures, third parties have the right to submit comments.

– Third parties may obtain a copy of any Commission decision on state aid which is not published.

– Third parties have the possibility of challenging state aid decisions which affect them under the conditions of Art. 173(4) of the Treaty.

It thus seems that sufficient protection of third party rights is already provided under the present system.

Secondly, one could also plead for more third party rights if it resulted (or were likely to result) in a more efficient control system. However, when looking at the alternatives to the status quo, this does not seem to be the case. The scenario most often requested by lawyers or enterprises would involve third parties during the preliminary examination. This system would necessarily imply the publication of all notifications as a way of informing third parties. This would be interpretted by third parties as an invitation to submit comments and, indeed, if that were not the objective the publication would serve no purpose. The possibility for third parties to intervene during the first phase would therefore result in an anticipation and duplication of the formal examination procedure, which would be contrary to the logic of the two-phase system as described above. Moreover, such additional publication would create practical difficulties in terms of resources and would make it impossible for the Commission to conclude the first phase within two months. It would thus also contradict the objective of speeding up decisions. It follows from an efficiency point of view that on balance such an extension of third party rights would not be favourable.

For these reasons – that is the absence of a direct need to enlarge third party rights and the lack of efficient alternative ways to increase their participation – the Regulation only codifies the status quo. The main difference between the Commission's proposal and the Regulation the Council agreed upon, is that for transparency reasons, the Council preferred to put the rights of third parties together in a separate title of the Regulation.[44] As to the substance, however, the Regulation does not change the present system, which grants certain rights to third parties, but within the context of a bilateral procedure.

4.3.5 Publication of decisions. The publication of decisions is probably the area where the conflicts between transparency and efficiency are most striking. It goes without saying that full publication of all decisions in all languages would be ideal from a transparency viewpoint. However, this option would seriously reduce the efficiency of the system.

The Commission took the view that under the present practice of publication, the balance was already somewhat weighed against efficiency. Until now, the Commission has published all decisions in the full text and in all languages with the exception of decisions not to raise objections, which are published in the form of a short summary notice. Delays caused by this practice jeopardise both the goal of efficiency and the objective of reaching quicker decisions.

As far as decisions to open a procedure are concerned, their full publication increases the total duration of the procedure significantly.[45] It was therefore proposed by the Commission that only the authentic language, together with a summary notice in other languages would be published. Third parties could still request a translation within 15 working days, so that their interests would be fully preserved.[46] The low number of comments in many cases seemed to indicate that the proposed system, where the Commission would only make translations on request, could save resources and speed up the decision.[47] A disadvantage of the proposed system, however, is the multiplication of time-limits it would introduce. The deadline for an interested party to submit comments would depend on the moment it received the translation made by the Commission after it had received a request. General doubts as to whether this complicated system could really increase efficiency in practice made the Commission and the Council reflect on a simplified solution. Both parties finally agreed to delete the right for third parties to request translations of a decision to open a procedure. In future, only the authentic language version and a meaningful summary in other languages will be published. Compared to the original proposal of the Commission this modification constitutes an improvement from an efficiency viewpoint. But it remains to be seen whether the final gains in terms of an acceleration of decisions will meet expectations.

As far as final decisions are concerned, their date of publication is essential for the legal certainty of beneficiaries, as the period for an action under Art. 173 starts from knowledge of the decision, which normally coincides with its publication. The Commission considered that continuing with the present system would soon no longer be feasible. Taking account of the number and length of decisions and of the prospect of enlargement, it proposed publishing only summary notices in the Official Journal, which would state that a copy of the authentic language version is available. This would considerably reduce the translation workload. However, the proposed system was unlikely to reduce the period for beneficiaries to obtain legal certainty. If one adds the time needed to translate and publish the summary notice, a reasonable period for an interested party to request and obtain a copy of the decision, and additional time to have it translated into that party's own language, the total period may not be very different from the time the Commission would have needed to translate and publish the full decision. Moreover, only in the latter case would a beneficiary be able to calculate the two-month time-limit of Art. 173.[48] Taking this into account, the proposed system did not seem to have struck the balance between transparency and efficiency. The Council, supported by the industry, therefore wanted to come back to the present situation, where the full text of all final decisions is published in all languages. For the Commission, this was an acceptable compromise, given the agreement on a reduced publication concerning decisions to open a procedure, which would have a direct effect on the duration of procedures and was thus considered as more important.

5. Conclusion

The Commission's initiative to make proposals under Art. 94 is a historical step in the development of state aid policy for several reasons.

First of all, the mere decision to use Art. 94 constitutes a complete change in the Commission's attitude, the importance of which should not be underestimated. For decades the Commission was determined not to use Art. 94 as it considered that there was no need to do so or that the risks involved were too high. However, a project of modernising state aid control was needed in order to adapt the system to the needs of a rapidly changing environment and although this could have been carried out by means of traditional instruments (guidelines, communications, etc.) it would then have remained a very modest reform which was likely to increase the lack of transparency of the system. Fortunately, the Commission decided to leave the traditional route and chose the modern way to reform state aid control: that of formal legislation, without which the required transparency and legal certainty could not have been ensured.

Secondly, the Enabling Regulation is historic because of the very principle it introduces. It lays down the foundations of a simplification of procedures, transforming the system of prior control into an *ex post* control. It had long been thought that in following such a simplification the Commission would be giving away part of its powers of control. It is true that it gives more responsibility to the national level (national administrations check themselves whether their projects meet the criteria of the group exemptions) and therefore contains certain risks. The challenge is to ensure that these risks are compensated by an efficient system of monitoring, not only by the Commission, but also by national jurisdictions which can directly apply the group exemption regulations. This was a necessary step, since it cannot be efficient for the Commission to continue to examine a considerable number of notifications of relatively low importance, which already correspond to the established compatibility criteria.

Finally, the adoption of a procedural regulation will complement this reform. Its main importance lies not so much in the new instruments it introduces to improve the effective enforcement of state aid control, but rather in the value of a codification itself. A streamlined and binding legal text setting out the different state aid procedures will finally put an end to the mixture of case law and soft law which is still dominating this field. It will increase the transparency and visibility of state aid rules and is a prerequisite for administrations, enterprises and academics increasing their knowledge of this area. It will also provide the required legal certainty which state aid is missing now. Therefore, its final impact can be expected to far exceed its contents.

NOTES

* The views expressed in this Chapter are the author's own; they should not be attributed to the EC Commission.

1. See also the guide to procedures in state aid cases, in: European Commission, *Competition law in the European Communities, Volume II A, Rules applicable to state aid*, Brussels, Luxembourg, 1995.

2. The consultation of the European Parliament was introduced with the Maastricht revision of the Treaty.

3. A first proposal on the basis of Art. 94 was submitted to the Council on 18 April 1966. It concerned, in particular, the exemption of certain categories of aid from the notification obligation. After years of fruitless negotiations, the Commission withdrew its proposal on 28 February 1975. The second proposal, submitted in 1972 and concerning a reporting system on important regional aid cases, was given up in 1976.

4. See e.g. the letter by which Commissioner Sir Leon Brittan informed the Italian President of the Industry Council in October 1990 of his conclusion that there was no apparent need for the Commission to make a proposal on the basis of Art. 94 (Agence Europe, Europe Documents No. 1656 of 19 October 1990).

5. Case T-95/94, *Sytraval* [1995] ECR 2651.

6. Proposal for a Council Regulation (EC) on the application of Articles 92 and 93 of the EC Treaty to certain categories of horizontal aid (OJ 1997 C 262/6).

7. Council Regulation (EC) No. 994/98 of 7 May 1998 on the application of Articles 92 and 93 of the Treaty establishing the European Community to certain categories of horizontal state aid (OJ 1998 L 142/1).

8. The first group exemption expected concerns aid to SMEs.

9. The Council reached a political agreement on the proposal at the Industry Council back on 13 November 1997. After the European Parliament had given its opinion, it was formally adopted at the Industry Council of 7 May 1998.

10. The Commission's proposal initially also included export credit insurance covering non-marketable risk in so far as it is harmonised by EC law and export credits, in so far as they are subject to precise rules established in international agreements (Art. 1 (c) and (d) of the proposal). These categories of aid were taken out during the negotiations in the Council.

11. e.g. because it exceeds the thresholds fixed in the group exemption or concerns an excluded sector.

12. See J-P. Keppenne, (R)évolution dans le système communautaire de contrôle des aides d'État, *Revue du Marché Unique Européenne*, 2/1998, 125 (at p. 143). Keppenne assumes that most horizontal aid will fall under group exemptions, so that notifiable aid will in future mainly consist of restructuring cases and aid coming under the multisectoral framework. That is not likely to be the case, as the group exemptions are only intended to exempt clear-cut cases, leaving the system unchanged for all other cases.

13. Commission notice on the *de minimis* rule for state aid (OJ 1997 C 68/9).

14. See e.g. J-Y. Chérot, "Les aides d'État dans les Communautés européennes",

Paris, *Economica*, 1998, p. 136.

15. The Commission proposal which stated that Member States should publish those summaries in their national official journals was modified in this respect.
16. The advisory committee on state aid (Arts. 7 and 8) is composed of representatives of the Member States and chaired by a representative of the Commission. It shall be consulted before a draft group exemption is published and before the adoption of such a regulation.
17. Such aid would be treated by the Commission as unlawful aid.
18. Some of the ideas in this chapter have been developed by the author in "Der Kommissionsvorschlag zu einer Verfahrensverordnung für die Beihilfenkontrolle", *Europäische Zeitschrift für Wirtschaftsrecht*, 1998, p. 268.
19. Proposal for a Council Regulation (EC) laying down detailed rules for the application of Article 93 of the EC Treaty (OJ 1998 C 116/13).
20. See e.g. the discussion concerning the Commission communication on the recovery of aid granted unlawfully (OJ 1995 C 156/5).
21. The Court of Justice has also repeatedly pointed to the lack of a procedural regulation, see e.g. in Case 84/82, *Germany v. Commission*, [1984] ECR 1451; Case C-301/87 *Boussac* [1990] ECR I-307; Case T-277/94 *AITEC* [1996] ECR II-351; Case T-189/97 *SFP* [1998] ECR II-335.
22. The Economic and Social Committee gave its opinion on 1 July 1998 (OJ 1998 C 284/10).
23. Possibly March 1999.
24. The following Section is based on the text of the Regulation as it was agreed upon by the Industry Council on 16 November 1998.
25. See also AG Lenz in Case 40/85 *Boch* [1986] ECR 2321.
26 Cf. supra.
27 See e.g. case C-39/94 *SFEI* [1996] ECR 3547.
28. See European Commission, *Competition law in the European Communities, Volume II A, Rules applicable to state aid*, Brussels, Luxembourg, 1995, p. 41, footnote 3, where a period of two weeks is suggested. The reasoning was that if no such possibility existed for the Commission, a notice *after* implementation of the proposal would have been sufficient.
29. See e.g. J-Y. Chérot, o.c., p. 146-147.
30. In this regard the final text of the Regulation differs from the Commission's proposal, which left the decision on whether a notification is complete entirely with the Commission. According to the Commission's proposal, Member States would only have had the right to ask the Commission to consider a notification as complete, but the Commission would still have decided whether or not it accepted that the requested information did not exist or had already been provided (see Art. 5 of the proposal).
31. The Member State will probably invoke *Lorenz* (Art. 4 (6) of the Regulation) after two months and put the measure into effect, while the Commission will probably consider that in the absence of complete notification it cannot take a decision and any implementation of the aid would be unlawful.
32. Two months for the preliminary examination, 18 months for the formal

examination procedure and two additional months from the request of the Member State.

33. See e.g. the recent case T-107/96 R *Pantochim* [1998] ECR II-311, which suggests that the Commission is denied this power.

34. Suspension injunctions are mainly useful for aid schemes and for individual aid which has not entirely been paid out yet.

35. The important difference is that, since the recovery injunction is entirely based on the procedural illegality of the aid, no *"fumus boni juris"* on the substance is required.

36. Depending on the Member State and on the type of aid, provisions of administrative law, civil law, insolvency law, fiscal law, company law, etc. may apply to a recovery procedure.

37. See e.g. Case C-24/95 *Alcan II* [1997] ECR I-1591.

38. One could argue, however, that the sentence was directly in line with the case law of the Court, since suspensive effect can be interpreted as a provision which makes the effective execution of recovery decisions impossible.

39. A disadvantage of the deletion is that the present text is less transparent. A clear, directly applicable provision excluding suspensive effect would have been easier to apply by national judges.

40. Although the Court has always rejected arguments based on principles such as proportionality or legitimate expectations, their application has never been generally excluded and one could perhaps invoke them in the kind of cases which come under the limitation period.

41. In principle, this obligation already exists. See Commission letter to Member States of 22 February 1994, in: *European Commission, Competition law in the European Communities, Volume II A, Rules applicable to state aid*, Brussels, Luxembourg, 1995, p. 73.

42. See e.g. the proposal of the European Association of Lawyers, *Europäische Zeitschrift für Wirtschaftsrecht*, 1996, p. 688.

43. Case C-367/95 P *Sytraval* [1998] ECR I-1719. Although the Court upheld the judgement of the CFI, in its motivation it fully confirmed the Commission's position on third party rights. See also the recent judgement in case T-371/94 and T-394/94, *Air France*, of 25 June 1998, point 59, not published yet, and the references to previous case law there.

44. In the Commission's proposal references to third party rights were spread over different articles: the obligation for the Commission to examine all the information it receives about alleged unlawful aid (Art. 10 (1) of the proposal); the rights of third parties to submit comments and to request that their identity is not disclosed to the Member State (Art. 5 of the proposal); the right of an interested party to obtain a copy of any Commission decision on state aid (Art. 25 of the proposal); the right for interested parties having submitted comments, and beneficiaries of individual aid, to be sent a copy of the final decision of a formal investigation procedure (Art. 25 of the proposal).

45. At present it takes ca. 100 days on average to translate and publish a decision to open proceedings.

46. See Art. 25 of the proposal.
47. However, this was far from sure, since under the present system the number of enterprises having read the decision to open a procedure must be higher than the number of comments received. Therefore, the number of future requests could also be higher than the Commission expects. Moreover, one could imagine that associations and confederations would have systematically requested translations. In that case, the proposed system would rather have increased the present workload and delayed the decision making.
48. Another long-term disadvantage is that the proposed reduced publication system would have made it very difficult, if not impossible, for academics to follow and study state aid policy in the Official Journal.

CHAPTER 12

UNEQUAL TWINS: REFORM OF THE STATE AID RULES UNDER ARTICLE 94[1]

Christian Ahlborn

1. Introduction

Recent years have seen a dramatic increase in activity in the area of state aid. This flood of notifications has come close to drowning the state aid control system and has finally triggered Commission proposals for a reform of the state aid rules under the dormant Art. 94. The aim of the proposed reform is twofold:

(i) to avoid spending Commission resources on cases of minor importance and to focus on important issues. This aim is supposed to be achieved via a block exemption enabling regulation from the Council ("the Enabling Regulation") and subsequent Commission block exemptions in areas such as SMEs and R&D;

(ii) to improve the assessment and enforcement mechanisms for important cases.

These improvements were to flow from a regulation laying down detailed rules for the application of Art. 93 of the EC Treaty ("the Procedural Regulation"). However, while the Enabling Regulation has passed the Council with no resistance, the proposed Procedural Regulation has been caught in the cross-fire and at the moment it is far from certain in what form, and indeed whether, it will finally be adopted.

2. The Enabling Regulation

The Enabling Regulation gives the Commission the power to draw up regulations defining categories of aid which are exempted from the notification obligation (so-called group exemptions). Areas where the Commission will

S. Bilal and P. Nicolaides (eds.), Understanding State Aid Policy in the European Community, 231–242.
© 1999 *Kluwer Law International. Printed in the Netherlands.*

be able to draw up group exemptions (Art. 1) to cover horizontal aid include:
- – aid to small and medium-sized firms (SMEs);
- – research and development (R&D);
- – environmental protection;
- – employment and training;
- – regional aid.

The Commission, through block exemptions, will be obliged to limit the scope covered by each of the above areas to specified categories of beneficiaries, types of aid and aid ceilings (either in terms of aid intensity or absolute volume).

The concept of block exemptions has been tested in the context of Art. 85 and is generally accepted as a means of focusing on important cases. As the Enabling Regulation provides just the bare bones of the system it has been fairly uncontroversial.

Whether the block exemptions will work satisfactorily in the context of state aid will depend first on the monitoring and reporting system to be established between the Commission and Member States and, second, on the precise nature of the individual block exemptions.

3.   The Procedural Regulation

3.1   THE STARTING POINT

The proposed Procedural Regulation is, at least potentially, the most important piece of competition legislation since the introduction of the Merger Regulation (its importance is only matched by the reforms related to the application of Art. 85 to vertical restraints). The success of competition policy is largely determined by the procedural rules and institutional structure of state aid control.

Efficient and transparent procedural rules will limit any political influence and are therefore likely to lead to a more consistent application of substantive state aid rules.

Many practitioners consider that the proposed Procedural Regulation offers an ideal opportunity to harmonise and streamline the state aid procedures, which have developed rather haphazardly through Court judgements and Commission guidelines and notices. The Commission, from the outset, was much more modest in its aspirations. It aimed for a codification of the status quo coupled with certain minor improvements. It took the view that any far-reaching procedural reforms would not pass the Council.

3.2 KEY POINTS OF PROCEDURAL RULES

The remainder of this paper will assess how the Commission's proposal of the Procedural Regulation (the "Commission Proposal")[2] will affect state aid rules (if at all) and where opportunities for reforms have been missed. It will also discuss certain amendments proposed by the Council. The analysis of the Procedural Regulation will focus on the following five key points of procedural rules:

– *Information gathering*: here, the question arises whether the procedural rules provide the Commission with sufficient access to information required for the efficient monitoring and assessment of state aid measures.

– *Time limits*: both in relation to preliminary investigations (Phase I investigations) and in-depth investigations (Phase II investigations) time limits are an important factor for the administrative efficiency of state aid control.

– *Third party rights*: although, formally, state aid control is a process between Member States and the Commission, third parties (such as competitors for trade acquisitions) play an important role in the assessment process. This is particularly true given the limited resources of the Commission. Third parties help the Commission to carry out monitoring services, they provide information and help the Commission withstand political pressure.

– *Publication obligations*: are closely linked to the issue of transparency. The procedural rules have to ensure that the state aid process is sufficiently transparent for the Member State concerned, as well as for the beneficiary or any complainant. A lack of transparency will not only affect legal certainty it will also facilitate the politicisation of state aid control.

– *Enforcement*: ultimately, the efficiency of the competition policy system depends on the effectiveness of its enforcement mechanisms. In the past, EC state aid control has shown particular deficits in this area, due to insufficient monitoring and cumbersome enforcement procedures.

4. Information gathering

Information gathering will be necessary both for the assessment of notified aid cases as well as the detection and assessment of non-notified aid cases. Given politicians general desire to advertise their state aid measures, detection is less of an issue than in cartel cases and so the emphasis is on the issue of assessment.

4.1 NOTIFIED AID CASES

Where aid is notified, the Commission will often be in a position to establish whether a measure amounts to state aid. The onus is then on the Member State to prove that any of the exemptions apply, with the threat of a negative decision being given on the basis of that information. As a result, there is an incentive for the Member States to provide sufficient information to obtain a positive decision.

Under the Commission Proposal, the Commission is entitled to regard a notification as withdrawn if its request for further information is not answered by a Member State, unless the Member State can convince the Commission that the information does not exist or has already been provided (Art. 5(3)).

In view of the uncertainty as to when a notification is complete (there are no standard forms), the concept of a deemed withdrawal is dangerous and should be limited to cases where the Commission cannot assess whether a measure amounts to state aid. Otherwise the threat of a negative decision on the basis of the information available should be sufficient to obtain the information required.

4.2 NON-NOTIFIED AID CASES

In the case of illegal (i.e. non-notified aid) or misuse of aid (i.e. enforcement of conditions) the situation is different. Here the Commission may be faced by a Member State which, for example, takes the view that a certain measure is outside the state aid rules altogether.

As a result the Commission and the Member State can play "silly games" for months, if not years. The Commission requests information to assess whether a certain measure contravenes the state aid rules, but the Member State may refuse to supply the information on the basis that the measure falls outside those rules.

The only option available to the Commission in this situation is an "information injunction". If this is ignored then all the Commission can do is refer the matter to the European Court of Justice (ECJ) and apply for a declaration that the failure to comply with the request constitutes an infringement of the Treaty. This procedure is not only lengthy, cumbersome and expensive, it is also politically highly embarrassing for Member States.

An obvious solution would be to give the Commission the right to obtain information directly from third parties (in particular the beneficiary) and to provide the Commission with powers similar to those contained in the Procedural Regulation for Art. 85 and 86 of the EC Treaty (i.e. Regulation 17/62 or the Merger Regulation).[3]

The Commission Proposal does not contain any provisions empowering the Commission to extract information from third parties with one surprising exception, namely the "on-site monitoring" provision. Art. 20 states:

"In cases where the Commission has serious doubts as to whether conditional decisions (under Article 7(4)) are being complied with, the Member State concerned shall allow the Commission to undertake on-site monitoring visits."

While there are good reasons for the Commission's on-site monitoring powers, it begs two questions:

(i) Why are these powers limited to only the cases of misuse of aid and not to the equally serious cases of unlawful aid? and

(ii) Why does the Commission Proposal not provide for less dramatic means of gathering information from third parties, such as requests for information?

The absence of any satisfactory answer may be explained by the fact that not all Member States are whole-heartedly in favour of an efficient state-aid control system.

5.   Time limits

5.1 TIME LIMITS IN PHASE I

As early as 1973 the ECJ imposed a time limit on the Commission in relation to preliminary investigations, namely the two month "*Lorenz* period".[4]

To soften the blow of strict time limits, the ECJ stated that the implementation of aid after the expiry of the two-month period would require a letter by the Member State to the Commission confirming its intention to grant the aid. Only if the Commission does not react to this letter will the Member States be allowed to go ahead and implement the aid measure.

This procedure is now contained in Art. 4(6) of the Proposal giving the Commission 15 working days following receipt of the Member State's notice. Not only has the Commission thereby extended the period to more or less three months (although apparently the Legal Service seems to think this still reflects the *Lorenz* judgement) but, more importantly, the question also arises whether the procedure of the *Lorenz* letter is still appropriate. In 1973, when strict time limits were something unheard of in competition cases, such a "wake-up call" may have been necessary. In the 1990s the *Lorenz* letter is an insult to the efficiency of the Commission. If a Member State notifies aid to the Commission one can reasonably assume that it intends to implement it.

Secondly, there are no particular skills involved in determining the end of a two-month deadline with the help of a calendar. Therefore the *Lorenz* letter increases the administrative burden without obvious benefit and therefore should be abolished.

Not only is the two-month time limit mitigated by the *Lorenz* letter, but also time only starts to run when a notification is complete. Given that state aid control does not operate with standard forms, the concept of complete information is more vague in state aid than in other competition areas.

In the past the Commission has made generous use of requests for information. The Procedural Regulation should contain a restriction on the use of information requests in order to avoid artificial extensions of the time limit. Furthermore, the use of standard forms, such as the Form CO for the notification of mergers, should also be developed in the field of state aid.

5.2 TIME LIMITS IN PHASE II

While the abolition of the *Lorenz* letter and a restriction on information requests would be helpful in streamlining procedures, the big issue is whether binding time limits for the formal investigation should be introduced.

There is little doubt that the introduction of time limits would increase administrative efficiency. As a general rule, people work more efficiently under time pressure (as long as the pressure is still bearable). The difference between Art. 85 and the Merger Regulation certainly illustrate this point. Moreover, deadlines force the Commission to take decisions in cases which are politically inconvenient. Apparently, there are still cases undecided which have been open since 1995 and which have no reasonable prospect of ever coming to a conclusion.

The Commission has taken the view that, given its lack of resources, it is not in a position to adhere to overall timetables and as a result the Commission proposal does not provide for time limits for Phase II investigations. As the Council insisted on time limits, a classical Community compromise was found, namely time limits which are so wide as to have no practical effect. The Council seems to be in favour of an 18-month time period at the end of which Member States can insist on a Commission decision within a further two months. The decision would then be taken on the basis of the information available.

Obviously, it is nonsensical to create procedural rules which the system will not be able to support. However, resource constraints are no excuse for the complete absence of time limits (or time limits which have no practical impact). If there is no capacity for operating all Phase II investigations on fixed time limits, then the Commission should at least work to time limits on important priority cases. The number of cases under fixed time limits should then be gradually increased as the block exemption will begin to ease the workload. Priority cases could be determined on the basis of aid intensity or the time pressure facing the beneficiary (e.g. in cases of rescue and restructuring aid).

6. Third party rights

6.1 THIRD PARTY RIGHTS IN PHASE I INVESTIGATIONS

The scope of third party rights in Phase I investigations was subject to considerable controversy. In *Sytraval*,5 a case concerning the transportation of monies and valuables by a subsidiary of the French post office, the Court of First Instance (CFI) came to the conclusion that, in certain circumstances, the EC Treaty (Art. 190) imposed the following two procedural obligations on the Commission during a Phase I investigation:

- "where the Commission decided to reject a complaint concerning a measure characterised by the complainant as unnotified state aid, without allowing the complainant to comment, prior to the adoption of the definitive decision, on the information obtained in the context of its investigation, it is under an automatic obligation to examine the objections which the complainant would certainly have raised if it had been given the opportunity of taking cognisance of that information";

- "the Commission's obligation to state reasons for its decision may in certain circumstances require an exchange of views and arguments with a complainant, since, in order to justify to the requisite legal standard its assessment of the nature of a measure characterised by the complainant as state aid, the Commission needs to know what position the complainant takes on the information gathered by it in the course of its enquiry."

The Commission appealed and found support with the ECJ, which rejected the reasoning of the CFI on both points.

As the Commission Proposal was published prior to the ECJ's Sytraval judgement, it is not surprising that it does not contain any provisions on third party rights in Phase I investigations. The Council apparently wants to bring the Procedural Regulation in line with the Sytraval judgement. That is for interested third parties to be entitled to submit comments to the Commission about possible illegal aid or abuse of aid. Where the Commission considered that the information provided was insufficient to take a view, it would have an obligation to inform the third party about this position. Moreover, they want third parties to be entitled to receive a copy of the decision in cases where they have submitted comments.

This minimalist approach clearly carries the risk of Commission decisions to approve a measure at the end of a Phase I investigation not being sufficiently scrutinised and of continuing to be influenced by political considerations.

6.2 THIRD PARTY RIGHTS IN PHASE II INVESTIGATIONS

Neither the Commission Proposal nor any subsequent Council amendments deal with the issue of third party rights in the Phase II investigations, which have been well established by the ECJ.

The Commission itself has always claimed that a codification of the status quo would greatly increase the transparency and legal certainty of state aid control. It is difficult to see why one of the main areas of state aid procedure, namely third party rights, should be excluded from this codification process.

However, a partial codification would reduce transparency and legal certainty. More importantly it would negatively affect the position of third parties, which has been one of the driving forces behind the transformation of state aid control from a cosy dialogue between the Commission and Member States to the outline of a proper competition policy.

7. Publication obligations

7.1 PUBLICATION OF NOTIFICATIONS

While publication of every state aid notification would not be justified, in certain cases, particularly in those involving complex issues, publication could be useful. An earlier draft of the Commission Proposal states:

> "The Commission may in cases of individual aid publish the fact of the notification in the Official Journal of the European Committees, at the same time indicating the Member State concerned, the names of the beneficiary, the form, purpose and amount or intensity of the aid and the economic sectors involved. The criteria for publication shall be established by the Commission."

Unfortunately, this paragraph has disappeared in subsequent drafts. It is, however, unclear whether this deletion reflects a policy decision not to publish any notifications or whether the Commission felt that the above paragraph states the obvious.

7.2 PUBLICATION OF A DECISION TO INITIATE A FORMAL INVESTIGATION

The Commission Proposal specifies in relation to the publication of Art. 4(4) decisions:

> "The Commission shall publish in the Official Journal of the European Communities the decisions which it takes pursuant to Article 4(4) in the authentic language versions. It shall also publish in all the other official languages of the Community a summary notice of those decisions. For the purpose of submitting comments pursuant to Article 6, a copy of the decision may be requested in any official language of the Community within a period of 15 working days following the date of publication of the summary notice."

The Council amendments on the other hand leave the publication of Art. 4(4) decisions unaltered but restrict the obligation to publish final decisions in languages other than the language of the case. In those languages a summary of the decision is deemed sufficient.

Clearly, in this case, there is a conflict between administrative efficiency (and in particular speed) on the one hand and transparency on the other, a conflict which arises not only in the field of state aid control but also in other areas of competition policy. With enlargement of the Union, the urgency for a solution to this conflict will increase. Whether the above Commission proposal strikes the right balance between administrative efficiency and transparency is rather doubtful. Transparency could certainly be enhanced (without loss of administrative efficiency) if decisions were not only published in the language of the case but also publicised (if not published) in at least one of the major Community languages.

8. Enforcement

Enforcement is the one area where the Commission has made an attempt to go beyond the status quo, particularly in relation to the recovery of illegal state aid and the enforcement of negative Commission decisions.

8.1 RECOVERY INJUNCTION

Art. 11 of the Commission Proposal states that:

"the Commission may, after giving the Member State concerned the opportunity to submit its comments, adopt a decision requiring the Member State provisionally to recover any lawful aid until the Commission has taken a decision on the compatibility of the aid with the common market".

The Commission takes the view that this paragraph merely reflects the present legal position following the *Boussac* judgement.[6] This view is highly contested and indeed the Commission so far has not made use of a recovery injunction.

The Council does not seem to be willing to accept the unconditional power of the Commission to make recovery injunctions. A compromise has been suggested where the recovery injunction would be limited to cases which satisfy certain conditions such as the absence of doubt that the measure amounts to aid and a serious risk of irreparable damage to a competitor.

A recovery injunction would be a major step forward in removing an incentive to provide illegal state aid and to create a level playing field between those Member States which are willing to respect the state aid rules and those which are not. The conditions attached to the recovery injunction which have been suggested by the Council, however, would deprive the recovery injunction of most of its impact: a serious risk of irretrievable damage to a competitor is difficult if not impossible to prove.

8.2 NO SUSPENSIVE EFFECT OF REMEDIES UNDER NATIONAL LAW

Having been faced with numerous cases where the effect of a negative decision was frustrated by lengthy national proceedings challenging the decision, the Commission inserted in Art. 14:

"Remedies under national law shall not have suspensive effect".

Again such a provision would make the grant of illegal aid less attractive. However, it seems unlikely that the Council will agree to this provision and in the latest Council amendments the above sentence has been deleted.

9.   Conclusion

The Enabling Regulation and the Procedural Regulation started as a twin reform project to achieve more focused, efficient and transparent state aid control.

As far as the Enabling Regulation is concerned, it is too early at this stage, to pass judgement on whether the right degree of focus will be achieved. The true test will come with the individual Commission block exemptions.

The conclusion on the Procedural Regulation must await the final outcome. However, on the basis of the latest Council amendments, the result is disappointing:

– The Commission's original (modest) aim of codification of the status quo will not be achieved. Major areas such as third party rights in Phase II investigations will operate outside the Procedural Regulation subject to non-codified rules. As a result the Procedural Regulation will increase rather than reduce legal certainty.

– The only area where the Commission has attempted reform of the existing system, in the area of enforcement, is likely to be blocked by the Council, either outright or through the attachment of conditions which will minimise the effect of the reforms.

– Certain changes will reduce transparency beyond what is necessary in order to achieve administrative efficiency.

– Changes which would have enhanced administrative efficiency without facing the resistance of the Council (such as a reform of time limits in Phase I) have not been attempted.

Should it not prove possible, in the present political climate, to preserve the proposed Commission reforms in the area of enforcement, i.e. the power of recovery injunctions (at least in the majority of cases of illegal aid) and the removal of the suspensory effect of national proceedings, then it may well be better to continue with the existing regime, with all its imperfections, rather than to introduce an even less perfect Procedural Regulation.

NOTE

1. This Chapter reflects the state of play as at the end of June 1998.
2. Proposal for a Council Regulation (EC) laying down detailed rules for the application of Art. 93 of the EC Treaty, Com (98) 73 final.
3. Such as the power to request information (Art. 11) or the power to carry out investigations (Art. 18).
4. C–120/73 [1973] ECR 1471, *Lorenz v Federal Republic of Germany.*
5. Case 367/95 2 April 1998, ECR I–1719, *Commission of the European Communities v Chambre syndicate national des entreprises de transport de fonds et valeur (Straval) and Brink's, France SARL.*
6. C301/87, [1990] ECR I–307, *France v Commission.*

ANNEXES

ANNEX I

PROPOSED APPLICATION OF ARTICLE 93:
A DIAGRAMMATIC OUTLINE OF THE DRAFT
PROCEDURAL REGULATION

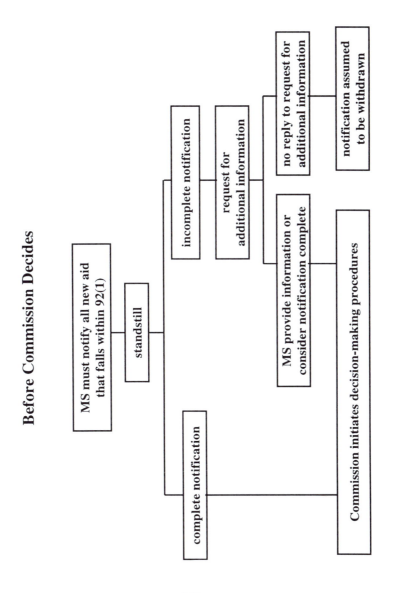

S. Bilal and P. Nicolaides (eds.), Understanding State Aid Policy in the European Community, 245–260.
© 1999 Kluwer Law International. Printed in the Netherlands.

Decision-Making Procedures

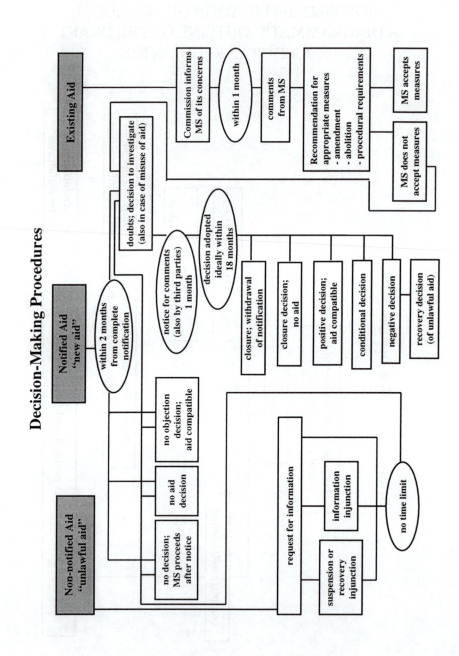

After Commission Decides

Publication in OJ of decision in authentic language; summary notices in other languages (copies of decision given to third parties that provided comments)

MS submit annual reports on all existing aid

Commission may undertake on-site monitoring

Commission may adopt implementing provisions on:
- notifications
- annual reports
- time limits
- interest rates

input

Advisory Committee on State Aid

ANNEX II*

Proposal for a

COUNCIL REGULATION (EC)

laying down detailed rules for the application of Article 93
of the EC Treaty

(Text with EEA relevance)

THE COUNCIL OF THE EUROPEAN UNION,

Having regard to the Treaty establishing the European Community, and in particular Article 94 thereof,

Having regard to the proposal from the Commission[1],

Having regard to the opinion of the European Parliament[2],

Having regard to the opinion of the Economic and Social Committee[3],

Whereas ...

HAS ADOPTED THIS REGULATION:

CHAPTER I: GENERAL

Article 1 Definitions

For the purpose of this Regulation, the following definitions shall apply:

(a)   *"aid"*: any measure fulfilling all the criteria laid down in Article 92(1) of the Treaty;

---

[1]   OJ C
[2]   OJ C
[3]   OJ C

---

*   Draft text agreed in the Council on 16 November 1998.

(b)   *"existing aid"*:

    (i)   without prejudice to Articles 144 and 172 of the Act of Accession of Austria, Finland and Sweden, all aid which existed prior to the entry into force of the Treaty in the respective Member State, that is to say, aid schemes and individual aid which were put into effect before, and are still applicable after the entry into force of the Treaty,

    (ii)   authorized aid, that is to say, aid schemes and individual aid which have been authorized by the Commission or by the Council,

    (iii)   aid which is deemed to have been authorized pursuant to Article 4(6) of this Regulation or prior to this Regulation but in accordance with this procedure;

    (iv)   aid which is deemed to be existing aid pursuant to Art. 15;

    (v)   aid which is deemed to be an existing aid because it can be established that at the time it was put into effect it did not constitute an aid, and subsequently became an aid due to the evolution of the common market and without having been altered by the Member State. Where certain measures become aid following the liberalisation of an activity by Community law, such measures shall not be considered as existing aid after the date fixed for liberalisation.

(c)   *"new aid"*: all aid, that is to say, aid schemes and individual aid, which is not existing aid, including alterations to existing aid;

(d)   *"aid scheme"*: any act on the basis of which, without further implementing measures being required, individual aid awards may be made to undertakings defined within the act in a general and abstract manner and any act on the basis of which aid, which is not linked to a specific project may be awarded to one or several undertakings for an indefinite period of time and/or for an indefinite amount;

(e)   *"individual aid"*: aid that is not awarded on the basis of an aid scheme and notifiable awards of aid on the basis of an aid scheme;

(f)   *"unlawful aid"*: new aid put into effect in contravention of Article 93(3) of the Treaty;

(g)   *"misuse of aid"*: aid used by the beneficiary in contravention of a decision taken pursuant to Article 4(3) or Article 7(3) or (4) of this Regulation;

(h)   *"interested party"*: any Member State and any person, undertaking or association of undertakings whose interests might be affected by the granting of aid, in particular the beneficiary of the aid, competing undertakings and trade associations;

CHAPTER II: PROCEDURE REGARDING NOTIFIED AID

Article 2 Notification of new aid

1.　Save as otherwise provided in regulations made pursuant to Article 94 of the Treaty or to other relevant provisions thereof, any plans to grant new aid shall be notified to the Commission in sufficient time by the Member State concerned.

　　The Commission shall inform the Member State concerned without delay of the receipt of a notification.

2.　In a notification, the Member State concerned shall provide all necessary information in order to enable the Commission to take a decision pursuant to Articles 4 and 7 ("complete notification").

Article 3 Standstill clause

Aid notifiable pursuant to Article 2(1) shall not be put into effect before the Commission has taken or is deemed to have taken a decision authorizing such aid.

Article 4 Preliminary examination of the notification and decisions of the Commission

1.　The Commission shall examine the notification as soon as it is received. Without prejudice to Article 8, the Commission shall take a decision pursuant to paragraphs 2, 3 or 4 of this Article.

2.　Where the Commission, after a preliminary examination, finds that the notified measure does not constitute aid, it shall record that finding by way of a decision.

3.　Where the Commission, after a preliminary examination, finds that no doubts are raised as to the compatibility with the common market of a notified measure, in so far as it falls within the scope of Article 92(1) of the Treaty, it shall decide that the measure is compatible with the common market ["decision not to raise objections"]. The decision shall specify which exception under the Treaty has been applied.

4.　Where the Commission, after a preliminary examination, finds that doubts are raised as to the compatibility with the common market of a notified measure, it shall decide to initiate proceedings pursuant to Article 93(2) of the Treaty ("decision to initiate the formal investigation procedure").

5.　The decisions referred to in paragraphs 2, 3 and 4 shall be taken within two months. That period shall begin on the day following the receipt of a complete notification. The notification will be considered as complete if, within two months from its receipt, or from the receipt of any additional information requested, the Commission does not request any further information. The period can be extended with the consent of both the Commission and the Member State concerned. Where appropriate, the Commission may fix shorter time-limits ("accelerated procedure").

6. Where the Commission has not taken a decision in accordance with paragraphs 2, 3 or 4 within the period laid down in paragraph 5, the aid shall be deemed to have been authorized by the Commission. The Member State concerned may thereupon implement the measures in question after giving the Commission prior notice thereof, unless the Commission takes a decision pursuant to this Article within a period of 15 working days following receipt of the notice.

Article 5 Request for information

1. Where the Commission considers that information provided by the Member State concerned with regard to a measure notified pursuant to Article 2 is incomplete, it shall request all necessary additional information. Where a Member State responds to such a request, the Commission shall inform the Member State of the receipt of the response.

2. Where the Member State concerned does not provide the information requested within the period prescribed by the Commission or provides incomplete information, the Commission shall send a reminder, allowing an appropriate additional period within which the information shall be provided.

3. The notification shall be deemed to be withdrawn if the requested information is not provided within the prescribed period, unless before the expiry of that period either the period has been extended with the consent of both the Commission and the Member State concerned, or the Member State concerned, in a duly reasoned statement, informs the Commission that it considers the notification to be complete because the additional information requested is not available or has already been provided. In that case, the period referred to in Article 4(5) shall begin on the day following receipt of the statement. If the notification is deemed to be withdrawn, the Commission shall inform the Member State thereof.

Article 6 Formal investigation procedure

1. The decision to initiate proceedings pursuant to Article 4 (4) shall summarise the relevant issues of fact and law, shall include a preliminary assessment of the Commission as to the aid character of the proposed measure, and shall set out the doubts as to its compatibility with the common market. The decision shall call upon the Member State concerned and upon interested parties to submit comments within a prescribed period which shall normally not exceed one month. In duly justified cases, the Commission may extend the prescribed period.

2. The comments received shall be submitted to the Member State concerned. If an interested party so requests, on grounds of potential damage, its identity shall be withheld from the Member State concerned. The Member State concerned may reply to the comments submitted within a prescribed period which shall normally not exceed one month. In duly justified cases, the Commission may extend the prescribed period.

Article 7 Decisions of the Commission to close the formal investigation procedure

1. Without prejudice to Article 8, the formal investigation procedure shall be closed by means of a decision as provided for in paragraphs 2 to 5 of this Article.

2. Where the Commission finds that, where appropriate following modification by the Member State concerned, the notified measure does not constitute aid, it shall record that finding by way of a decision.

3. Where the Commission finds that, where appropriate following modification by the Member State concerned, the doubts as to the compatibility of the notified measure with the common market have been removed, it shall decide that the aid is compatible with the common market ("positive decision"). That decision shall specify which exception under the Treaty has been applied.

4. The Commission may attach to a positive decision conditions subject to which an aid may be considered compatible with the common market and lay down obligations to enable compliance with the decision to be monitored ("conditional decision").

5. Where the Commission finds that the notified measure is not compatible with the common market, it shall decide that the aid shall not be put into effect ("negative decision").

6. Decisions taken pursuant to paragraphs 2, 3, 4 and 5 shall be taken as soon as the doubts referred to in Article 4(4) have been removed. The Commission shall as far as possible endeavour to adopt a decision within a period of 18 months from the opening of the procedure. This time-limit may be extended by common agreement between the Commission and the Member State concerned.

7. Once this time-limit has expired, and should the Member State concerned so request, the Commission shall, within two months, take a decision on the basis of the information available to it. If appropriate, where the information provided is not sufficient to establish compatibility, the Commission shall take a negative decision.

Article 8 Withdrawal of notification

1. The Member State concerned may withdraw the notification within the meaning of Article 2 in due time before the Commission has taken a decision pursuant to Articles 4 or 7.

2. In cases where the Commission has initiated the formal investigation procedure, the Commission shall close that procedure.

Article 9 Revocation of a decision

The Commission may revoke a decision taken pursuant to Article 4(2) or (3), or Article 7(2), (3) or (4), after having given the Member State concerned the opportunity to submit its comments, where it was based on incorrect information provided during the procedure which was a determining factor for the decision. Before revoking a decision and taking a new decision, the Commission shall open the formal investigation procedure pursuant to Article 4(4). Articles 6, 7, 10, 11(1), 13, 14 and 15 shall apply *mutatis mutandis*.

CHAPTER III: PROCEDURE REGARDING UNLAWFUL AID

Article 10 Examination, request for information and injunction for information

1. Where the Commission has in its possession information from whatever source regarding alleged unlawful aid, it shall examine that information without delay.

2. If necessary, it shall request information from the Member State concerned. Article 2(2) and Article5(1) and (2) shall apply *mutatis mutandis*.

3. Where, despite a reminder pursuant to Article 5(2), the Member State concerned does not provide the information requested within the period prescribed by the Commission, or where it provides incomplete information, the Commission shall by decision require the information to be provided ("information injunction"). The decision shall specify what information is required and prescribe an appropriate period within which it is to be supplied.

Article 11 Injunction to suspend or provisionally recover aid

1. The Commission may, after giving the Member State concerned the opportunity to submit its comments, adopt a decision requiring the Member State to suspend any unlawful aid until the Commission has taken a decision on the compatibility of the aid with the common market ("suspension injunction").

2. The Commission may, after giving the Member State concerned the opportunity to submit its comments, adopt a decision requiring the Member State provisionally to recover any unlawful aid until the Commission has taken a decision on the compatibility of the aid with the common market ("recovery injunction"), if the following criteria are fulfilled:

   – according to an established practice there are no doubts about the aid character of the measure concerned;

   – there is an urgency to act;

   – there is a serious risk of substantial and irreparable damage to a competitor.

   Recovery shall be effected in accordance with the procedure set out in Article 14(2) and (3). After the aid has been effectively recovered, the Commission shall take a decision within the time-limits applicable to notified aid.

The Commission may authorise the Member State to couple the refunding of the aid with the award of rescue aid to the firm concerned.

The provisions of this paragraph shall be applicable only to unlawful aid put into effect after the entry into force of this Regulation.

Article 12 Non-compliance with an injunction decision

If the Member State fails to comply with an injunction decision as referred to in Article 11, the Commission shall be entitled, while carrying out the examination on the substance of the matter on the basis of the information available, to refer the matter to the Court of Justice direct and apply for a declaration that the failure to comply constitutes an infringement of the Treaty.

Article 13 Decisions of the Commission

1. The examination of possible unlawful aid shall result in a decision pursuant to Article 4(2), (3) or (4). In the case of decisions pursuant to Article 4(4), proceedings shall be closed by means of a decision pursuant to Article 7. If a Member State fails to comply with an information injunction, that decision shall be taken on the basis of the information available.

2. In cases of possible unlawful aid and without prejudice to Article 11 (2), the Commission shall not be bound by the time-limit set out in Article 4(5), 7 (6) and 7 (7).

3. Article 9 shall apply *mutatis mutandis.*

Article 14 Recovery of aid

1. Where negative decisions are taken in cases of unlawful aid, the Commission shall decide that the Member State concerned shall take all necessary measures to recover the aid from the beneficiary (" recovery decision"). The Commission shall not require recovery of the aid, if this would be contrary to a general principle of Community law.

2. The aid to be recovered pursuant to a recovery decision shall include interest at an appropriate rate fixed by the Commission. Interest shall be payable from the date on which the unlawful aid was at the disposal of the beneficiary until the date of its recovery.

3. Without prejudice to any order of the Court of Justice pursuant to Article 185 of the Treaty, recovery shall be effected without delay and in accordance with the procedures under the national law of the Member State concerned, provided that they allow the immediate and effective execution of the Commission's decision. To this effect and in the event of a procedure before national courts, the Member States concerned shall take all necessary steps which are available in their respective legal systems, including provisional measures, without prejudice to Community law.

Article 15 Period of limitation

1. The powers of the Commission to recover aid shall be subject to a limitation period of ten years.

2. The limitation period shall begin on the day on which the unlawful aid is awarded to the beneficiary either as individual aid or as aid under an aid scheme. Any action taken by the Commission or by a Member State, acting at the request of the Commission, with regard to the unlawful aid shall interrupt the limitation period. Each interruption shall start time running afresh. The limitation period shall be suspended for as long as the decision of the Commission is the subject of proceedings pending before the Court of Justice of the European Communities.

3. Any aid with regard to which the limitation period has expired, shall be deemed to be existing aid.

CHAPTER IV: PROCEDURE REGARDING MISUSE OF AID

Article 16 Misuse of aid

Without prejudice to Article 23, the Commission may in cases of misuse of aid open the formal investigation procedure pursuant to Article 4(4). Articles 6, 7, 9, 10, 11(1), 12, 13, 14 and 15 shall apply *mutatis mutandis*.

CHAPTER V: PROCEDURE REGARDING EXISTING AID SCHEMES

Article 17 Cooperation pursuant to Article 93(1) of the Treaty

1. The Commission shall obtain from the Member State concerned all necessary information for the review, in cooperation with the Member State, of existing aid schemes pursuant to Article 93 (1) of the Treaty.

2. Where the Commission considers that an existing aid scheme is not or is no longer compatible with the common market, it shall inform the Member State concerned of its preliminary view and give the Member State concerned the opportunity to submit its comments within a period of one month. In duly justified cases, the Commission may extend this period.

Article 18 Proposal for appropriate measures

Where the Commission, in the light of the information submitted by the Member State pursuant to Article 17, concludes that the existing aid scheme is not or is no longer compatible with the common market, it shall issue a recommendation proposing appropriate measures to the Member State concerned. The recommendation may propose, in particular:

(a)   substantive amendment of the aid scheme, or

(b)   introduction of procedural requirements, or

(c)   abolition of the aid scheme.

Article 19 **Legal consequences of a proposal for appropriate measures**

1. Where the Member State concerned accepts the proposed measures and informs the Commission thereof, the Commission shall record that finding and inform the Member State thereof. The Member State shall be bound by its acceptance to implement the appropriate measures.

2. Where the Member State concerned does not accept the proposed measures and the Commission, having taken into account the arguments of the Member State concerned, still considers that those measures are necessary, it shall initiate proceedings pursuant to Article 4(4). Articles 6, 7 and 9 shall apply *mutatis mutandis*.

CHAPTER VI: INTERESTED PARTIES

Article 20 **Rights of interested parties**

1. Any interested party may submit comments pursuant to Article 6 following a decision of the Commission to initiate the formal investigation period. Any interested party which has submitted such comments and any beneficiary of individual aid will be sent a copy of the decision taken by the Commission pursuant to Article 7.

2. Any interested party may inform the Commission of any alleged unlawful aid and of any alleged misuse of aid.

    Where the Commission considers that on the basis of the information in its possession there are insufficient grounds for taking a view on the case, it shall inform the interested party thereof.

    Where the Commission takes a decision on a case concerning the subject matter of the information supplied, it shall send a copy of that decision to the interested party.

3. At its request, any interested party shall obtain a copy of any decision pursuant to Article 4, 7, 10 (3) and 11.

CHAPTER VII: MONITORING

Article 21 **Annual reports**

1. The Member States shall submit to the Commission annual reports on all existing aid schemes with regard to which no specific reporting obligations have been imposed in a conditional decision pursuant to Article 7(4).

2. Where, despite a reminder, the Member State concerned fails to submit an annual report, the Commission may proceed in accordance with Article 18 with regard to the aid scheme concerned.

Article 22 **On-site monitoring**

1. In cases where the Commission has serious doubts as to whether decisions not to raise objections under Article 4 (3), positive decisions under Article 7 (3) or conditional decisions under Article 7(4) with regard to individual aid are being complied with, the Member State concerned, after having been given the opportunity to submit its comments, shall allow the Commission to undertake on-site monitoring visits.

2. The officials authorized by the Commission shall be empowered, in order to verify compliance with the decision concerned:

   (a) to enter any premises and land of the undertaking concerned;

   (b) to ask for oral explanations on the spot;

   (c) to examine books and other business records and take or demand copies.

   The Commission may be assisted if necessary by independent experts.

3. The Commission shall inform the Member State concerned, in good time and in writing, of the on-site monitoring visit and of the identities of the authorized officials and experts. If the Member State has duly justified objections against the Commission's choice of experts, the experts shall be appointed in common agreement with the Member State. The officials of the Commission and the experts authorized to carry out the on-site monitoring shall produce an authorization in writing specifying the subject-matter and purpose of the visit.

4. Officials authorized by the Member State in whose territory the monitoring visit is to be made may be present at the monitoring visit.

5. The Commission shall provide to the Member State a copy of any report produced as a result of the monitoring visit.

6. Where an undertaking opposes a monitoring visit ordered by a decision of the Commission pursuant to this Article, the Member State concerned shall afford the necessary assistance to the officials and experts authorized by the Commission to enable them to carry out the monitoring visit. To this end the Member States shall, after consulting the Commission, take the necessary measures within eighteen months after the entry into force of this Regulation.

Article 23 **Non-compliance**

1. Where the Member State concerned does not comply with conditional or negative decisions, in particular in cases referred to in Article 14, the Commission may refer the matter to the Court of Justice direct in accordance with Article 93(2) of the Treaty.

2. If the Commission considers that the Member State concerned has not complied with a judgement of the Court of Justice, the Commission may

pursue the matter in accordance with the provisions of Article 171 of the Treaty.

CHAPTER VIII: COMMON PROVISIONS

Article 24 **Professional secrecy**

The Commission and the Member States, their officials and other servants, including independent experts appointed by the Commission, shall not disclose information which they have acquired through the application of this Regulation and is covered by the obligation of professional secrecy.

Article 25 **Addressee of decisions**

Decisions taken pursuant to Chapters II, III, IV, V and VII of this Regulation shall be addressed to the Member State concerned. The Commission shall notify them to the Member State concerned without delay and give the Member State concerned the opportunity to indicate to the Commission which information it considers to be covered by the obligation of professional secrecy.

Article 26 **Publication of decisions**

1. The Commission shall publish in the *Official Journal of the European Communities* a summary notice of the decisions which it takes pursuant to Article 4(2) and (3) and Article 18 in conjunction with Article 19 (1). The summary notice shall state that a copy of the decision may be obtained in the authentic language version or versions.

2. The Commission shall publish in the *Official Journal of the European Communities* the decisions which it takes pursuant to Article 4(4) in the authentic language version. In the Official Journal published in languages other than the authentic language version the authentic language version will be accompanied by a meaningful summary in the language of that Official Journal.

3. The Commission shall publish in the *Official Journal of the European Communities* the decisions which it takes pursuant to Article 7.

4. In cases where Article 4(6) or Article 8(2) applies, a short notice shall be published in the *Official Journal of the European Communities*.

5. The Council acting unanimously may decide to publish decisions pursuant to the third subparagraph of Article 93(2) in the *Official Journal of the European Communities*.

Article 27 **Implementing provisions**

The Commission acting in accordance with the procedure laid down in Article 29 shall have the power to adopt implementing provisions concerning the form, content and other details of notifications, the form, content and other details of annual reports, details of time-limits and the calculation of time-limits, and the interest rate referred to in Article 14(2).

Article 28 **Advisory Committee**

An advisory committee, hereinafter referred to as the Advisory Committee on State Aid, shall be set up. It shall be composed of representatives of the Member States and chaired by the representative of the Commission.

Article 29 **Consultation of the advisory committee.**

1.   The Commission shall consult the Advisory Committee on State Aid before adopting any implementing provision pursuant to Article 27.

2.   Consultation of the Committee shall take place at a meeting called by the Commission. The drafts and documents to be examined shall be annexed to the notification. The meeting shall take place no earlier than two months after notification has been sent.

   This period may be reduced in the case of urgency.

3.   The Commission representative shall submit to the committee a draft of the measures to be taken. The committee shall deliver an opinion on the draft, within a time limit which the chairman may lay down according to the urgency of the matter, if necessary by taking a vote.

4.   The opinion shall be recorded in the minutes; in addition, each Member State shall have the right to ask to have its position recorded in the minutes. The Advisory Committee may recommend the publication of this opinion in the Official Journal.

5.   The Commission shall take the utmost account of the opinion delivered by the committee. It shall inform the committee on the manner in which its opinion has been taken into account.

Article 30 **Entry into force**

This Regulation shall enter into force on the twentieth day following that of its publication in the *Official Journal of the European Communities*.

This Regulation shall be binding in its entirety and directly applicable in all Member States.

Done at Brussels,   For the Council
                                                                  The President

Recent and Forthcoming EIPA Publications

All prices are subject to change without notice.

La face nationale de la gouvernance communautaire: L'élaboration des "positions nationales" des Etats membres sur les propositions d'actes communautaires
Current European Issues Series
Franck Petiteville
IEAP 1999, environ 111 pages
(La version anglaise sera publiée plus tard cette année)
NLG 40

Internal Management of External Relations: The Europeanization of an Economic Affairs Ministry
Adriaan Schout
EIPA 1998, 360 pages
(Only available in English)
NLG 65

European Environmental Policy – A Handbook for Civil Servants
Christoph Demmke/Birgit Schröder
EIPA 1999, 385 pages
(Only available in English)
NLG 50

Schengen's Final Days? The Incorporation of Schengen into the New TEU, External Borders and Information Systems
Monica den Boer (ed.)
EIPA 1998, 174 pages
(Mixed texts in English, French and German)
NLG 65

L'Euroformation des administrations régionales et locales d'Europe (Actes de la Conférence interrégionale; Barcelone, juin 1998) /
Eurotraining for Regional and Local Authorities in Europe (Proceedings of the Interregional Conference; Barcelona, June 1998)
Sous la direction de Eduardo Sánchez Monjo
IEAP 1998, 409 pages
(Pour faciliter la compréhension de cet ouvrage et lui assurer une large diffusion, les textes sont publiés dans la langue originale mais aussi en traduction française et anglaise)
NLG 65

An Institution's Capacity to Act: What are the Effects of Majority Voting in the Council of the EU and in the European Parliament?
Current European Issues Series
Madeledine O. Hosli
EIPA 1998, 26 pages
(Only available in English)
NLG 15

Taming the Third Pillar. Improving the Management of Justice and Home Affairs Cooperation in the EU
Current European Issues Series
Monica den Boer
EIPA 1998, 44 pages
(Only available in English)
NLG 15

Competition Policy and the WTO: Is there a need for a multilateral agreement?
(Working Paper)
Sanoussi Bilal and Marcelo Olarreaga
EIPA 1998, 18 pages
(Only available in English)
NLG 15

Coping with Flexibility and Legitimacy after Amsterdam
(Current European Issues Series)
Monica den Boer/Alain Guggenbühl/Sophie Vanhoonacker (eds)
EIPA 1998, 259 pages
(Only available in English)
NLG 65

Guide to Official Information of the European Union
3rd Edition
Veerle Deckmyn
EIPA 1998, 65 pages
(Available in both English and French)
NLG 30

Regionalism, Competition Policy and Abuse of Dominant Position
(Working Paper)
Sanoussi Bilal and Marcelo Olarreaga
EIPA 1998, 19 pages
(Only available in English)
NLG 15

The Senior Civil Service: A comparison of personnel development for top managers in fourteen OECD member countries
Research carried out under the authority of The Office for the Senior Public Service in the Netherlands
EIPA 1998, 99 pages
(Only available in English)
NLG 25

Openness and Transparency in the European Union
Veerle Deckmyn/Ian Thomson (eds)
EIPA 1997, 169 pages
(Only available in English)
NLG 60